To Dougie
A fellow military enthusiast

Ken [signature]

28ᵗʰ December 2010
Southampton

MAILED FIST

MAILED FIST

6th Armoured Division at War, 1940–1945

Ken Ford

SUTTON PUBLISHING

First published in the United Kingdom in 2005 by
Sutton Publishing Limited · Phoenix Mill
Thrupp · Stroud · Gloucestershire · GL5 2BU

Copyright © Ken Ford, 2005

All rights reserved. No part of this publication may be reproduced, stored in a retrieval system, or transmitted, in any form or by any means, electronic, mechanical, photocopying, recording or otherwise, without the prior permission of the publisher and copyright holder.

Ken Ford has asserted the moral right to be identified as the author of this work.

British Library Cataloguing in Publication Data
A catalogue record for this book is available from the British Library.

ISBN 0-7509-3515-4

To my Mother
Evelyn Gladys Ford 1907–89

Typeset in 11/13pt Photina MT.
Typesetting and origination by
Sutton Publishing Limited.
Printed and bound in England by
J.H. Haynes & Co. Ltd, Sparkford.

Contents

	List of Maps	vii
	Introduction and Acknowledgements	ix
One	Raising the Division	1
Two	Blade Force	9
Three	Bou Arada	28
Four	Kasserine and the Defence of Thala	49
Five	Fondouk	69
Six	The End in Tunisia	89
Seven	Italy: The First Winter	115
Eight	The Liri Valley	129
Nine	The Chase Begins	145
Ten	The Advance through Italy	159
Eleven	Italy: The Second Winter	171
Twelve	The Final Battle	183
	Appendix	193
	Notes	195
	Bibliography	203
	Index	205

List of Maps

Map 1	Tunisia	10
Map 2	Blade Force	15
Map 3	Bou Arada	28
Map 4	Kasserine and the stop line at Thala	50
Map 5	The Battle of Fondouk and Kairouan	70
Map 6	Tunisia: The final offensive, May 1943	90
Map 7	The Liri Valley	130
Map 8	The advance through Italy	160
Map 9	The mountain line, September–October 1944	172
Map 10	The final battle, April 1945	184

Introduction and Acknowledgements

Unlike most other British divisions, there was no history of 6th Armoured Division produced after the Second World War. This was a great pity, for the people most suitably qualified to write such a history were the men of the division who made the decisions and fought the battles, but they are, for the most part, now long gone. This history therefore can only be a partial one, put together with all the disadvantages that the passing years bring. Nonetheless, I have been most fortunate in being able to contact some veterans of the division who were able to offer help and advice.

First and foremost I should like to single out Allan Waterston for thanks, for it was he who started me on this project and was able to offer a wealth of personal details of his service with the Lothians and Border Horse and general information about the division. Without this initial impetus, I doubt whether this book would have been written.

My good fortune continued when I made contact with two surviving armoured regiment commanders, Col Gordon Simpson of the Lothians and Border Horse and Lt Col Val ffrench Blake of 17th/21st Lancers. Through correspondence, interviews and their private papers I was able to gain a valuable insight into the actions of 26th Armoured Brigade. The value of the information they were able to provide was boundless and I do thank them both most sincerely for allowing me to have access to it.

I should also like to thank these other veterans of 6th Armoured Division who were kind enough to contact me: Frank Beckett, Bob Crichton, David Fulton, Francis Hepburne-Scott, George Martin and George Turnball. A special thanks goes to Frank Beckett and George Martin for allowing me to quote from their books *Prepare to Move* and *Cassino to the River Po*.

This history is only able to give the briefest outline of the actions fought by 6th Armoured Division. I hope that it might act as a spur to the reader to widen his knowledge of this fine division. There have been many regimental histories that include accounts of battalions and armoured regiments which served in 6th Armoured. Those that have been most useful are listed in the Bibliography at the end of this book. Two of these are recognised as being among the very best of the genre: *A History of the 17th/21st Lancers 1922–1959*, by Lt Col Val ffrench Blake and *The Proud Trooper: The History of the Ayrshire (Earl of Carrick's Own) Yeomanry* by Maj W. Steel-Brownlie. My thanks go to Val ffrench Blake and to Maj George Hay of the Ayrshire Yeomanry Museum for allowing me to quote from these titles.

The role of infantry in support of an armoured brigade is vividly described in the late Lt Gen Sir James Wilson's memoir, *Unusual Undertakings*. General Wilson's book should be read by all who wish to experience a more intimate description of life within the division. I am also most grateful that he allowed me to quote from his book.

My thanks are also offered to the National Archives at Kew and to the Imperial War Museum for giving me access to their archives. All the illustrations are published courtesy of the Trustees of the Imperial War Museum. Finally, and certainly not least of all, I should like to thank my wife Valda for having to forgo leisurely weeks in our apartment in France through the summer while this book was being completed.

Ken Ford
Southampton
October 2004

Chapter One

RAISING THE DIVISION

The Second World War revolutionised the way that war was fought. It was a time when the use of armour influenced the course of all campaigns. A single tank could sometimes turn the course of a battle; an armoured column could often halt a complete division. It may therefore come as something of a surprise to those interested in the war to discover how few armoured divisions were actually employed in the British Army during that period.

Between 1935 and the end of the war, Germany raised and put into the field eighty-six panzer and *panzergrenadier* divisions. During the same period, Britain formed just eleven armoured divisions, two of which – 9th and 42nd Armoured Divisions – remained in the UK and never saw action. The 6th Armoured Division was the fourth of these armoured formations to come into service, 1st, 2nd and 7th being raised earlier. Of the eleven divisions that came into being during the hostilities, the 6th was one of only five that survived until the end of the war; the other six were all disbanded well before the German surrender. In May 1945, in Italy, the 6th was the only British armoured division which remained in service in a theatre outside north-west Europe. The other four survivors – the Guards, 7th, 11th and 79th Armoured Divisions – were engaged in the more newsworthy struggles in France, Belgium and Germany.[1]

There were of course many reasons why so few armoured divisions were raised and deployed, some of which had nothing to do with strategy or the tactics of how they were employed. The fact was that, apart from North Africa, there was rarely a battlefield on which British forces were engaged that was suitable for them to act as armoured divisions. Most of the time they went into action not as divisions, but as a collection of armoured regiments in support of the infantry.

As the war progressed more and more independent armoured and tank brigades were formed. These smaller formations were more easily deployed in the support of infantry, especially in the confines of the rural countryside of north-west Europe. In contrast, the Germans were able to deploy large numbers of panzer divisions and even panzer corps in the wide open plains of Russia. The story of 6th Armoured Division during the Second World War illustrates some of the problems faced by complete armoured divisions when being used in actions for which their composition was often unsuitable.

The 6th Armoured Division was raised in September 1940 by Maj Gen John Crocker. For its divisional sign it chose a clenched mailed gauntlet in white on a square black background – a symbol that was to earn it the name of the 'Mailed Fist Division'. Maj Gen Crocker was a veteran of the First World War and a man with a great deal of armoured experience, the ideal person to create a new tank division from scratch. Crocker had volunteered for service in the previous war and joined the ranks of 28th London Regiment, the Artists' Rifles. He served with some distinction on the Western Front, earning himself a commission into the Machine Gun Corps, and was awarded both the Distinguished Service Order and Military Cross. After the war he left the army, but a year later he was back in uniform when he rejoined the services. This time he transferred to the fledgling Tank Corps. Throughout the 1930s, Crocker was at the heart of the pioneering work associated with armoured forces, serving as Percy Hobart's brigade-major and eventually joining the staff of Maj Gen Alan Brooke's newly formed Mobile Division as his GSO1. When war broke out, Crocker was in command of 1st Tank Brigade – later rechristened 3rd Armoured Brigade. In September 1940, after the fall of France and the withdrawal of the British Expeditionary Force, he was promoted to major-general and given the task of raising 6th Armoured Division.

Crocker was not destined to take the division which he had created to war, for in 1942 he was promoted to corps command. He served in this capacity in North Africa and north-west Europe, eventually finishing the conflict as the highest-ranking British commander from the Royal Tank Corps. After the war he continued his service career, eventually attaining the rank of full general.

When 6th Armoured Division was raised in 1940 it conformed to Basic Organisation III, which meant that it comprised two armoured brigades, one support group and an armoured car regiment. These were 20th and 26th Armoured Brigades, the 6th Support Group and the Derbyshire Yeomanry (armoured cars). This type of formation was not found to be successful. Experience showed that having two armoured brigades in a division was the wrong balance and created a slow-moving administrative tail which stretched for miles. More infantry were needed to make the armoured formation self-supporting on the battlefield, so 20th Armoured Brigade left the division in April 1942 and was replaced by an infantry brigade to conform with the new Basic Organisation V.

The 26th Armoured Brigade and the Derbyshire Yeomanry armoured car regiment then remained with the division without change. The 6th Support Group was disbanded in June 1942 and its component parts – 12th (Honourable Artillery Company) Royal Horse Artillery,

72nd Antitank Regiment RA, 51st Light Antiaircraft Regiment RA and the brigade HQ – were all absorbed by 6th Armoured Division as divisional troops. To these units were added a second artillery regiment – 152nd (Ayrshire Yeomanry) Field Regiment RA – and several Royal Engineer formations – 5th and 8th Field Squadrons and 144th Field Park Squadron. These additions brought the division up to the recommended Basic Organisation V.

The incoming infantry formation resulting from the reorganisation was 38th (Irish) Infantry Brigade, containing 1st Royal Irish Fusiliers, 6th Inniskilling Fusiliers and 2nd London Irish Rifles, which established the division with the structure it would eventually take into battle. The division was now a manageable amalgamation of armour and infantry, supported by artillery and engineers, capable of mobile operations. The tank arm of the division was 26th Armoured Brigade with a mix of cavalry and yeomanry regiments. It comprised 16th/5th Queen's Royal Lancers, 17th/21st Lancers and 2nd Lothians and Border Horse. The armoured brigade also had an infantry component in the shape of the motorised riflemen of 10th Rifle Brigade.

The combination of one armoured brigade and one infantry brigade made the division into a powerful fighting force. In theory each brigade was organised and deployed to support the other. The weight of firepower and the mobility of the tanks would enable the armoured brigade to break through enemy defences and seize ground; then the infantry brigade would move forward and hold the ground. That was the theory and in practice it worked, provided that the terrain was suitable for the deployment of large numbers of tanks.

The individual units that came together to form the division in 1940 had a mix of experience. Some were Territorial and yeomanry battalions, others were from the Regular Army who had seen service abroad, or, in the case of 1st Royal Irish Fusiliers, had seen action in France in 1940. The two cavalry regiments in 26th Armoured Brigade, 16th/5th Queen's Royal Lancers and 17th/21st Lancers, both had long pedigrees dating back to 1759, with a great list of battle honours to their name, including Blenheim, Salamanca, Waterloo, Balaclava and the Somme. Both had been in India in the late 1930s, undertaking expeditions against tribesmen in the North West Frontier mounted on horses and indulging in the gentler pastimes of polo and 'pigsticking'. Mechanisation came slowly and their horses were given up with great regret. Indeed, 16th/5th Lancers was still a mounted regiment in India when war actually broke out in September 1939 and did not get its tanks until the following year. The third armoured regiment in the brigade was 2nd Lothians and Border Horse. It was formed in May 1939 from a yeomanry regiment that could trace its ancestry back to the Napoleonic Wars. It was raised by the recruitment of volunteers, covering all trades and professions, from the

Edinburgh area. The lorry-borne infantry component of 26th Armoured Brigade was 10th Battalion Rifle Brigade (10 RB). This battalion was part of the Territorial Army and comprised a few regular soldiers together with conscripts and volunteers, all of good London stock.

In July 1942, Lt James Wilson, later Lt Gen Sir James Wilson, joined 10th Rifle Brigade as a junior subaltern. He was impressed with the battalion and its London roots as he later explained in his memoirs:

> 10 RB had developed from a second line Territorial battalion, the Tower Hamlets Rifles, formed in 1939 as part of the Hore-Belisha campaign to 'Double up and Double the TA'. Its first set of officers came from the city, the riflemen from Mile End, Hoxton and Stepney. All were volunteers, the great majority of whom joined the Territorial Army because they saw that war was inevitable and they preferred to face it in the company of their friends. If the officers varied in quality, the standard of riflemen was outstanding. In 1939 there had been no dilution of the Cockney stock from East London. Apart from a talented Jewish element, the remaining riflemen were Cockneys to a man, younger 'mirror images' of Stanley Holloway in *My Fair Lady*. They were tough, loyal and sensible; importantly, they were young, with an average age of 20 or so in 1939, which meant that by 1942 they had matured enough to be the right age for service in an active battalion. They were also streetwise, pleasantly cynical, and with a wit and sense of humour which permeated the battalion and maintained its morale until 1945.[2]

The infantry brigade of the division, 38th (Irish) Brigade, was formed in January 1942 at the insistence of Winston Churchill. He proposed the creation of an Irish Brigade, which would 'draw together battalions of the Irish line regiments in which men from all over Ireland could serve'. There was some opposition from the Northern Ireland government, but Churchill got his way.[3] The brigade consisted of one Regular Army battalion, one wartime battalion and one Territorial Army battalion: 1st Royal Irish Fusiliers, 6th Inniskilling Fusiliers and 2nd London Irish Rifles, respectively.

The 6th Armoured Division contained two regiments of artillery. The 12th (HAC) RHA supported 26th Armoured Brigade, while 152nd Field Regiment RA supported 38th Brigade. The 12th RHA was formed in May 1939 from the most senior regiment in the Territorial Army, the London-based Honourable Artillery Company. The 152nd Field Regiment RA had equally impressive antecedents, coming as it did from the Ayrshire (Earl of Carrick's Own) Yeomanry, the senior regiment of Scotland's auxiliary forces. When the yeomanry regiment was mobilised in September 1939, its troopers assembled complete with rifle and sword. Initial training continued with riding school, sword drill and schemes over the Carrick hills, with stable work three times a day. While Hitler was preparing to launch his 'Blitzkrieg' armoured thrust across France and the Low Countries, A and B Squadrons were giving a display of a cavalry charge with drawn swords for the Pathé newsreel cameras. Early in 1940 the Ayrshire (Earl of Carrick's Own) Yeomanry was absorbed into the Royal Regiment of Artillery and in April 1940 it was divided into 151st and 152nd Field Regiments RA.[4]

In October 1941 Maj Gen John Crocker left 6th Armoured Division for promotion to a corps command. He was replaced for a short while by Maj Gen C.H. Gairdner who began the process of restructuring the division to comply with Type V Organisation. On 19 May 1942, Gairdner was replaced by Maj Gen Charles Keightley, a cavalryman from 5th Royal Inniskilling Dragoon Guards. At only 41 years old, Keightley was a relatively young man for divisional command and showed great promise of further promotion. He had served on the staff of 1st Armoured Division in France in 1940 and had a sound understanding of armoured tactics. Keightley arrived at an opportune moment, for the division had been earmarked for service in North Africa in the autumn, and he now had several months in which to make his mark on the division before it saw action.

Experience gained in France and in North Africa, and reports coming back from Russia, showed that the Germans were equipped with good tanks. Their Panzer IIIs (50mm gun) and the newer Panzer IVs (short 75mm gun) at the head of crack panzer divisions were gaining impressive reputations. In reply, British tank design was found to be rather pedestrian. By 1942, the Matilda tank was obsolete, the Valentine (2-pounder 40mm gun) was significantly under-gunned and the Crusader (6-pounder 57mm gun) was mechanically unreliable. Maj Val ffrench Blake served with 17th/21st Lancers in 1942 and he later commented on the design and performance of the Valentine and Crusader tanks:

> The Valentine was armed with a 2 Pounder gun. The idea of arming a tank with a gun firing high explosive had not yet emerged as being of supreme importance in support of infantry. The 2 Pounder was purely an antitank weapon. The Valentine was also provided with a coaxial Besa machine gun for engaging infantry, guns or 'soft' vehicles. The 7.92mm Besa looked like being a good weapon; air-cooled with a heavy and simple mechanism, it seemed reliable and not subject to the many possible stoppages which made the Vickers training so long and complicated. Though mechanically reliable the Valentine had a faulty type of track pin, and the number of breakages we experienced was enormous; in fact the supply of track pins was always smaller than the demand for them, and all our tactical moves or marches were bedevilled

by broken tracks. In one exercise twenty Valentine tracks broke in a march of eighty-six miles. Later mark Valentines were fitted with an excellent American two-stroke diesel engine which made it faster, quiet and wonderfully reliable. The other tank we used in 1942 was the Crusader which was armed with a 6-pounder gun. Each squadron headquarters also had two Crusaders equipped with a three-inch howitzer for close support. This little gun had a maximum range of about 3,000 yards and fired either smoke or a small HE shell. It was to prove invaluable in battle. The Crusader was fast but lightly armoured. It was fitted with a petrol engine and had acquired a bad name from the desert with Eighth Army. It had certain mechanical troubles which were never satisfactorily cured; it had unreliable steering worked by compressed air; it was liable to petrol stoppages and was not a certain starter. When it ran well it had an impressive cross-country performance, but too often it failed mechanically.[5]

Lt Allan Waterston of 2nd Lothians and Border Horse was the commander of a troop of Crusaders in Tunisia and recalled some of his experiences with this type of tank: 'The Crusader was the first tank I actually did any fighting in. We were very critical about the tank. It had a complicated system of starting up with a thing called Kigas. You had to put your hand right down inside the back of the turret and give it so many pumps before the engine could start. It was petrol driven, which made it vulnerable; when it was hit it often went up like a Ronson lighter. It had a very thin skin which would just about keep out a rifle bullet, but not a shell. When you stopped it was a very debatable affair as to whether or not it would start again when you wanted it to.'[6]

Life inside a tank was claustrophobic, smelly and very noisy at the best of times. In action the heat, the noise and the fumes made life almost unbearable. Each member of the crew had specific tasks on which he concentrated to help drown out the reality that each second might bring a deafening clang and a sheet of flame and prove to be his last. The 2nd Lothians' history described the role of each man inside the Sherman tank, which later became the standard fighting vehicle for the armoured brigade, beginning with the gunner:

From the point of view of visibility the tank gunner is not the best placed among the crew. While other members of the crew can traverse their periscopes at will to obtain a picture of the surrounding terrain and of what is happening to right and left, the gunner can see only what lies dead ahead of him unless he traverses the whole turret, a practice not encouraged by crew commanders. Thus the gunner remains wistfully perplexed as to what is going on on each side of him. As action becomes imminent he locks his adjustable seat and sits erect, his forehead in the telescope pad, his hands on the brass handles of the elevating and traversing gears. Immediately behind the gunner, head and shoulders exposed out of the turret hatch, stands the crew commander, dividing his attention between map, binoculars, wireless and intercom. Protruding far into the turret, the buffers, breech and guard of the 75mm gun separates the gunner from his loader, whose duty varies, as circumstance dictates, between operating the wireless set and feeding the guns. These three, crew commander, gunner and loader, form the crew of the fighting compartment. In front of, and below them, sit the driver and co-driver, their shoulders barely level with the floor of the turret. To the rear of the turret are the engines, while both in and around the turret are ammunition racks, each with its allocated proportion of smoke, HE (high explosive) and AP (armoured-piercing) shells.[7]

In late September 1942 orders were received for the division to prepare for service overseas. Maj Gen Keightley was also instructed to form an independent regimental group within the division, to be known as Blade Force. This group would embark in advance of the rest of the armoured division for a special duty. No one knew the destination, or the task, although most people expected the force would land somewhere in North Africa. They were right in one sense, for their destination, and that of the whole division, was North Africa, but not to join Monty's Eighth Army: they were to land with Lt Gen Kenneth Anderson's new First Army as part of an Anglo-American invasion force, under the command of Gen Dwight D. Eisenhower. America's entry into the fighting war was to begin with joint landings with the British in Morocco and Algeria, codenamed 'Operation Torch'.

The name 'Blade Force' at first had little significance, but later it was realised that it referred to the parent unit it would be fighting with after the landings. The force would come under the command of 78th Division whose divisional badge was a crusader's battleaxe in yellow. Blade Force was to be the armoured cutting edge of the Battleaxe Division.

The regimental group was organised to contain all that it required to act independently from the rest of the division. It was to be a self-contained battlegroup able to undertake missions against the enemy, well in front of any support. The CO of 17th/21st Lancers, Lt Col Richard Hull, was promoted to full colonel and placed in command of the force. The armoured body of his new command was his old regiment, 17th/21st Lancers. In support were a mix of 6th Armoured Division's support groups: B Squadron 1st Derbyshire Yeomanry (armoured cars); C Battery 12th RHA (25-pounder field guns); A Battery 72nd Antitank Regiment RA (6-pounder guns); G Troop 51st Light Antiaircraft Regiment RA (Bofors guns); B Company 10th Rifle Brigade (motorised infantry company); one troop of 5th Field Squadron RE (engineers); two sections of 165th Field Ambulance; detachments of 26th Armoured Brigade Company RASC and RAOC (fitters and armourers); a section of 6th Armoured Division Provost Company and a detachment of 9th Tank Transporter Company. Everything was planned down to the last detail.[8]

The remainder of 6th Armoured Division was to embark in slow convoys bound for Algeria after Blade Force had left. The division was to join First Army in the follow-up phase of the Torch landings. The term 'Army' was rather a grand title for Lt Gen Anderson's forces, for when First Army began its campaign on the African continent, it contained only 78th and 6th Armoured Divisions. Much less than an army, it was barely a corps!

Chapter Two

BLADE FORCE

With the remainder of 6th Armoured Division assembling in Scotland ready for embarkation, the ships carrying Blade Force left the River Clyde on 2 November 1942 as part of a giant invasion convoy. Their destination was unknown until the convoy was well out to sea three days later. Sealed orders were then opened to reveal that it was to be Algiers.

Sailing with the convoy were the follow-up troops of 78th 'Battleaxe' Division; its leading two brigades, 11th and 36th Brigades, had left earlier on a previous convoy as part of the initial assault force. An even greater armada was en route from the USA to join with the British to carry out the operation, bringing 107,453 troops to land at Casablanca, Oran and Algiers.

The leading British troops from 78th Division came ashore on the eastern flank of the invasion zone on 8 November, carrying out their assault landings close to Algiers with the US 34th Division. The Anglo-American assault force quickly established a beachhead, then moved out to seize port facilities and the airfield at Maison Blanche, so as to provide a firm base and allow the follow-up forces to come ashore.

The assault parties met with some opposition after landing from forces allied to the cause of the Vichy regime in France. Wherever possible, the Allied force tried to withhold its fire and not to get involved in any shooting matches with the Vichy French. It was hoped that the occupation could take place without protracted fighting. This was achieved for the most part, since the local military were loath to engage the Anglo-Americans, but were, nonetheless, still hostile in principle to what was an invasion of their country. By the time Blade Force arrived a few days later on 12 November, the area had been totally subdued and the local civilians were starting to become friendly.

Although the Allied forces had landed in French Morocco and Algeria, Tunisia was their real objective. Early possession of this French colony would cut off German supply routes to Libya and enable the Allies to strike eastwards to meet up with Montgomery's Eighth Army advancing from Egypt. However, between Algiers and Tunis were 560 miles of mountainous roads, French troops of unknown loyalty and the possibility

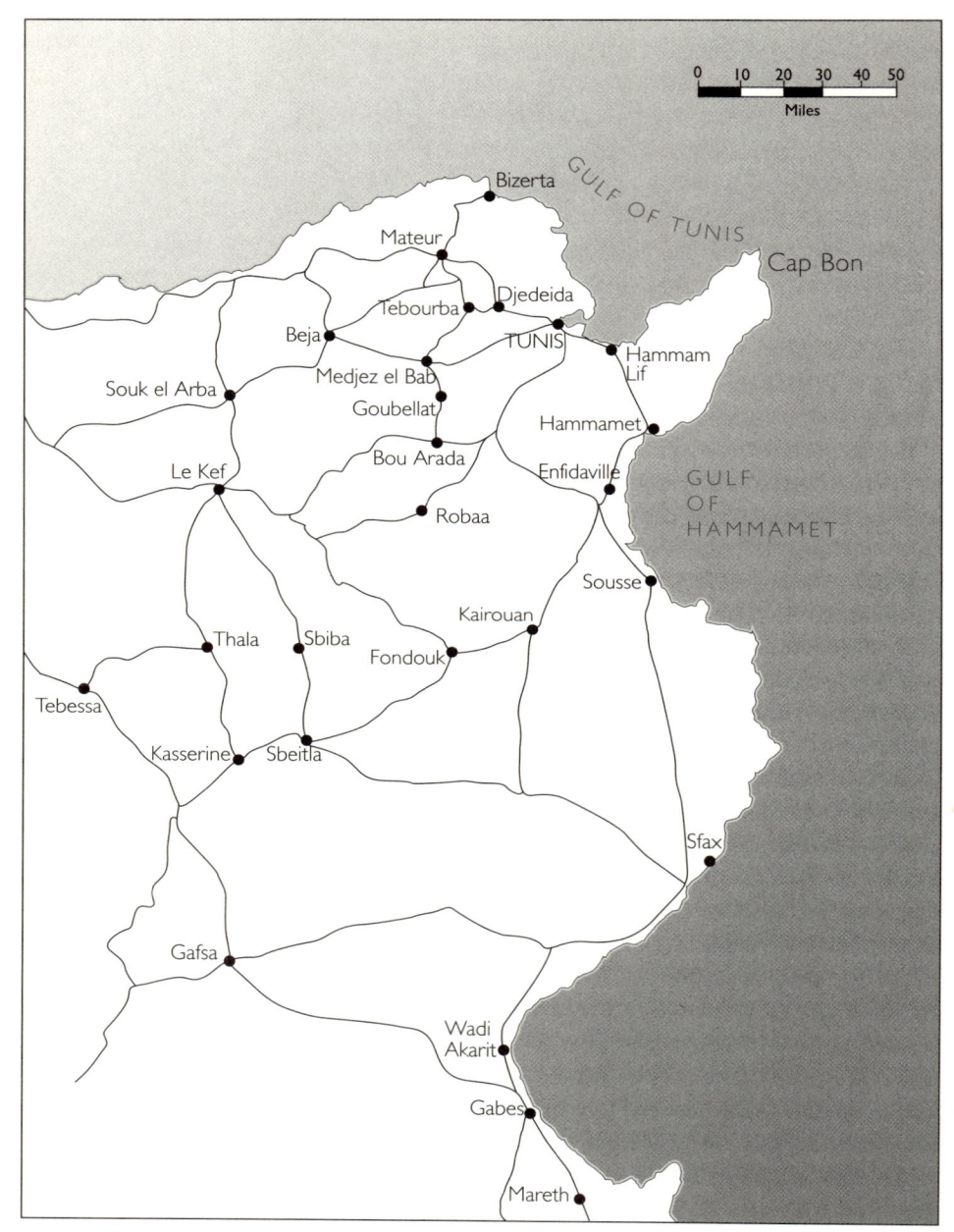

Map 1. Tunisia

of meeting German forces, who were being rushed into the country to deny it to the Allies. Gen Evelegh's 78th Division, with Blade Force under command, was now unleashed to lead the drive eastwards towards the Tunisian border.

The advance on Tunis was undertaken along three main routes: 36th Brigade along the route closest to the coast, passing through Sedjenane and then swinging down on Tunis through Mateur from the north; 11th Brigade in the south would advance through Beja and Medjez el Bab and then proposed to wheel up into Tunis along the road from Massicault; Blade Force would take the middle road through the mountains at Sidi Nsir, to the Chouigui Pass which led down through Tebourba and into the capital. Col Hull's orders were to create 'a tank infested area' in the hills to the south-west of Chouigui, so that 78th Division's flanks were covered and it could concentrate on capturing Tunis and the port of Bizerta. As the move progressed, some American armoured units coming up from Oran might be available for support.

The advance of Blade Force was led by the armoured cars of the Derbyshire Yeomanry. The main body moved by road, but C Squadron of 17th/21st Lancers took a quicker route, moving as far forward as possible by train. The French in Algiers were reasonably cooperative and allowed their rolling stock to be used for the purpose. Two days after landing, Maj Val ffrench Blake had begun to organise C Squadron's move, overseeing the loading of the tanks onto flats in the rail sidings. When the task was complete it became clear to the major that the tanks would be all too obvious from the air. He decided that the loads would need to be camouflaged: 'I went to Army HQ in the evening to ask for hay-bales or tarpaulins to conceal the character of the loads. I found the staff at dinner by candlelight, and not interested in the problem. I availed myself of their loo, and left, having confirmed the value of the vow I had made myself, never to take a staff appointment until I had seen action. The attitude, "Pass the port, Brigadier, the troops have got their ground sheets," was still prevalent.'[1]

On 15 November, Col Hull's force from the Mailed Fist Division began its move, led by the armoured cars of the Derbyshire Yeomanry. That same day, C Squadron of 17th/21st Lancers left by train, the tanks loaded onto flats and the men in cattle trucks in the rear. Over the following days the remainder of Blade Force moved out as they became organised. The distance to be covered was too far for the tanks to complete driving on their tracks, so a detachment of 9th Tank Transporter Company had been included in the group, and B Squadron and Regimental Headquarters now left by road loaded on the trailers of the tank transporters.

The route ahead of Hull's battlegroup was not all enemy country. There were no German troops in Algeria and only a few in Tunisia at the time of the Torch invasion. Those Germans who were there were from rear echelons organising supplies for Rommel's forces who were engaging Montgomery much further east in Libya. Tunisia was under French control, administered by the Nazi-friendly regime at Vichy in France. Once the Allied landings had taken place in Algiers and Morocco, the Germans took over the country and the French Resident General in Tunis, Adm Estéva, obeyed instructions from Vichy HQ to put no obstacle in their way. Similarly, Adm Derrien in Bizerta allowed his 14,000 men to stand tamely by while the Germans seized the port. On the other hand, the Tunisian land force commander, Gen Barré, decided to hedge his bets and see how the invasion fared. He withdrew his forces from Tunis and Bizerta into the mountains and waited for the arrival of the Allies.

The Germans reacted to news of the landings with remarkable speed, seizing Tunisia's ports and airfields and rushing troops, tanks and aircraft across the Mediterranean to garrison the country. With systematic efficiency, they organised a force ready to confront the threat from the west. Hitler ordered that the bridgehead in Tunisia should be on as short a front as possible, making maximum use of defensible terrain. To guard Tunis, this 'defensible terrain' was the range of hills to the west of the capital, the very ones on which Blade Force was aiming to create 'a tank infested area'. The first German units to arrive in the country were directed on to these hills, and plans were made to fortify them. Of course Allied high command knew that the Germans would react in this way, but gambled on getting more troops ashore quicker than the enemy could, then seizing and holding Tunis before the Germans could take control. It was a very tall order and one that was lost almost before it began.

Throughout the war the Allies were to experience the ability of German commanders to improvise and move quickly when the occasion required them to do so. The Allies remained ponderous and slow, relying to a great extent on wishful thinking. The plan to seize Tunis relied on a main force of two infantry brigades, one independent armoured regimental group and a battalion of paratroopers, with virtually no air support and supply lines that stretched back 600 miles over land and thousands of miles over sea routes. In contrast, the Germans had to negotiate relatively short sea crossings from Italy and Sicily, protected all the way by aircraft, able to land their troops at Tunis and Bizerta and drive directly onto the battlefield. So it was not surprising that, in the three weeks following the invasion, the Germans managed to land 15,000 fighting troops, 100 tanks, 60 field guns and 30 antitank guns, and organise a makeshift corps, XC Corps, under the accomplished command of *General der Panzertruppe* Walther Nehring, before the Allies had even begun to gather a strike force in Tunisia.

The roads eastwards from Algiers were through olive groves and prosperous French farms. Dotted along the roadside were colonies of Arab huts, swarming with children, goats and mongrel dogs and, in the distance, the majestic snow-capped peaks of the Atlas mountains.[2] The force was travelling through a countryside as yet untouched by war and this tranquillity continued until well inside the Tunisian frontier.

When B Squadron of the Derbyshire Yeomanry arrived at Beja in their Humber armoured cars, they found that 1st Parachute Regiment had beaten them to the town. The paratroopers had dropped unopposed at nearby Setif to make contact with French forces and persuade them to join the Allied cause. The Paras were also ordered to carry out harassing operations to the east against any Germans who moved into the area. When the Derbyshire Yeomanry arrived their CO was requested to send a troop of armoured cars on to Medjez el Bab to support the French who were having a stand-off with German troops over the possession of the bridge there. At the time, Barré's French troops were still not in conflict with the enemy. However, on 19 November, with signs that the Allies were arriving in some force, the general declared himself for the Allies and within a short time the Germans attacked his forces at Medjez el Bab to secure the crossing over the River Medjerda.

This action closed the approach road to Tunis allocated to 11th Brigade of 78th Division and it became clear that the brigade would now have to fight its way through. It was vital that Blade Force quickly got up into the hills in the centre to outflank Medjez el Bab and to capture the Chouigui Pass, which led down to Tebourba, just 15 miles from Tunis. This would put them behind the Germans in Medjez el Bab. The paratroopers had already driven along this road as far as Sidi Nsir and captured a German patrol, but the area was still thought to be relatively free of the enemy.

German air activity was by this time also starting to make itself felt. Gen Nehring's forces had the use of good all-weather airfields with concrete runways around Tunis, a short distance from the leading British troops. The RAF and USAAF were operating out of landing strips hundreds of miles in the rear. By the time the Allied aircraft had reached the leading Allied units, their fuel levels were so low they could spend only minutes over the front. In contrast, the German Luftwaffe had several squadrons of Me 109 fighters and Stuka dive-bombers within a few miles of the front and were employing these aircraft aggressively wherever they could, carrying out bombing raids on Beja and Medjez el Bab and on vital road junctions, as well as attacking convoys and even individual transports along the roads. The closer Allied troops got to Tunis, the greater was the danger from German hit-and-run, low-level fighter sweeps.

Before Blade Force set out from its final concentration point at Souk el Arba, Col Hull had the good news that his battlegroup was being reinforced by the arrival of an American battalion of light Stuart tanks, known to the Americans as Honeys. Lt Col John Waters had brought his 1st Battalion of the US 1st Armoured Regiment all the way from Oran to join the British drive on Tunis. The Stuarts were armed with small 37mm guns which were similar to the 2-pounders of the Valentines.

By 25 November Blade Force had reached Beja and was continuing towards its first objective among the hills along the Tine valley, a road junction 10 miles south of Mateur and 5 miles west of the Chouigui Pass. Tracked vehicles took to the countryside while wheeled vehicles moved along the winding road through the hills past Sidi Nsir station. Lt Col Waters and his American Stuarts were ordered to move along the high ground to the right of the road and to make for the area of the Chouigui Pass. The 17th/21st Lancers, led by C Squadron, were on the left of the advance. Maj Val ffrench Blake recalls the move: 'The route, up a maze of shallow valleys, was not easy to find – several units subsequently lost the way on the same journey – but to my relief, the T-road junction appeared at the right moment, together with a message that 10th Rifle Brigade, who had come by the road, were in contact with the enemy in two farms overlooking the road junction.'[3]

The enemy position had been located earlier by the armoured cars of the Derbyshire Yeomanry who were scouting ahead of the main column. B Squadron had come under fire from an antitank gun and some infantry located in the two farms. They returned this fire with their Besa machine guns. Contact had now been made with the enemy and the Mailed Fist Division's first action was about to take place.

Two troops of the armoured cars kept up spasmodic fire on the enemy buildings while plans were made for the attack. It looked just like a problem from an exercise. The enemy were holed up in and around a farm to the right of the crossroads and were also holding another farm along a ridge away to the left. A plan of attack was formed: the buildings were to be shelled by C Battery of 12th RHA while B Company of the Rifle Brigade put in an infantry assault. The 17th/21st Lancers would sweep round either flank as required and shoot the riflemen in, just as they had done so many times during training. The exercises they had performed endlessly back in the UK were rehearsals for this event.

The attack started with an assault against the right-hand farm and the action opened with the field guns of 12th RHA's W Troop landing their third round in the farm among the enemy infantry. Further salvoes bracketed the farm buildings and smoke was laid by some of the Lancers' tanks to cover the assault.[4] The men of the Rifle Brigade were by then nearing the T-junction in carriers. They dismounted several hundred yards short of the junction and continued the approach on foot, advancing along the ditch parallel to the road. The artillery was now targeting the area around the farm and the building itself with plunging shellfire. Machine guns from the armoured cars were also raking the area. Maj ffrench Blake and his squadron of tanks now joined in the assault: 'I was ordered to attack and seize the farms. I sent two troops round the right flank, and, rather unwisely, sited myself on the road junction and was promptly bracketed by two shells from enemy artillery. I moved off smartly and the third shell fell exactly on the T-roads. One of my Crusaders was hit by a shell and had a track broken, so the driver kept going round and round in circles to avoid being hit again.'[5]

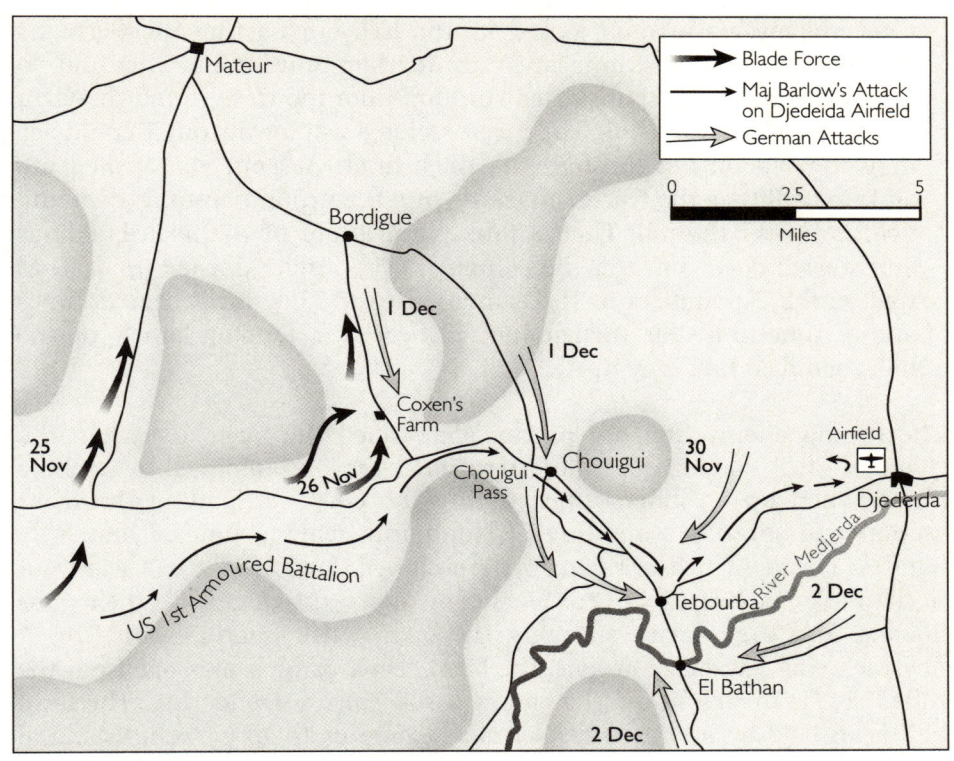

Map 2. Blade Force

Near the road junction the Rifle Brigade switched to an arrow formation and advanced on their objective, textbook style. The German defenders were now facing a set-piece attack from all angles: artillery fire pounded their positions; to their front, closing inexorably on the farm, was the steadfast approach of determined infantry; and to their rear, tanks were circling waiting to swoop. It was all too much for them. Their return fire stopped abruptly, to be replaced by 'a mass of fluttering white handkerchiefs. Then down the hill trooped sixty unhappy Italians, most of them disarmed and all clearly intent on surrender,' recalls Lt James Wilson of the Rifle Brigade.[6]

Maj ffrench Blake's tanks continued up the hill towards the second farm, and the leading Crusader rounded a hedge to find an Italian self-propelled gun turning the other corner about 70 yards away. The tank's gunner hit the enemy gun with his first 6-pounder shot, smashing its steering and killing the driver. The Crusader then drove past it and shot it from behind, seriously wounding the rest of the crew.[7] The other troop of tanks from C Squadron had by then got behind the left-hand farm and were on the ridge. Coming up the hill to attack the building was 7 Platoon of the Rifle Brigade, led by Lt Tony Naumann:

I got out my glasses and looked up the hill, hoping that the Germans would give their positions away by further movement. They did so rather unexpectedly, and started running from the trees round the farm up to the top of the hill. They were a long way away, but I could see they were labouring through the thick mud. A scout car opened fire and we could see the tracer smacking into the ground around them and flying off over the hill. Then a tank plunged out of the farm buildings and started down towards the column. A 6-pounder opened up at it, as well as the 2-pounders in the armoured cars. They hit it several times and it came to a stop, turned and crawled back, limping lamely up the hill, then died half way up.[8]

The fleeing enemy had not in fact abandoned the farm, for when the riflemen of 7 Platoon had almost reached the outbuildings, a machine gun opened up at short range, killing the corporal leading the front section and severely wounding Lt Naumann, leaving him permanently blind. For a moment the riflemen were pinned down and a call went out to the tanks for help. Two Crusaders came down the ridge with their guns blazing and their Besas spraying the farm with machine-gun fire. A haystack was set ablaze, as was the farm. Then came a message from the Rifle Brigade to stop firing: the enemy inside were surrendering. The farm had been held by a section of Germans, some of them parachutists, and they were more determined than the Italians to put up a fight. Some, however, had got away and Lt James Wilson watched through his field glasses as two Italian tanks made their escape along the road to Mateur. It had been a very successful action and spirits soared among those involved in the fighting as Lt Wilson relates: 'So easy had our triumph been that, despite 7 Platoon's misfortune, Sergeant Bert Coad and I felt we could have captured Mateur single-handed with just 6 Platoon (and a tank or two in support, of course).'[9]

This first action, completely successful with few casualties, gave Blade Force just the boost it needed to start the campaign. The haul from the action was 4 SP guns, about 100 Italians and 40 Germans, 2 good lorries and a great deal of equipment. B Squadron of the Lancers now pushed up the road towards Mateur. After two miles the leading tanks came up to an isolated farm and met the enemy. The tanks attacked immediately, firing into the farm with high explosive. Once again a stream of thirty Italian infantry came out readily, surrendering without a fight.

While this action was taking place, A Squadron of the Lancers had pushed on eastwards for five miles to another T-junction just before the Chouigui Pass. Here the tanks turned north in the direction of Mateur and were met with fire from a farm building on the right, later to be known as Coxen's Farm. An attack was put in by A Squadron. Its commander, Maj Strang Steel, later described the attack:

We moved round to the east to get on high ground, and the Valentine troops attacked the farm under covering fire from Squadron Headquarters, and what remained of the two Crusader troops (three tanks). The farm was properly shot up, a number of Germans killed, and six lorries set on fire, one of which went up with a big explosion. This silenced the enemy; all that was required was the infantry to go in and mop up the farm buildings. I was told by the CO that none were available. The squadron rallied north of the farm with three tanks left scattered about, ditched or bogged. While waiting for the infantry, a wave of Stukas came over three or four times. We thought each time we were 'for it', but the enemy in the farms, on seeing their own aircraft, each time sent up a stream of Verey lights which had the satisfying effect of bringing bombs down among themselves – while we stood back and watched.[10]

Without infantry the farm could not be cleared and the only infantry with Blade Force, 10th Rifle Brigade's B Company, were engaged back down the valley. The squadron therefore abandoned the attack, rescued its three bogged-down tanks and returned to regimental harbour for the night, leaving one of their number who had disappeared somewhere in the gathering darkness.

Over on the right of the advance the American 1st Battalion of 1st Armoured Regiment had also made contact with the enemy that day. Moving along rough goat tracks on the southern side of the Tine valley, the Stuarts had come up against a large farm surrounded by an impressive stone wall. Italian infantry were established in and around the compound and opened up on the light tanks with machine-gun fire. Lt Col Waters' armour made a swift assault on the buildings, circling the farm like Indians around a wagon train. Fire from their 37mm main weapons made little impression on the stone and concrete perimeter; machine-gun fire killed a few of the Italians but failed to provoke a surrender. Without infantry support the attack could not be pressed home to a conclusion and Waters pulled his battalion back down the valley.

Waters did not recall all his tanks into harbour after the attack, but sent C Company under Maj Rudolf Barlow further east to check out the Chouigui Pass and to reconnoitre the ground beyond. The light tanks made good going and reached the pass without incident. Once through the gap in the hills they descended on to a flat plain that led to Tunis 20 miles away. They left behind the rocky outcrops and bare hillsides of the Tine valley and motored along good roads meeting no resistance. They hurtled through orchards and orange groves of the fertile valley at speeds of up to 35 miles an hour, sweeping past surprised farmers and Arabs, but meeting none of the enemy. At Tebourba they swung around the village and drove southwards for a mile to check out the river crossing at El Bathan. At the bridge they surprised a party of Germans and dispersed them with a few rounds of well-aimed fire. When the action had died down, Maj Barlow discovered that he had taken possession of a crossing over the River Medjerda, 22 miles downstream of the heavily defended German bridge at Medjez el Bab. His swift advance had got his company deep behind the enemy line.

Flushed with his success and emboldened by his unopposed cavalry dash, Maj Barlow pushed his company on down the left bank of the Medjerda for 7 miles to the village of Djedeida. He was now just 9 miles from Tunis. While he deliberated on the route of his next bound forward, an enemy plane rose into the air a few hundred yards ahead of him from behind a ridge. The major ordered his tanks into the relative seclusion of an olive grove and sent a platoon ahead to reconnoitre the ground. Within minutes the platoon commander, Lt Hooker, came roaring back and excitedly told his commander that a German airfield lay on the other side of the ridge, packed with aircraft and seemingly undefended by sentries. The enemy were unaware of the American approach.

Maj Barlow radioed his news back to Lt Col Waters and was told to attack the airfield immediately. All seventeen Stuarts now made their way up to the ridge and, on a signal from the commander, crested the rise and swept down on the unsuspecting enemy. German fighters, bombers and dive-bombers lay dispersed in front of them, some taxiing for take-off, some being refuelled and rearmed and some standing idle between sorties. Once onto the airstrip the American tanks fanned out and roared down the runway, all guns blazing. The Messerschmitts and Stukas made easy targets; it was a killing ground of the most spectacular kind. Within a few minutes the airfield was covered with burning wrecks and exploding fuel tanks. A few aircraft tried to get airborne but were pulled back to earth in a hail of machine-gun fire, cartwheeling into the ground trailing smoke and streaming flame. Barlow's company attacked targets with impunity; one tank drove down a row of static aircraft shearing off their tails with its armoured turret. Once over the initial shock of the attack, some enemy managed to return fire and strafed the tanks with heavy machine guns and light cannon.

After half an hour of unbridled mayhem, Barlow pulled his tanks back off the airfield. Behind the ridge he checked his company and counted the cost of the action: one tank destroyed, several damaged and two men killed. Behind them at least twenty aircraft had been wrecked, scores of German bodies littered the runways, fuel bunkers were burning and ammunition dumps were exploding all across the blazing Luftwaffe station.[11] A few miles away in headquarters and operations rooms, enemy commanders were reaching a state of near panic. The Allies were almost at the gates of Tunis and the garrison at Medjez el Bab had been outflanked.

As the winter evening began to close in over the plain before Tunis, the light tanks of Barlow's company made their way back along the Medjerda valley, up over the Chouigui Pass and into safe harbour for the night with the rest of the battalion. It had been a good day; Blade Force had succeeded in carving out a tank-infested area as planned.

The next day, 26 November, Blade Force began to reap the whirlwind it had sown the day before. German forces were now well aware of its presence in the Tine valley and reacted accordingly. While breakfast was being cooked among the dispersed tanks and dug-in infantry the first air attack of the day came in. Six Me 109s swept down the valley and strafed the tanks and their support vehicles. These attacks continued spasmodically throughout the day and those that followed. The Luftwaffe had almost total command of the sky and Blade Force was to see a good deal more of its aircraft as the campaign progressed.

The American attack on the airfield at Djedeida and the temporary capture of the bridge at El Bathan had certainly worried Gen Nehring. He complained bitterly to his superior *Generalfeldmarschall* Albert Kesselring, German C-in-C Mediterranean, that the Allies were virtually at the gates of Tunis and he had little with which to stop them. Kesselring told him to be calm and to hold firm, assuring him that the Allies were inclined to be cautious and rarely made bold tactical gambles.[12] Nonetheless, Nehring decided to reduce his perimeter and to concentrate his sparse forces closer to Tunis. He ordered Medjez el Bab to be given up and the forces there to be withdrawn to Tebourba and the next bridge lower down the River Medjerda at El Bathan. He also pulled back men and tanks from the positions to the west of Mateur.

This contraction of the German line allowed the two brigades of 78th Division to move further along their line of advance. The sound of the bridge at Medjez el Bab being blown was heard by 11th Brigade; when they sent patrols into the town, the enemy had gone. Maj Gen Evelegh then ordered 11th Brigade to advance down the Medjerda valley and make for Tunis through Tebourba. The move met no opposition, and 1st East Surreys made it to Tebourba without loss. The next day they were counterattacked by infantry and tanks.

In the north 36th Brigade set out from Djebel Aboid along the road to Mateur. In the afternoon, just west of Jefna, its leading battalion, 8th Argyll and Sutherland Highlanders, had to pass through a gap between two high hills, later named Green and Bald Hills. Here they were ambushed by German Luftwaffe troops under the command of a brilliant young paratroop engineer officer, Maj Witzig, hero of the storming of the Belgian fort of Eben Emael in 1940. Witzig's paratroopers stopped 36th Brigade's advance dead and threw it back with considerable losses. These two hills then became the northern front line, past which no Allied troops were to venture for many months.

GenFM Kesselring was quite right when he reassured Nehring that it was not in the Allies' nature to do anything spectacular. Maj Gen Evelegh, backed by Lt Gen Anderson, had chosen to continue the advance on Tunis with his force split into three groups. The tactical opportunity which arose with Maj Barlow's raid with light tanks was never exploited, nor was it even considered worth exploiting. It was too late to change an inflexible plan at that stage. The decision to dilute the forces available for an advance along three routes had been made long before. The Napoleonic maxim of always concentrating force ready to make a blow of maximum strength had been ignored. Evelegh's command was split into penny packets to probe the enemy in several places, each hoping to make a breakthrough, even though such a breakthrough could not be exploited with any strength.

Blade Force continued this probing the next day, with the American 1st Armoured Battalion returning to the Chouigui Pass and 17th/21st Lancers pushing up the two roads that led from the Tine valley towards Mateur. Both once again bumped into the enemy, the most violent clash being near Coxen's Farm on the easternmost road. Here on 26 November the Lancers received word that Lt Col Waters's tanks were being engaged by German armour. C Squadron was sent to help, advancing eastwards towards a column of black smoke.

A troop of 25-pounder field guns from 12th RHA was also sent in support but the column was hit by Stuka dive-bombers and its towing vehicles were knocked out. Now immobilised, the guns tried to go into action where they remained, but found that they were unable to reach the limit of C Squadron's advance.

The Americans had engaged a strong column of tanks and infantry pushing down the road from Mateur which passed close to Coxen's Farm. Three German companies including tanks from 190th Panzer Regiment were moving southwards to reinforce the troops in Tebourba. Lt Col Waters's 75mm assault guns mounted on armoured half-tracks had opened up on the Germans with little effect, but had received accurate enemy fire in return. While the enemy was being engaged by these guns, the CO of 1st Armoured Battalion dispersed his companies for the attack.

The first German–American tank battle of the Second World War was a David-and-Goliath struggle. The light Stuart tanks were attacking a formidable enemy, for as chance would have it, some Panzer IVs among the German armour sported the new 75mm, long-barrel gun. With a muzzle velocity double that of the guns on the American tanks, these Panzer IV 'Specials' had twice the range and twice the penetrating power. Not only could the Germans engage the Americans at a range beyond the reach of their Honeys, but at closer quarters the Panzer IVs were seemingly invincible.

The US 1st Armoured Battalion attacked the enemy from the right flank. Closing to just a few hundred yards in a mad charge, twelve Stuarts from Maj Siglin's A Company engaged the enemy with their puny 37mm main guns. At such range they couldn't miss, but their shells just bounced off the front plates of the Panzer IVs. One Italian armoured car was hit and burst into flames. Then the German tanks replied and the long barrels of the Panzer IVs swept in a menacing arc to lock on to individual targets. The flames that erupted from the muzzles were immediately followed by a deep roar and just a few hundred yards away an American tank flared like a volcano. Lt Freeland Daubin later described the violent deaths of these vulnerable Stuarts as German shells slapped into them: 'Long searing tongues of flame erupted from every hatch of the shattered tank and silver rivulets of aluminium puddled beneath the engine block. Sparks spouted from the barrel as ammunition began to cook. Thick black smoke boiled from the burning rubber tracks and bogey wheels.'[13] In ten minutes of battle, six of the Stuarts had been destroyed.

It was then that Col Waters sprang his trap. While the German armour had been engaging A Company to their front, B Company had been manoeuvring behind a ridge to the panzers' left. This company, led by Maj Tuck, now hit the flanks of the enemy at just 100 yards' range. At that distance even the diminutive 37mm armour-piercing shot that they fired could not fail to penetrate the thin sides and engine covers of the German tanks. Taken completely by surprise, the Germans reacted too late. The twelve American tanks fired a barrage of solid iron at the enemy just as fast as the loaders could service their guns. The enemy tried to wheel around to engage them, but the Americans had beaten them to the draw. Dozens of rounds slammed into the German tanks and it was their turn to face annihilation. Seven Panzer IVs were knocked out, including six of the new long-barrelled 'specials'. The remainder took flight, roaring down the valley and through the pass on to Chouigui and Tebourba, pursued by some Stuarts nipping at their heels.

Two of the surviving German tanks and all of the supporting infantry withdrew back up the Mateur road, some taking refuge in Coxen's Farm. The Americans attacked them at once, charging through the gates and machine-gunning anything that moved. But here they were vulnerable to the German infantry and they withdrew, continuing to chase and attack those of the enemy who were making an escape northwards.

It was about this time that the Lancers joined the Americans. They were asked to help clear the enemy from Coxen's Farm. They attacked down the valley of the River Tine and approached the farm from its left flank. At a range of about 1,000 yards, the two troops of Valentines took up hull-down positions on a hill and engaged the Germans with their machine guns. Then the troop of Crusaders came forwards with their 6-pounder guns. They, too, joined in the battle but got a little too far forward and two Crusaders were hit right through the mantlet by enemy tank fire. It was amazingly accurate shooting by the enemy from 1,000 yards, another example of the potency of the new Panzer IV 'specials'. The Lancers and the Americans shot up the farm and machine-gunned the enemy, but once again lacked the infantry necessary to take the position. Both groups later withdrew up the valley to harbour for the night, towing out their damaged tanks behind them. The Americans had done well in this their first battle, accounting for eight tanks for the loss of fifteen of their own. The numbers might seem to show just the opposite, but considering that it was light tanks with 37mm guns against medium tanks with 75mm 'specials', it was surprising that the score did not read 15–nil.

Twice in two days, Coxen's Farm – overlooking the Mateur road – had been there for the taking, except there had been no infantry available to seize it. This was at last rectified when 1st Parachute Regiment was sent down the Tine valley to join Blade Force. The next day, 27 November, the farm was raided again by 17th/21st Lancers with paratroopers in support. They found the buildings abandoned. The enemy had given up the position and withdrawn up the Mateur road to new positions around a farm at Bordjgue. The mixed force of tanks and paratroopers attacked this new strong point, but were driven off by a powerful 88mm gun and dug-in infantry. This heavy antitank gun outranged the Valentines by several thousand yards.

The next day all was quiet in the Tine valley, for the focus of attention had been shifted over to the Medjerda valley about Tebourba. The 11th Brigade was in possession of the village and had pushed troops almost as far as Djedeida only to meet fierce enemy resistance and an armoured counterattack. Gen Nehring had pulled his forces back from Medjez el Bab, shortened his line around Tunis and put a defensive line in front of Djedeida. The next day he was visited in Tunisia by GenFM Kesselring. The C-in-C did not approve of the moves and implied that Nehring had overreacted. He ordered him to push the British back from Tebourba and enlarge the Tunis bridgehead at least to its original position. Kesselring reassured Nehring that more troops were to arrive through Bizerta and Tunis daily and Axis strength was beginning to outstrip that of the Allies before the capital. Also available for immediate use were the advance units of *Generalmajor* Fischer's 10th Panzer Division.

GenMaj Fischer's division was being enlarged by the attachment of four 'Marsch' battalions and a variety of guns. The plan was to split the force into four battlegroups for the operation: 'Hudel', 'Lüder', 'Koch' and 'Djedeida', and to create enveloping movements against the British 11th Brigade and Blade Force. Battlegroup Hudel would attack the British around Chouigui with forty tanks and then join Lüder with its twenty tanks and move on Tebourba from the north-west. Battlegroup Koch would attack El Bathan from the south-east and then move down the Medjerda valley to eliminate the rear areas of 11th Brigade. Battle group Djedeida, with the bulk of the German infantry, would attack 11th Brigade head-on down the Tunis road. The attack was planned for 1 December with all available units of the division which had thus far arrived in the capital.

The 11th Brigade had reached Tebourba on 28 November. Its leading battalion, 1st Surreys, were told to hold the village and the bridge at El Bathan. However, even before it had got itself established, the battalion was attacked by the hastily formed Battlegroup Lüder and, although it successfully beat off the enemy, it incurred some losses in the process. The 5th Northamptons had then twice tried to advance further east on Djedeida, supported by a few American tanks from 2nd Battalion of 13th Armoured Regiment, but each time had received a bloody rebuff from the Lüder group. The Northamptons had then been withdrawn and replaced by 2nd Hampshires of 1st Guards Brigade, who arrived just in time to withstand an enemy attack on 30 November.

Maj Gen Evelegh, commander of 78th Division, now gathered his strength and paused for two days to be ready for a final push on Tunis. He planned a new attack, with 2nd Parachute Regiment dropping at Dipienne to attack the enemy landing ground at Oudna and then linking up with Blade Force to support an armoured thrust on Tunis. The 11th Brigade would then strike down the Tebourba–Djedeida–Tunis road for the capital. In preparation for this attack, Evelegh told Col Hull to withdraw 17th/21st Lancers to the west of Tebourba, leaving its C Squadron in the Tine valley with 1st Parachute Regiment to hold that flank. Evelegh's well-laid plans, however, were not put into effect, for his arrangements were interrupted on 1 December by an enemy attack.

Guarding 11th Brigade's northern flank was B Company of 10th Rifle Brigade. It was dug into a defensive arc just south of Chouigui, blocking the road to Tebourba from the north. In support were B Squadron of the Derbyshire Yeomanry, A Battery of 72nd Antitank Regiment and Lt Col Waters' American Stuarts. They had occupied the position since just before dawn; a few hours later, this flank guard was disturbed by the noise of moving tanks. Trundling down a track from Mateur came part of Battlegroup Hudel, with twelve tanks and some motorised infantry; at the head of the group was GenMaj Fischer himself. First to spot the Germans were the armoured cars of the Derbyshire Yeomanry, who, immediately outgunned by a massive margin, withdrew through the Rifle Brigade's defences. From their dug-in position the riflemen watched in horror and fascination as the enemy tanks deployed in front of them from line ahead to a shallow V-shaped battle formation, able to bring all of their guns to bear simultaneously on Blade Force.

The Germans had little artillery with them for they were depending on the assistance of much heavier support from the Luftwaffe; only a few shells whined overhead towards the riflemen. At about 1,500 yards short of the British line, the tanks halted and took up 'hull-down' positions behind a low rise. Here they waited, unmolested by the American Stuarts at a range too great for their 2-pounder guns. The wait was not a long one, for the pause in the advance was to allow aircraft to soften up the target. Soon a dozen Stukas flew in from the east and circled overhead. Targets identified, they came screaming down one after the other to drop bombs on the static trenches and tanks of Blade Force.

By this time 17th/21st Lancers had been called forward into the battle from their maintenance area. Once the air raid had passed the enemy tanks continued forward, drawing fire from the Americans and from the first of the Lancers who had moved up in support. It was the same old story, a flash from the enemy guns and a Valentine, Crusader or Stuart burst into flames. C Battery of 12th RHA now trained their 25-pounder guns on the enemy and opened fire. Forward Observation Officers from 78th Division came into position and passed ranges and bearings back to 132nd Field Regiment's guns in Tebourba for them to join in the shoot. Before long the 3.7in howitzers of 457th Light Battery RA located in the Tebourba Gap were lobbing shells onto the enemy. From the flanks, 6-pounder antitank fire from Blade Force's 72nd Antitank Regiment flared across the battlefield to join the 2-pounder fire from 10th Rifle Brigade's own antitank guns. Determined stuff, but not very effective. Fischer urged his battlegroup onwards.

B Squadron and RHQ of the Lancers advanced to meet the enemy. Five of their tanks were quickly knocked out one after the other. The position of the infantry blocking the road was quickly recognised as being untenable against such a force. B Company of 10th Rifle Brigade was told to withdraw while the antitank guns and tanks held off the enemy. Lt Bliss, 17th/21st Lancers' Intelligence Officer, described the action of his tank and that of Maj Dugdale – second in command of the regiment – in the battalion history.

> Just in front of me Nigel Dugdale is blazing away with his two-pounder, but I'm damned if I can spot his target. We'll go and have a better look. 'Driver advance.' The whole tank shudders and a red flame seems to shoot out from the front. For a moment I think my gunner has started firing without orders, and I curse him through the intercom. 'We've been hit, sir' – it's the driver's voice in my 'phones. 'OK, can you reverse? – get turret down – halt.' At the same time, Nigel's tank is hit and three figures bale out of the turret. They climb on the front of the tank, evidently trying to extricate the driver. Some HE comes down and all three are blown off the tank, but they're up and have another go. Some more HE, and this time one of the figures doesn't rise. The other two bend over him and then come running back. Nigel's face is streaming with blood and I haul out our first aid box. 'Are you OK?' I ask. 'Yes, but Dawson and Flanagan are killed. Turret's jammed, transmission jammed, we couldn't get Dawson out of the cab.'[14]

Alongside the Lancers the US 1st Armoured Battalion fought the enemy with its Stuarts. Neither unit could stop the attack, for even as they bravely fired their ineffectively small guns at the larger tanks the scales tipped further against them. From the north-east, Battlegroup Lüder now came on the scene, joining Fischer's group with another twenty tanks. Even more armour was at that time coming down the road from Mateur past Coxen's Farm and running headlong into 1st Parachute Regiment and C Squadron of the Lancers. Twenty more tanks of Battlegroup Hudel advanced along this road into a barrage of fire from a nearby field battery of 12th RHA. Two tanks were knocked out and the remainder swung across the hills to their left to work their way around to join the attack on Tebourba.

With no hope of victory, all of Blade Force drew back, carrying out a fighting withdrawal in the face of an inexorable enemy force. Among those of the Rifle Brigade heading for the rear was Lt James Wilson. He was trying to extricate his No. 6 Platoon: 'The riflemen as usual reacted superbly when it came to quick movement; soon we were all in the dead ground behind our ridge, jumping on our trucks like a load of football supporters leaving a lost match. Thank God, too, I had remembered my training; the trucks were parked facing the exit, so we could drive straight out of our area and on to the Tebourba road. We bumped agonisingly over the rough field between us and the tarmac, followed by our antitank guns; once on the firm surface Rifleman Gough and the others put their feet down. It had been a near thing. As we drove into Tebourba we passed a 5.5 inch medium gun, sighted to fire down the road in an antitank role.'[15]

Not all the riflemen got out: 8 Platoon had been overrun by a Panzer III accompanied by a group of *panzergrenadiers*. The road back to Tebourba was quickly filled with lorries, armoured cars and tanks escaping from the German onslaught. Lt Wilson thought that the retreat was so headlong as to constitute a rout. In the village itself all was chaos, for another German battlegroup was also attacking the area from the east. Battlegroup Djedeida had attacked 2nd Hampshires on the eastern side of Tebourba with infantry and tanks and was steadily forcing them back. Battlegroup Koch was driving down the Medjerda valley against 1st East Surreys in El Bathan. Koch's tanks could not break through their line so they veered to the south and headed for the Medjez road, attempting to pinch off this escape route to the rear at a narrow defile called the Tebourba Gap.

When Blade Force arrived west of Tebourba they found that they had entered an area almost under siege; German forces were everywhere. Battlegroups Hudel and Lüder had followed the retreating units down the road and had virtually surrounded the village. The Derbyshire Yeomanry were chased by enemy tanks and had to take them on with their 2-pounder guns to allow their support transport to withdraw towards

Medjez. Their battalion history describes the scene: 'For a brief moment the situation looked nearly in hand, then SSM Perry, who was withdrawing with our soft vehicles, came on the air to report that the road behind us had been cut and was under heavy fire from rifles and machine guns. All traffic was stopped and some lorries were burning. It looked as though the enemy tanks had only to come on for all of us to be in the bag.'[16]

Pte Laverack of 11th Field Ambulance RAMC was on that road dealing with a wounded American and remembers the action: 'We were dressing the Yank's stomach when all hell broke loose. All around us men were running down the road shouting, "Jerry is behind us." We had to stay put to deal with the wounded man, but an American Jeep came alongside us and took us off at great speed.'[17] Panic began to take hold when German tanks got to within 500 yards of 11th Brigade's HQ. The road through the gap soon became full of vehicles streaming westwards out of the way of the advancing German armour.

In Tebourba, the Hampshires, the Surreys and the support guns from 78th Division were also in danger of being cut off. Fighting there went on for most of the day without the enemy being able to break through the British perimeter. As gaps started to open they were closed down by artillery and antitank fire. Pressure on the defences from the German tanks and infantry gradually increased and the line inevitably began to shrink. In one orchard on the northern flank all eight guns of a battery of 132nd Field Regiment were knocked out, the last 25-pounder succumbing to a Panzer IV at 20 yards' range. In the late afternoon the Germans withdrew, unable to break through the British line.

Those units of Blade Force that had regrouped were concentrated outside Tebourba along the road back to Medjez, just in front of the Tebourba Gap. Here the remaining tanks of 17th/21st Lancers, just five Crusaders and eleven Valentines, were sited as antitank guns, scattered among the infantry and armoured cars to form a roadblock in front of the gap. The next day Combat Command B of the US 1st Armoured Division moved up to help in the defence of Tebourba. Its Grant tanks came forward into the area to the south-west of the village and were in action against another attack by 10th Panzer Division. Once again the enemy sent in battlegroups of tanks and infantry to break the British hold on Tebourba and once again the Hampshires and East Surreys fought with unbelievable determination. Inevitably, the perimeter shrank even more and the list of casualties rose higher and higher. Several sorties by the Lancers went into Tebourba and El Bathan to harass the German positions and to help relieve the pressure on the infantry, each time losing a few more tanks to enemy fire.

German armour broke through to the Medjez road a number of times and almost made it into the Tebourba Gap, but each time they were flung back by tank, antitank and artillery fire. On 3 December the Tebourba position had become hopeless. Those elements of Blade Force that had survived were ordered back far in the rear to Oued Zarga for refitting and replenishment. In Tebourba itself the fighting went on. The order for withdrawal was given, but so closely were the Hampshires engaged by the enemy that they found it almost impossible to draw back. Behind them, 11th Brigade HQ and the forces holding open the gap withdrew. Then the East Surreys began to pull out, but the Hampshires fought on. In a heroic, but ultimately senseless, counterattack, Maj Le Patourel won the Victoria Cross trying to clear the enemy from an important hill feature. The Commanding Officer of the Hampshires, Lt Col Lee, ordered his men to fall back into the centre of Tebourba. When they got there they found everyone had gone; they had been abandoned. The road back to Medjez had been cut by the enemy and Lee's troops were isolated. The CO gave orders for his men to break through the German cordon individually and make their own way back to Medjez el Bab. It was each man for himself. Two days later, just 194 men reported back to the British lines out of the 800 who had entered Tebourba a few days before.[18]

Back in the Tine valley, C Squadron of 17th/21st Lancers was still supporting the paratroopers holding the two roads that led south from Mateur. On 1 December the group had been attacked by part of Battlegroup Hudel and clashes with German armour occurred throughout the day. On 2 December the positions in the Tine valley were reinforced by the arrival of the infantry of 2nd Lancashire Fusiliers from 11th Brigade. Over the next few days, the tank/infantry force consolidated their hold on the roads from Mateur and the route leading up to the Chouigui Pass, fighting sporadic skirmishes with local German forces. The remainder of the Lancers came up to rejoin C Squadron on 4 December to strengthen Blade Force's hold on the area.

On 6 December, after assisting 1st Parachute Regiment and 2nd Lancashire Fusiliers withstand another German attack against the T-junction, Blade Force was withdrawn to Munchar and disbanded. Col Hull's force had been in continual contact with the enemy for twelve days. The situation on First Army's front had stabilised somewhat after the Germans had driven down the Medjerda valley from Tebourba and been stopped by a firm Anglo-American defence line before Medjez el Bab. More of the British follow-up troops had been landed and were now moving up the line. Their task completed, the units of Blade Force now looked to be reunited with the rest of 6th Armoured Division.

Chapter Three

BOU ARADA

A month after the invasion of North Africa the focus of Eisenhower's Allied forces had shifted to Tunisia. The troops who had landed in Morocco and Algeria were now concentrating along a line stretching north–south down the eastern side of the country. French forces had joined the British and Americans to hold this front. In many places 'front' was too important a word for what was in reality a loose line covered by patrols and reconnaissance units, with hundreds of miles of open territory still devoid of any troops from either side. This state of affairs would gradually change over the coming months as more divisions were shipped across from the USA and from Britain. The enemy's hold on Tunisia would tighten, too, as Rommel continued his long retreat from Egypt and pulled his armies into the Tunisian battlefield.

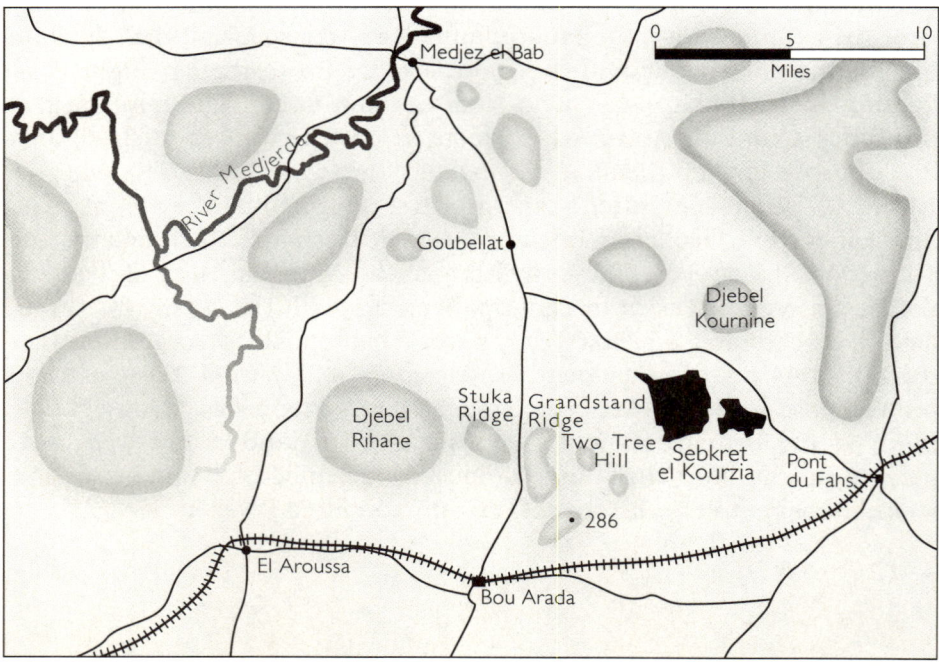

Map 3. Bou Arada

When the whole of 6th Armoured Division had finally arrived with First Army in late December 1942, V Corps was activated under the command of Lt Gen Allfrey. The corps included 6th Armoured and 78th Divisions. Lt Gen Anderson could now contemplate launching another effort to capture Tunis. The first attempts made by Blade Force and 78th Division did not have enough weight behind them and they ran out of steam in the face of increasing German resistance. The arrival of a full armoured division and the increased participation of the Americans led Eisenhower and Anderson to believe that a thrust on Tunis by this more powerful force might now be successful. Such optimism was, however, misplaced, for two factors now conspired to frustrate the move, both of which were beyond the Allied commanders' control.

First, the winter weather had set in and December brought with it heavy and prolonged rainfall, which turned all off-road terrain into liquid mud. Second, the enemy had reinforced his forces in Tunisia at a faster rate than the Allies. The result was that First Army was faced with a more powerful opponent than they expected, in a period when the state of the ground did not favour the attacker. 'Mud was everywhere,' wrote the Lothians' historian. 'Great, ponderous clods of it adhered to boots. It caked and dried on trouser legs and gaiters. In tank turrets it gathered on floors, smothered the rear ammunition racks and stuck to the seats. Not even our bedding could escape it.' [1]

In late December, Lt Gen Allfrey was ordered to mount an attack towards Tunis with V Corps from the Medjez area. In this operation, 6th Armoured Division was to strike from the low ground to the east of Medjez through Massicault towards the capital. Prior to this move, the Battleaxe Division would assault up the Medjerda valley towards Tebourba, supported by the Americans.

The 78th Division began the battle on 22 December in driving rain, with the high ground of Longstop Hill, overlooking the Tebourba road, its first objective. The 2nd Coldstream took the hill the next day and 1st Battalion of the US 18th Regiment then came forward to take over the position, only to lose it almost immediately to a German counterattack. The Coldstream were recalled and ordered to return to Longstop to seize the hill again from the enemy. By this time both sides realised that Longstop had a greater significance than first thought. It was a key position overlooking the Medjerda valley and the enemy was desperate to keep it under his control. The Coldstream attacked and regained the feature, but lost it soon afterwards in a counterattack of even greater force than the first. By that time, days of continual rain had reduced the ground to a quagmire, which made further operations impossible. The armoured attack towards Tunis was called off and both Eisenhower and Anderson realised that a further major attack could not now be launched until the end of the winter.

The Allies in Tunisia were now confined to a programme of defence, forced to spend a long winter jostling for position with the enemy, preventing him from seizing territory or engineering a breakthrough, while they themselves gained good ground from which to mount a strong offensive when the weather improved. Within just six weeks of the invasion, the Allies had been forced into a stalemate. The armoured division had arrived on a battleground that had a great need for infantry, but had little immediate use for an armoured strike force.

Once the Germans had stabilised their line in front of Tunis, they strengthened the lightly held ground to the south by shifting 10th Panzer Division beyond Pont du Fahs. Anderson met this threat by ordering Keightley to extend his division's line southwards into the open terrain beyond Goubellat to link up with the French corps about Bou Arada. The first units of the division to move were 38th (Irish) Brigade and 17th/21st Lancers. Other units followed later. To help bolster the poorly armed French troops beyond Bou Arada, two troops of armoured cars from the Derbyshire Yeomanry, a troop of antitank guns from 72nd Antitank Regiment and a troop of Bofors guns from 51st Light Antiaircraft Regiment RA were detached to assist Gen Barré's corps.

The area south of Medjez was semi-desert although it had been very fertile land in the time of the Romans. The decline was due in part to the climate and in part, as Maj John Horsfall of 1st Royal Irish Fusiliers later remarked, on the neglect of the Berber inhabitants.[2] Below Goubellat was a wide-open plain which ended with a row of hills just before Bou Arada. Further south from here were more hills, some of great height, held by very light French forces.

The Irish Brigade now moved into positions on the Goubellat plain. The vast area of ground to be covered dictated that a great number of infantry and tanks would be needed to occupy it completely. Since such resources were unavailable, the company of the Irish Brigade that was holding each area would have to operate as an individual battlegroup and contain the opposition by a simple show of strength, even if there was nothing behind it to back it up. 'The area assigned to us was too large to hold in safety at night and we stood off in any farm buildings that were available,' noted Maj John Horsall of 1st London Irish.[3] Patrols were sent out to find just where the enemy were. Initially, all was peace and the patrols probed eastwards across the plain without finding a sign of human activity, enemy or otherwise.

During the daytime the companies just lay up in the buildings out of sight and studied the vast, rolling plain around them. It seemed to Maj Horsfall that there was enough cover to his front in the middle distance to conceal an enemy division, and in the background there was a series of rolling ridges on the far side of the plain that could shield even more. These were the effective limits to his vision. It would be nice, he thought, to know just who was the other side of the hills.[4]

On the other side of those hills was, as expected, the enemy and as the Irish Brigade held one side of the plain, the Germans moved across on to the other. Within a few days they came into view, probing forward and establishing defences of the same style as the British – strung along the foothills, widely spaced and thinly held. Ground which could have been easily taken a few days before if sufficient troops had been available would now have to be fought for.

The enemy began to establish himself under the watchful eyes of the Irishmen, seemingly oblivious to their presence. More patrols were sent out by 38th Brigade to glean information about who was holding the German line and what his strength was. Some of these patrols were successful, some not; some passed off without incident while others developed into fire-fights. One such patrol managed to capture an enemy prisoner and it was learned that the area was being reinforced ready for an attack. Lt Col Pat Scott, commander of 1st Irish Fusiliers, realised that his battalion's widely spaced positions would be vulnerable and their best defence would be to remain mobile so that the enemy could not identify any fixed targets. He also decided to get his blow in first and attack the enemy before they were too well established, just to let them know who was in control of the area.

The next morning B and D Companies moved out over the open ground. For most of the men it was their first action. Very soon they came under fire from German outposts, but the screen of enemy troops defending them soon took flight as the Irishmen pressed resolutely forward. A short distance ahead the main German line opened up on the Irish troops, criss-crossing the low scrub with machine-gun fire. Just as though on an exercise the attacking infantry went to cover, then edged forward firing back, raking the enemy positions with their own counter-fire. It was too much for the Germans; most of them picked up their weapons and retired, moving a mile back up into the hills, spurred on their way by shells from the guns of the Ayrshire Yeomanry. 'It was only the briefest fire fight,' recalls Maj Horsfall, 'but our fusiliers knew they had won it.'[5]

With these small-scale attacks things had changed. The Irish Brigade could no longer be left on the flat valley floor vulnerable to sudden enemy counterattack. German reaction to its presence would inevitably mean that action would be taken against its widely dispersed positions. The three battalions were now pulled back westwards on to the hills that overlooked the plain.

During that first week in January, the area around Bou Arada to the south of the Irish Brigade was still devoid of Germans. The 15 miles of road from Goubellat to Bou Arada was frequently patrolled by the armoured cars of the Derbyshire Yeomanry, who kept watch to ensure that it was still free of the enemy. Bou Arada itself was originally held by a small French outpost until the first week in January, when 10th Rifle Brigade took control, with 17th/21st Lancers and two batteries of 12th RHA in support. The village was an important crossroads and was dominated by a number of hills all around it. The local French knew the tactical significance of Bou Arada and its importance was now impressed on the British, for it became the southern outpost of V Corps's front. The Rifle Brigade sent patrols out each night along the road towards Pont du Fahs and occupied observation points (OPs) on the surrounding hills by day. The area towards German-occupied territory was overlooked by a high feature a few miles to the north-east of the village. A daily watch was kept by a scout car of the Derbyshire Yeomanry perched near the top of this hill, supported by a picket of riflemen. This excellent OP gave a commanding view across the Goubellat plain almost to the sea. On its summit were two lone pines and they gave rise to its name – Two Tree Hill.

On 10 January the men occupying Two Tree Hill were surprised to see a great column of vehicles moving quickly towards them from the north-east. It soon became clear that a whole battalion of the enemy were set on occupying the hill. The picket withdrew and raised the alarm, but it was too late to stop the move and Two Tree Hill fell to the Germans without a fight. No sooner had the hill been lost than Gen Keightley decided that he wanted it back again, for the feature overlooked all other hills in the immediate area, dominated the roads from Bou Arada to Goubellat and Pont du Fahs and had a command of the village itself. However, before this could be organised, worse was to come when the enemy continued westwards, crossed the Goubellat–Bou Arada road and began occupying the string of hills on either side. By then they were beginning to overstretch themselves and A Company of 10th Rifle Brigade, supported by A Squadron of 17th/21st Lancers, drove them off their forward posts and pushed them back over the road towards Two Tree Hill before they could become established.

The next day an attempt was made to recapture the feature, this time with D Company of the Rifle Brigade and C Squadron of the Lancers. The riflemen were carried as far as possible into the attack on the back of the tanks with the intention that they would dismount as soon as the armour came under fire. The tanks would then assault the hill with the infantry following behind. None of this worked out according to plan for the approaches to Two Tree Hill were littered with natural antitank obstacles and the hill itself was too steep for the armour to climb. The tanks then became the targets of concealed 50mm antitank guns and the infantry were pinned down by heavy fire. Into all of this confusion the enemy launched their own counterattack with about two companies of infantry. This was beaten off by fire from the Lancers' Valentines. Eventually it became clear that the attack against the hill was going nowhere and, under cover of smoke, the infantry and tanks withdrew towards Bou

Arada, fortunately having suffered only fairly light casualties and two tanks damaged.

It was clear that the arrival of German troops close by Bou Arada threatened not only the southern flank of First Army, but the whole of its line. An enemy breakthrough here would get behind the British front and then be able to roll it up from south to north. Anderson ordered Lt Gen Allfrey to move the whole of 6th Armoured Division further southwards to create a firm bastion about Bou Arada and to remove the enemy from the hills above the village. To do this he needed more infantry, so the Irish Brigade was now gradually shifted southwards to the area to the east of the Goubellat–Bou Arada road along a ridge which faced across part of the valley floor towards Two Tree Hill. The long escarpment had a good view of the German positions and was not surprisingly named Grandstand Ridge. Brig Nelson Russell established the Royal Irish Fusiliers along the ragged escarpment, kept the London Irish in reserve and warned 6th Inniskilling Fusiliers to prepare to launch yet another frontal attack against Two Tree Hill.

The new attack was similar to the previous two efforts save that it was to be a battalion action supported by 17th/21st Lancers. The assault was also to have the backing of the whole of the divisional artillery, which was now all concentrated around Bou Arada.

Just arrived with the Lancers were three new Grant tanks. The Grants were a departure for British armoured units as they were built in the United States. They were armed with a variety of weapons, their main gun being a sponson-mounted 75mm piece on the right-hand side of the tank. This gun had a much greater punch than any of the weapons in a British tank, able to fire a good-sized high-explosive shell or a solid armour-piercing shot, but its fixed position next to the driver gave it a very limited traverse. In the turret was a 37mm gun, together with a 0.5in Browning machine gun which was supplied primarily for antiaircraft use. It also carried two 0.3in machine guns. The tank had a very high profile which Maj Val ffrench Blake of 17th/21st Lancers likened to a wedding cake, with its main weapon on the ground floor, a turret with 37mm gun at the next level and an antiaircraft Browning on the top. The Grant towered above the desert floor when going into the attack.

The operation to take Two Tree Hill by 6th Inniskilling Fusiliers has been heavily criticised, not for the way the battalion carried out its orders, for the 'Skins' attacked with much bravery and determination, but for the fact that it was ordered in the first place. The Irishmen were asked to assault a position that had been heavily fortified and reinforced by the enemy, who were a little quicker than the British in realising the strategic significance of the hill. Two previous frontal attacks over ground impassable to armour had failed to close on the summit and dislodge a weaker garrison; it was not clear why this renewed attack would be any more successful. Even if the hill were captured, it would be unlikely that the Inniskillings could hold it against an inevitable counterattack backed by the German armour which was known to be in the rear.

The 6th Inniskilling Fusiliers' assault on Two Tree Hill began on 13 January and was backed by the whole of 6th Armoured Division's artillery. In support were Maj ffrench Blake's C Squadron, which included the three Grant tanks. In the face of withering enemy machine-gun fire and plunging shells from German guns behind the hill, the 'Skins' advanced across the valley floor and on to the forward slopes of Two Tree Hill. Here they were held up by some German machine guns in a stone hut. A few HE rounds from ffrench Blake's Grants brought the Germans running out and the advance continued. The ground, however, was difficult for the armour, with deep, steep-sided gullies providing natural obstacles for the tanks. Maj ffrench Blake decided to move his tanks around to the right to try to get behind the enemy positions as he later described:

> We headed for a small farm, beyond which was a great wide expanse of open plough-land. Some German infantrymen in long grey coats appeared out of the ground on our left and ran away. We fired a round or two of our grapeshot at them, without effect. We had reached the farmhouse, with the other two Grants following, when my operator said, 'Number Two is burning.' A wisp of smoke was coming out of the turret and the crew were bailing out. A moment later: 'Number three is burning now.' We were sheltered by the farm, over the top of which I scanned the open plain with my binoculars. About 2,000 yards away I saw a big blast of dust as a gun fired. We could not return the fire since our gun was below the level of the building. Next moment I received a terrific blow on the right elbow and looking down saw a hole in my jersey through which I could see the white bone of my elbow joint. My arm still seemed to be working. I got down inside the tank and the crew put a field dressing on the wound. I got up again to have another look and soon after had the sensation that someone had hit me on the neck with a cricket bat. My head swam, I felt faint and baled out of the tank. I lay on the ground looking up at the blue sky. I realised that I was probably dying and thought of my father, shot in 1917 during the first battle of Gaza.[6]

All three of the Grants had been knocked out by an 88mm gun. Support from the artillery was patchy, for contact with the guns in the rear by the Forward Observation Officers (FOO) was soon lost as telephone lines were repeatedly cut by enemy fire or by the tracks of infantry carriers. With no tanks up with the leading troops and sporadic artillery fire in support, the Inniskilling Fusiliers fought a lonely battle.

Throughout the morning the Irishmen pushed forwards, creeping from rock to rock and crawling through the thin scrub, pressing themselves into the dirt at the approach of each shell. They were facing an entrenched enemy three times their number and their casualties began to mount. Up ahead the steep slopes of the enemy hill were riddled with the bright white and red flashes of machine guns, sending bullets cracking through the air above the men lying prone in the wet earth. By early afternoon it was a case of hanging on as best they could until, towards dusk, someone had the good sense to call them back off the hill and into the relative safety of the rear. Under the cover of smoke and through showers of stinging cold rain, those tired fusiliers who were able trudged wearily back from Two Tree Hill, one hundred fewer than when they had set out earlier that morning. As a parting gesture, the Germans cut down the two trees on top of the hill to prevent them being used as a ranging point by the artillery.

Val ffrench Blake of 17th/21st Lancers had not been killed in his Grant tank and his crew had managed to get him back to safety. 'We soon reached the medical post,' he later recalled, 'after almost running over Gen Keightley and his staff who were watching the battle from below the crest of the hill behind us. They had to smartly hop out of our way. By the time I reached the medical post the wound in my neck was bleeding freely and even noisily. My wounds were dressed and I lost consciousness.' Maj ffrench Blake spent the next nineteen months recovering from his wounds, but was eventually able to rejoin his regiment in September 1944, when he took over command.[7]

For the next few days, both sides shelled each other intermittently and sent out patrols to harry their enemy, satisfied to hold their main positions while they worked out their next moves. For the British it was to be, unimaginatively, the same again; this time 1st Royal Irish Fusiliers (the 'Faughs') would carry out the frontal attack, supported by even more artillery through the addition of 17th Field Regiment RA to the division, from the nearby 78th Division, and a battery of medium guns from corps. Concentrated artillery fire was deemed to be the new deciding factor in the attack. The 2nd Lothians and Border Horse were also brought down from south of Goubellat to give cover. The 'Faughs' would go in behind a heavier barrage, but just three field regiments and a battery of medium guns trying to concentrate their fire over such a wide valley and a number of interlocking peaks was hardly an overwhelming force.

Gen Kenneth Anderson, Commander First Army, had earlier briefed his intentions for the conduct of his small force in Tunisia while it gained strength ready for the spring. He dictated a policy of 'containing the enemy through constant pressure and by limited attacks to seize ground to facilitate a later offensive'.[8] The requirement for the Royal Irish Fusiliers to mount a third attack on Two Tree Hill fell within this brief. To the officers and men on the ground before the hill, such an attack was a waste of resources at a time when the whole front was held by just a thin line of infantry strung out along the hill tops like a necklace of pearls. Everything that Keightley had was virtually in the line; there was no real reserve. And if the hill were taken and held, what then? The Germans would still be there a mile away on another line of hills, threatening all the while to counterattack and break through the shallow Allied front. Perhaps the attack was just a case of showing offensive spirit.

On the other side of the hill, the enemy had a better plan. *Generaloberst* Jürgen von Arnim was now in command of Tunisia with his Fifth Panzer Army. Gen Nehring's forces had halted First Army's drive on Tunis in the defensive actions around Tebourba and Medjez and had forced the Allies to halt and hold their ground. Kesselring then appointed von Arnim to inject some spirit into the operations and ordered Fifth Panzer Army to go over to the offensive, even though the Allies deemed the conditions did not favour the attack. Gen von Arnim devised Operation *Eilbote*, which would involve launching attacks through the main gaps of the long line of mountains called the Eastern Dorsal. Starting in the north against the British at Bou Arada, he would then push through the mountain passes at Kairouan, Fondouk and Faid further to the south against the French and the Americans. Von Arnim was not attacking merely to secure ground, he was attacking to break through the invasion forces.

Opposite 6th Armoured Division were some very good German units, a mix of elite troops, panzer battalions and *panzergrenadiers*. Primarily the parent unit was 10th Panzer Division, commanded by GenLt Wolfgang Fischer.[9] Also under control of 10th Panzer Division were 5th Parachute Regiment, commanded by *Oberstleutnant* Walter Koch – light troops from the Luftwaffe – and the Jäger Regiment Hermann Göring of the Hermann Göring Division.[10]

On 17 January Lt Col Pat Scott readied his battalion for the attack the following day. The 1st Royal Irish Fusiliers had been pulled back off Grandstand Ridge and replaced by 6th Inniskilling Fusiliers, who would hold the feature as a jumping-off point for the 'Faughs'' attack. These moves came to nothing, however, for von Arnim chose 18 January to launch Operation *Eilbote*, thus saving the Royal Irish Fusiliers the trouble of having to mount their own assault on Two Tree Hill.

The German operation opened with a battlegroup of tanks and infantry from 10th Panzer Division's 7th Panzer Regiment advancing on Bou Arada along the road from Pont du Fahs. Warning of the approaching Germans was given by the two companies of the Rifle Brigade who held some high ground overlooking the road 4 miles to the east of Bou Arada. Lt James Wilson of B Company was called from his early-morning cup of tea by a rifleman claiming to have seen a large number of tanks advancing down the road towards them. Wilson went forward to look and was confronted by the sight of a column of tanks – Panzer IIIs and IVs – followed by infantry in lorries, stretching back as far as he could see. At the small bridge over a wadi below his position, the leading tanks had halted and were preparing to deploy off the road onto open ground on either side, no doubt fearing that the bridge was mined.[11]

Up with the Rifle Brigade was an OP from 12th RHA, whose Forward Observation Officer (FOO) quickly contacted the artillery to relay details of the range and bearing of the enemy column. In a matter of minutes this German advance guard was broken up by the simultaneous arrival of seventy-two shells fired by the three regiments of field guns in the rear. The enemy infantry debussed and fanned out onto open ground to begin their attack, with the tanks likewise seeking to put distance between each other in order to offer a smaller target to the British guns.

Once the alarm was raised 2nd Lothians were ordered from their leaguer to the west of the village. They had arrived in the area only a short time before and their crews were at breakfast when the urgent order came to move out. Leaving fires, food, blankets and everything that had been unpacked, they piled aboard their tanks and within a few minutes were drumming along the main road to Bou Arada. In one of the tanks was Sgt David Antonio, who later remembered the drive:

Ahead, a grey cloud hung over the battle area. 'That,' remarked the crew commander, 'is what is officially known as the smoke of battle.' It rose from a mixture of bursting shells, smoking haystacks, burning tanks and occasional smoke bombs. B Squadron was engaging the enemy, whose impetus had been checked by artillery fire. From a hull-down position on a ridge we looked down on them. The German tanks had halted. Shell bursts blossomed around them. Our squadrons below, their troops spread out, would edge forward, trying to close the range with the more heavily gunned panzers. From their slender 2-pounder guns would come a yellow flash and a tiny red spark would wing its way towards the enemy.[12]

The two artillery regiments of 6th Armoured Division, the Ayrshire Yeomanry and 12th RHA, were located behind Grandstand Ridge and on another smaller feature to the north called Stuka Ridge. Closer to the advancing panzers was 17th Field Regiment from 78th Division and as the German tanks pressed on towards Bou Arada they began to approach its gun lines. The regiment's 25-pounders soon engaged the enemy armour over open sights and sent one after another erupting into balls of flame and pillars of smoke. The guns followed the enemy tanks wherever they went, forcing them to cover and then flushing them out again. The infantry who should have been supporting the tanks were likewise shelled by the other field regiments and machine-gunned by the tanks of the Lothians and the Brens of the Rifle Brigade.

With the Lothians and Border Horse that day was Lt Allan Waterston. He had arrived with the regiment only two weeks before and this was his first action. When B Squadron advanced against the attacking panzers, Waterston's troop was in the rear. After a very short time he was ordered up to join the squadron's Valentines, which were being engaged by enemy tanks. They were armed with 2-pounder guns and their shells were carrying only about halfway to the enemy. Lt Waterston was told to come forward with his troop and have a go with his Crusader's 6-pounder. 'Up we came to a small ridge well covered with scrub,' he later recalled, 'and there they were, several enemy tanks bold as brass standing out clearly in the centre of the plain as if to challenge us to do our worst.'[13]

The young lieutenant was all set for some gunnery practice. He gave the order to engage and off went the first round. A near miss, but a good shot. The next was also good and he gave orders for a third, but the crew demurred. They insisted that they had all been told not to fire more than two rounds from any one position as the enemy would then spot where they were and fire back. The new troop leader was ready to go on firing as his position was well screened with bush, but fearing a mutiny agreed to reverse out of his position and move. As the Crusader manoeuvred to the rear, disaster struck, for the tank tipped over in a wadi and shed a track. While the crew baled out and assumed the infantry role, Waterston followed usual practice and went across to dispossess the troop corporal of his tank in order to continue the battle. Worse was to come as he later recalled:

> I had now learnt my lesson about firing from the hull down position so this time we backed up to the ridge and fired two rounds over the stern of the tank with no apparent effect. The enemy was not even provoked into replying to our fire. However, I was not to be caught in the same way twice and gave the order to draw off the ridge. Nothing happened. I repeated the order very loud and clear, but still nothing happened. Then a voice from the depths of the driving compartment announced: 'Sorry, sir, I am afraid we are stuck.' The Troop Sergeant was now summoned and towed us off the ridge. His face plainly showed his opinion of the ineptitude of the new troop leader. The fitters were on the scene in a few minutes and informed us that firing over the stern of a Crusader had ruptured the petrol system in several places and that it would take time to repair the damage.[14]

Not long after the attack by 7th Panzer Regiment had begun that morning, another attack was put in on the other side of 6th Armoured's positions. GenLt Fischer sent a force of about three battalions of infantry, the 1st and 3rd Jäger Battalions and the equivalent of three squadrons of tanks against positions of the Irish Brigade. The bulk of the tanks and infantry pushed across the plain heading for Bou Arada, just skirting the lower slopes of Grandstand Ridge; the Hermann Göring Jägers went straight for the ridge itself. The German assault came just at the moment that 1st Royal Irish were along the high ground to the west of the road preparing to make their own attack, so the full force of the assault fell on the depleted Inniskilling Fusiliers who were holding the ridge.

The elite Luftwaffe troops were soon among the trenches and positions of the 'Skins' on the northern part of the ridge and close hand-to-hand fighting broke out. Others of the enemy passed over and down towards the road, between the Inniskillings and the 'Faughs'. The confused fighting on Grandstand made it difficult for support to be given to those Fusiliers surrounded near the summit. The Royal Irish tried to force the Germans off the hill with machine-gun fire, but the enemy kept low, crawling among the rocks, tossing grenades on the trapped Inniskillings. The 'Faughs' on the hill behind were under intense shellfire and their positions were now under threat, but their own fire was also keeping the Jägers pinned down, making it difficult for them to push beyond the road. The Ayrshire Yeomanry joined in the battle and shelled the enemy and their rear positions.

On the southern end of the ridge the group of German tanks and infantry were pressing into the area held by 2nd London Irish Rifles. The shock of the attack carried the enemy forward through a storm of artillery fire from the guns of 12th RHA. In a slit trench up with the London Irish was Maj Hughes, an FOO from 12th RHA. Coming straight towards his position was almost a battalion of the enemy. Hughes called for fire from the eight guns of his battery and still the enemy came on. He then called for all of the guns of the regiment and twenty-four field guns brought shells crashing into the Germans. Still they came on. Maj Hughes and his crew then had to use their own small arms to try to defend the position, and still the advancing Germans pressed forward. The artillery officer joined with the Irish riflemen and they began to fall back, firing as they went.

The enemy was now getting very close to the field guns, for D Battery was sited behind a slight hill close to the southern end of Grandstand Ridge. Normally field gun positions are located well behind the lines, but the speed of the German advance was bringing D Battery almost into the front line. Frank Beckett was with the battery that day and remembers the attack:

> The enemy was only eight hundred yards from our guns. We then received orders from the command post to stand by with our small arms, and were given a range from our observation post of only six hundred yards. Only two guns in our troop could clear the crest in front of us at this range, and Z Troop's four guns were already out of action at such short range. Sergeant Jack Hanson told me later that when he

received the range of six hundred yards, his crew laid the gun and he took a sighting up the barrel before it was loaded to make sure his shell would clear the crest where our infantry were dug in. One German tank actually penetrated our position and shot up one of the gun quads, setting it on fire. Sergeant Harris of Z Troop turned his gun 180 degrees, and firing over open sights, scored a direct hit.[15]

Watching the action from an OP on the hills was the CO of the RHA, Lt Col Barstow. Below him a force of around twenty tanks was driving across his front trying to turn the right flank of Grandstand Ridge and move on Bou Arada. He could see that D Battery was being engaged at close range fighting for its life, so he ordered the other two batteries to concentrate on the German tank force. At the same time his adjutant asked the division's Commander Royal Artillery (CRA) to arrange for all the artillery and the battery of mediums also to concentrate on this force. Within minutes, just as they had done earlier that morning, all the guns on call to the division delivered a barrage of shells among the enemy tanks, all arriving in a tight concentration of bursts, sending plumes of smoke skywards, merging into one great pall, 'so pleasing to a field gunner's eye'.[16]

Again and again the guns fired in unison, sending salvo after salvo into the armoured German force. Other artillery closer to hand concentrated their fire on individual tanks. Groups of German infantry were likewise singled out by the field guns and also raked with fire by the Irish machine guns. Gradually the battle on this southern side of Grandstand began to swing in favour of the armoured division. The attack began to falter and then retreat.

On the northern end of the ridge, the assault by the Jäger battalions was halted amid the positions of the Inniskillings and before those of the Royal Irish Fusiliers. It now became an infantryman's battle, rifle and bayonet, machine gun and hand grenade, each side pressing the other to give way. The turning point came when A Company of the 'Faughs' was ordered to put in a flanking attack on the enemy round the right end of the ridge, to come in at the enemy from their rear. The move was to be supported by tanks. Maj Peter Murphy led his men in line across the open area beneath the view of both sides, into a frenzy of enemy fire from their front and from their flanks. Resolutely the major and his company pressed the attack home, to the amazement and admiration of all who watched. It was a bold move and one that deserved victory. The enemy took flight and withdrew in front of the 'Faughs'. The rout continued all along the line and gradually the Jägers pulled back off Grandstand across the plain to their own lines. At the moment of triumph, Maj Murphy was shot dead with his piper beside him. His second in command was shot through his temple and blinded.[17]

Over to the south, things were still going badly for GenLt Fischer's panzer regiment. Confronted by accurate artillery fire, antitank fire and opposition from the Lothians' tanks, 7th Panzer Regiment and their *panzergrenadiers* started to fade. They fought on for most of the morning, but amid mounting casualties began to withdraw during the afternoon, leaving eight tanks destroyed and six bogged down on the battlefield. Their departure signalled the arrival of a flight of Stuka dive-bombers who attacked Bou Arada, setting many of the buildings on fire and forcing gun crews and the staff of rear headquarters to take cover.

The enemy's withdrawal was followed up with a chase by part of B Squadron of the Lothians, to harry them on their way and to pick off any stragglers. The move was instigated without preparation by order of Gen Keightley himself. The Valentines roared off, following the line of the road to Pont du Fahs with a composite group of five Crusaders, including the tank of an artillery FOO, keeping abreast and covering the right flank. Dipping in and out of the undulations of the foothills which spread down towards the centre of the valley from Djebel Medjanine, the Lothians dashed after the retreating enemy. Their squadron leader had been wrong-footed by Keightley's order and was way behind, trying to catch up with the leading tanks. After several miles, just as it was nearing nightfall, they ran into a German ambush.

Behind the cover of a ridge, the German tanks opened fire at short range on the Valentines of B Squadron. Within just a few minutes many of the British tanks were burning fiercely. When the commander of B Squadron, Maj Gordon Simpson, got up with the leading tanks he could locate only two survivors. He later wrote of his experience:

> We gathered in a small wadi out of sight of the enemy, about 600 yards from the Germans on the ridge, and had a little conference where I was told what was supposed to be happening. It was beginning to get dusky so I decided to creep up the hill and see if it was at all possible to get nearer the German tanks. Suddenly, I saw the turret of a tank with a gun pointing at me (most of the tank was hull down). What happened next has been etched in my mind ever since. The tank fired at me. I saw the shell racing towards me because the tracer on its base was visible in the gloaming. My reaction was to duck my head a split second before the shell hit the turret almost at the top so that it skidded off into the air. The noise was appalling and dust and smoke filled the turret; meantime the left side of my face was hit by a number of small splinters probably from the turret rather than the shell. I was also stone deaf for a while. I had the luck to be able to get my driver to get into reverse just before the second shot was fired and it just missed us.[18]

In one of the Crusaders on the right flank was Lt Allan Waterston. His troop crossed over a wadi by means of a small bridge and fanned out on the far side on a slope which had an Arab village towards its crest. They then saw an enemy tank close by some huts and engaged it with several rounds from their 6-pounder guns. They made little impression and provoked no reply. It was then that Waterston received an order for the troop to retire at once. 'For God's sake, come back fast. The enemy are behind you', came the message.

The tanks withdrew down the rocky slope as fast as the ground permitted and as they neared the wadi at the foot, armour-piercing shot began to flash past unpleasantly close to them. It was coming from the flank where they expected the Valentines of the squadron to be, but the Valentines had been caught by the enemy. Waterston could see a line of five German tanks, hull-down along a ridge which commanded the whole of the valley, the turrets showing menacingly over the ridge just a few hundred yards beyond the little bridge. The flash of their guns was clear and distinct. Allan Waterston later recalled his predicament:

> I made a 'rapid appreciation of the situation'. To go straight on meant crossing the wadi and this would mean bottom gear with a slow crawl down and then up the steep banks, all to be carried out broadsides on to the enemy who had already found the range and was making things unpleasant. The alternative was a four hundred yard dash straight at the enemy, sharp left over the bridge, and then away from them as fast as possible on the opposite bank of the wadi. This had the advantage of presenting our front to the enemy, disconcerting him by an unexpected charge, changing our range, and above all it allowed us to use maximum speed throughout. The latter seemed the best, and, quicker than it takes to tell, we were dashing headlong at the enemy, any one of whose tanks should have been more than a match for us. The artillery officer's tank followed my lead and the two of us shot over the bridge in a cloud of dust and back along the opposite bank of the wadi as fast as we could motor. As we came level with our starting point we were greeted by the unpleasant sight of the three other tanks holed and burning in the wadi after an unsuccessful attempt to cross by the direct route. We slowed down to see whether any of the crews could be picked up. Two figures dashed up towards us from the wadi which was under machine-gun fire, but the enemy had now got over his surprise at our unorthodox behaviour and turned his attention on us. Any pause would have been fatal and in order to save the remaining two tanks we were forced to make our best speed up the hill towards safety. A hard decision to have to make in one's first action and we were far from happy as we made our way up the slope in low gear followed by the curses of our deserted friends and the red trace of the enemy armour piercing shot.[19]

After the events of the morning Waterston knew he could not fire back over the stern of the tank; such action was liable to stop the engine completely. The enemy continued shooting at the two fleeing tanks and Waterston's tank received two hits: one AP shell passed through the open hatch cover, drilling a neat, round hole in the steel lid, while the other went through the bin on the back of the turret, destroying the blankets and rations stowed inside. When Waterston finally got back to his squadron's HQ he found out that up to that time his was the only tank out of sixteen to return. A few others came in later that night.

As darkness fell on 18 January, the realisation sank in that the division had successfully beaten off the first major German attack made against it. The line had held in the face of determined assault by very experienced enemy units. Devastating artillery and accurate antitank fire had turned back and scattered German tanks and infantry. GenMaj Fischer's attack in the Bou Arada area was, however, just one of the enemy thrusts being put in by von Arnim's forces through the Eastern Dorsal Range as part of Operation *Eilbote*. To the south of 6th Armoured Division in the French sector, Gen Georges Barré's Tunisian and Moroccan troops were pushed back 6 miles along the road from Pont du Fahs towards Robaa. All that separated Maj Gen Keightley's division from the French in the Robaa valley was the massive heights of Djebel Mansour. The French were in a desperate state, for they had few modern weapons with which to counter the German attack, relying on antiquated equipment and the belligerent nature of the mountain tribesmen to hold the enemy at bay. Keightley was now asked to attack the enemy forces in front of him to try to divert some of the German pressure from the French. Lt Gen Allfrey, V Corps's commander, decided that the enemy should be evicted from Point 286 a mile to the south-east of Grandstand as a precursor to making a fresh attack against Two Tree Hill. Keightley chose the as-yet uncommitted 2nd London Irish Rifles for the task.

The attack was launched by the London Irish the next day, with its G Company assaulting a lesser hill, Point 279, adjacent to Point 286. F Company was then to follow and establish itself on the reverse slopes of the hill to attack the target, while H Company would put in its attack on Point 286 from the left flank. The operation began without any preliminary bombardment as it was thought that Point 279 was not held in strength by the enemy and an artillery barrage would alert him to an impending attack in time to allow him to bring up reinforcements. G Company made a successful move towards its initial goal, setting out into the darkness at 0440 and meeting such little opposition on Point 279 that it went on to Point 286. F Company followed up, but immediately lost direction and began attacking Point 351 to the left of the main objective. Here the Germans were strongly entrenched and the company ran into stiff opposition. G Company had meanwhile realised that it was on the slopes of Point 286 and withdrew to its original objective. F Company did the same. By this time it was daylight and the two companies now reformed, ready to launch the main attack.

Covered by fire from the men of G Company dug in on the forward slopes of Point 279, F Company stormed up Point 286 and took the hill at the point of the bayonet. When the riflemen reached its summit they found it abandoned; the enemy infantry had fled, giving up the strategic hillside with little fight. It was, however, a false victory, for almost immediately the Germans employed their usual tactics of counterattacking ground that they had given up before the new occupiers had time to dig in. Enemy tanks and armoured cars now led a force of infantry back up the hill, while mortars and artillery plastered the exposed summit.

The enemy fire took its toll on the company of Irishmen; its commander and two other officers were killed, along with many of the other ranks. As the morning wore on, just one officer was left standing and the company's strength was so reduced that it was pulled off the hill, allowing the enemy to resume occupation of the heights. E Company was told to ready itself to retake the hill, but a German mortar landed among the company during an orders briefing, killing three men and disrupting the preparations. When E Company finally put in its attack it stormed the exposed slopes but was unable to reach the summit. Now roused into concerted action, the enemy beat off this assault, mortaring and shelling Point 279 so severely that G Company had to withdraw down to a wadi at the base of the hill, where it was joined by battalion HQ and the men of E Company who had survived their attack.

Lt Col Jeffreys and his battalion were now back close to their starting point, with little ground taken. The Commanding Officer reported his predicament to Brig Russell at Brigade, explaining the situation and the growing enemy resistance his riflemen had met during the attacks. Russell was sympathetic but emphasised the need to secure Point 286 that day and the importance that Army Headquarters placed on the heights. Before the attack, Russell himself had expressed his objections about the move to the Corps Commander, Lt Gen Allfrey, feeling that the hill was untenable by either side.[20] Both Grandstand Ridge, held by the Irish Brigade, and Two Tree Hill, held by the enemy, had good observation across Point 286. Both were also sufficiently close to Point 286 to be the launch pads for surprise attacks to try to evict whoever's forces were in possession. Once taken, it would always be vulnerable.

Lt Col Jeffreys was ordered to try again for Point 286. This time H Company went into the attack, supported by artillery, mortars and machine guns. The new attack and the shelling provoked the enemy to counter with even greater efforts. The battalion area of the London Irish and the advancing troops were now subjected to a dive-bombing raid by Stukas. H Company lost its commander wounded and its second in command killed. The remainder of the company pressed on over ground swept by machine-gun fire and plastered by mortar bombs. Some riflemen actually managed to climb over the rock-strewn slopes up on to the summit, but they could not establish themselves in the face of intense enemy fire. Reluctantly, Lt Col Jeffreys called them down off the hill and back into the battalion area in the wadi.

All four companies of the London Irish had now tried to gain Point 286, each suffering considerable casualties in the attempt. The area to the north of Bou Arada was proving to be a nightmare battlefield. The nature of the terrain allowed troops dug in on the tops of the numerous ridges of high ground to dominate the flat plain between them, sweeping all approaches with fields of interlocking fire.

During the afternoon, the realisation that the height was untenable had obviously come to the enemy, for word came through that it was withdrawing from Point 286. Maj W. Swiny, second in command of the battalion, was ordered to take all that remained of H Company forward to seize the heights once more. The advance on to the abandoned hill was described in the battalion history: 'They went up as unobtrusively as possible, a section at a time, and despite constant mortaring, they occupied the hilltop. They remained there for the rest of the day, gaining such cover as they could on the bald, rocky hill, where the ground was so hard that they could not dig in. Firing died down in the afternoon and desultory shelling and mortar fire was the only sign of enemy activity to break the uneasy silence of the battlefield.'[21]

The battle was not over, however, for shortly after midnight an attack was put in on Point 279 behind Point 286 by enemy tanks and infantry. The Germans overran the posts on the hill and fired on battalion HQ and rear parties in the wadi below. The London Irish companies were scattered and communications between them disrupted. In the pitch darkness bouts of chaotic and noisy fighting broke out everywhere. Then, almost as suddenly as it started, the attack was over and the enemy melted away into the night, leaving a dispersed and confused battalion of Irishmen behind. At daylight all seemed normal, with Point 286 held in some strength and the enemy gone back behind Two Tree Hill.

The Germans had given up Point 286 only after 2nd London Irish Rifles had almost exhausted themselves and taken crippling casualties. Nearly all of the officers had been killed or wounded; F Company had no officers left. The final tally of casualties for the day's fighting showed that the London Irish had lost 26 officers and men killed and 227 wounded and missing. Such losses prompted Brig Russell to comment: 'I never hope to see a battalion fighting and enduring more gallantly. Nor do I want to witness again such cruel casualties. But the job was done.'[22]

The rebuff of GenMaj Fischer's attack on Bou Arada and the actions fought by 2nd London Irish for Point 286 had contained the enemy's forces north of the Bou Arada–Pont du Fahs road. To the south, in the French sector in front of Robaa, the situation remained precarious.

Gen Barré's corps desperately needed more infantry and better equipment with which to hold back the enemy. The German attacks had captured over 4,000 French troops and 70 guns. Limited help was at hand for Barré's northern section of the line, for the British 46th Division was at that moment arriving in Tunisia and its leading brigade had begun to take over the sector held by 36th Brigade of 78th Division. The result was that some seasoned infantry from the Battleaxe Division were available to be moved south into the line with the French. These troops were to come under the command of 6th Armoured Division and were to be supported by a battery of guns from both the division's 72nd Antitank Regiment and 12th RHA.

First to arrive were D and F Batteries of 12th RHA. As they approached Robaa they met with crowds of Frenchmen heading west away from the town. It was clear that the attack by German armour had disorganised Gen Barré's corps, driving through its positions with impunity, halting only when their accompanying infantry had been met with determined resistance from native troops. The guns of the Honourable Artillery Company were hastily dug in astride the road in an antitank position, ready to confront any further German attacks. The next day a squadron of 17th/21st Lancers joined the guns and awaited the arrival of infantry from 36th Brigade. When 5th Royal East Kent Regiment (the Buffs) reached Robaa the composite force was ready to advance to a position of their own choosing where they could organise a more effective defensive line.

The group moved on down through the near-empty town and out along the road towards Pont du Fahs, finally taking up a position seven miles in front of Robaa. The 25-pounder field guns of 12th RHA and the 6-pounder antitank guns of 72nd Antitank Regiment were sited to cover the road and the hills on either side. A screen of infantry was dug in around these positions. Joining the group during the night were more infantry from 6th Royal West Kents. These troops were sent up into the hills on the right among the positions of some Moroccan Goums. The cosmopolitan nature of the brigade group was further enhanced when an American battalion took the place of the third battalion of 36th Brigade. This polyglot group from several commands now barred the way to Robaa and prepared itself to meet the next German onslaught.

Early in the morning of 31 January, the clanking noise of tanks echoed up through the hills in the darkness and warned 36th Brigade of an impending attack. Capt Douglas Hughes, an FOO with 12th RHA, was in the most forward position of the infantry, alongside D Company of the Buffs. They were dug in on the reverse slope of a hill and Hughes was watching the road expectantly through his field glasses. In the half-light he could see the unmistakable outline of a German tank nosing its way over the crest of the hill in front of him. At first all that was visible was the outline of a massive turret. Then the menacing shape of a large gun came in view, followed by the solid hull of a monster. Hughes and the Buffs were facing the approach of Germany's new super heavy tank, the Panzer VI Tiger. On either side of this main tank, the two Panzer IVs accompanying it seemed minute by comparison. Capt Hughes radioed back details of the targets to the guns of D and F Batteries and almost immediately the valley echoed to the resounding crash of shells. The artillery fire had little effect on the enemy armour and they continued to lumber forward to the top of the hill. Here they stopped and began to slew their guns looking for targets. They then commenced fire at the forward infantry positions.

The division's two troops of 6-pounder antitank guns from A Battery of the 72nd Antitank Regiment were dug in on either side of the road. Capt S. Edwards' troop was the most forward on the left of the road, while Lt Heslop's guns were sited 500 yards further back on the right-hand side. Capt Edwards had planned to allow the first wave of any tank attack to pass his position and be dealt with by Lt Heslop's troop, while he would take on the next wave which was bound to follow. That was the plan, but the Germans were refusing to come forward past Edwards' guns and were starting to make a nuisance of themselves, belching enfilade fire along the lead positions of the Buffs. It was too much for the artillery officer to bear and Edwards ordered his guns to open fire with armour-piercing shot. Heslop's troop immediately joined in.

In just two minutes, struck by a welter of solid shot, the two Panzer IVs were ablaze. Further shots bounced off the sloping armoured front of the Tiger, but two struck its flanks and blew off one of its tracks, immobilising the monster. Soon the next wave of armour had arrived. This time Capt Edwards put his original plan into action as he later recalled: 'Over the hill came a Tiger, followed by two Mark IVs, at great speed. Unhesitatingly they passed their knocked-out colleagues and came straight on. In spite of the shouts of horror from the infantry, the tanks were allowed to pass, and within two or three minutes were met by a hail of 6-pounder tracer from the wood and immediately "brewed up". The groans from the Buffs changed to cheers. The enemy were having an expensive morning without getting anywhere.'[23]

It was a great start to the battle and the French were mightily impressed. For the first time in their sector German tanks had been shown not to be invincible. This initial setback had forced the enemy attack off the road and into the hills. Behind the leading tanks the road was crammed with other Panzer IIIs and IVs and a great number of half-tracks and 3-ton trucks carrying the infantry. Capt Hughes now brought his regiment's guns to bear on these new targets, dispersing the enemy infantry into the hills and sending their vehicles roaring in all directions frantically seeking cover. Great palls of smoke rose as one after another the trucks and half-tracks were hit by high explosive. The dispersed enemy infantry pressed forwards, trying to break into 36th Brigade's defences and at one time Capt Hughes was under fire from front, side and rear. The besieged FOO stuck to his task and directed the guns onto new targets as they appeared, as did other FOOs with the West Kents and the Americans. Ammunition expenditure was enormous: 3,600 rounds in just a few hours.

For the rest of the day the fighting settled down into an infantryman's battle, with mortar, machine guns and rifle fire ricocheting backwards and forwards as the Germans tried to get through or around the brigade group's positions. On the flanks the Goums fought in their usual determined vicious way, giving no quarter to any of the enemy they captured, and cutting off the ears of the dead as trophies.

While the fighting was in progress, the Germans put a defence cordon around the rearmost Tiger, for they were keen to ensure that their new weapon did not fall into British hands. After dark they managed to get the tank away, but the other Tiger was firmly under British control. It was the first of these machines to be captured and every high-ranking Allied officer was keen to inspect it. Gen Sir Giffard Martel, Commander of the Royal Tank Corps, was even flown out from England to examine it. The 17th/21st Lancers tried to tow the Tiger back into a safe zone, but found the giant tank to be immovable. The presence of Tigers in Tunisia had been identified since late November the previous year, but their deployment had been carefully controlled by German high command. The two Tigers knocked out by 72nd Antitank Regiment that day were from 2nd Company of 501st Heavy Tank Battalion, part of a battlegroup commanded by GenMaj Friedrich Weber, GOC 334th Motorised Infantry Division.

Chapter Four

KASSERINE AND THE DEFENCE OF THALA

January 1942 saw Gen von Arnim's Fifth Panzer Army concentrating on seizing the mountain tops and passes in front of First Army along the Eastern Dorsal, while Rommel's Panzer Army Africa was retreating towards Tunisia before the all-conquering British Eighth Army. Rommel planned to hold Montgomery's forces along an old French colonial system of fortifications just inside Tunisia called the Mareth Line. To hold the line initially and improve its defences required just the minimum of his forces, which allowed the German field marshal to look to make mischief elsewhere. He now contemplated launching a mobile thrust deep into Tunisia, via Tebessa, to get behind First Army's rear. Bolstered in his intentions by less than impressive reports of American fighting ability, Rommel planned to use his panzers against the area held by the US II Corps, commanded by Maj Gen Fredendall.

Rommel's attack, Operation *Frühlingswind*, hit the Americans at the Faid Pass on 14 February and brushed aside the small force holding the gap. The German 10th Panzer Division pushed through the pass to Sidi bou Zid and then on to Sbeitla, dispersing the Americans in front of them. On its left, 21st Panzer Division attacked simultaneously, sweeping across scattered defences to join 10th Panzer in Sbeitla on 17 February. Here the force split, with 21st Panzer heading for Sbiba and 10th Panzer Division driving for the village of Kasserine to meet up with Gen Buelowius's Afrika Korps, which had advanced up through Gafsa. American resistance to the move was patchy, with some units taking immediate flight and others putting up a very spirited resistance. The swift gains made by the advance gave Rommel confidence to continue the attack with great vigour. His next target was to get through the high pass over the Grand Dorsal mountain range above Kasserine. Once through he could drive on for Tebessa and Le Kef and thrust an armoured wedge into the rear of the Allied forces.

The gradual disintegration of the American defences caused great concern to Lt Gen Anderson. His forces were already stretched, but a catastrophe was developing that had to be prevented. Rommel had to be

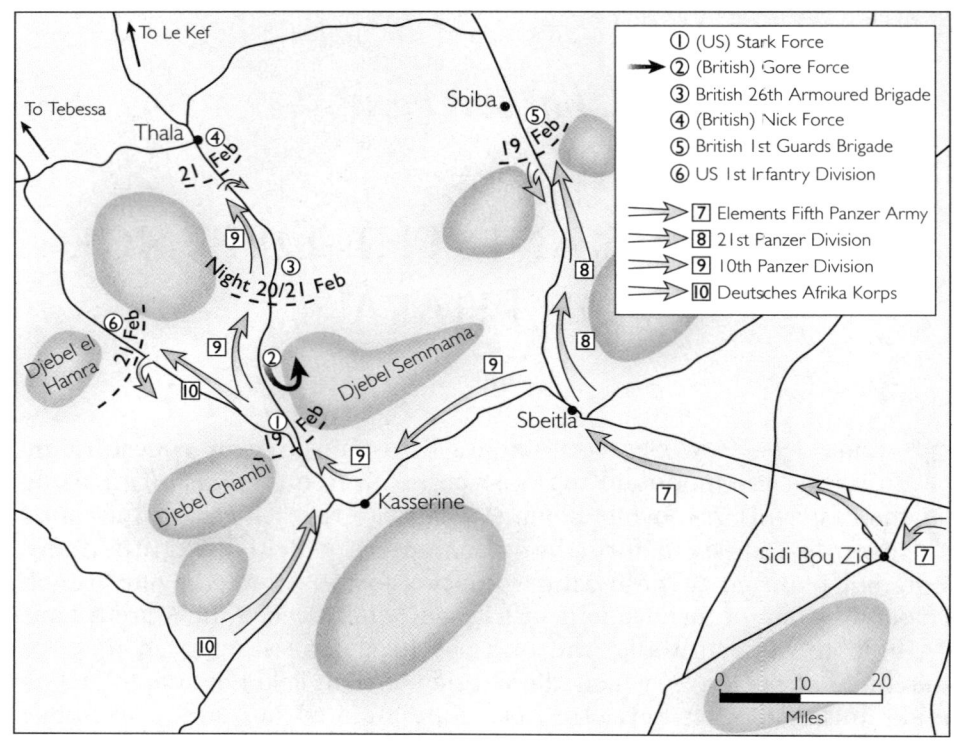

Map 4. Kasserine and the stop line at Thala

stopped well before Le Kef and it looked as though the Americans were unable to do it alone. Lt Gen Allfrey of V Corps was ordered to collect what forces he could gather and send them to Thala and Sbiba to form a block across the two roads up which Rommel's panzers were advancing.

The order gave Allfrey some problems, for his corps had no mobile reserve; everything he had was in the line. His front would have to be diluted and a scratch force gathered to meet the threat in the south, while still leaving sufficient troops in the line to prevent a collapse in the north. He decided to dispatch 26th Armoured Brigade to the Thala area and use 1st Guards Brigade from 78th Division to hold Sbiba, putting them both under the command of Maj Gen Keightley. To increase the infantry support of the armoured brigade, 2nd/5th Leicesters of 46th Division, newly arrived in Tunisia, were also sent to Thala. The Irish Brigade was left holding the area of Bou Arada.

Maj Gen Keightley instantly headed south with his HQ, entrusted with the critically important defence of the Sbiba Pass. Leaving the commander of 26th Armoured Brigade, Brig Charles Dunphie, to control the action at Thala, Keightley picked up the US 18th Regimental Combat Team on the way and immediately brought the two battalions of the Guards Brigade under command as they arrived. To this force was added the tanks of 16th/5th Lancers and three battalions from the US 34th Division. Once Keightley had established this force at Sbiba, he assembled a formidable entrenched position, overlooking the ground through which 21st Panzer Division must pass.

The enemy attacked him on 19 February and tried to manoeuvre around the Anglo-American force, but was stopped by a hastily laid minefield and heavy artillery concentrations. The ground off-road was waterlogged and the enemy tanks found it difficult to get into a fighting position. Keightley's force observed every attempt to regroup made by the enemy from good positions on the high ground and broke each of them up with strong artillery fire. At one point 16th/5th Lancers sallied out against the panzers, but a few quick losses soon made them realise that their Crusaders and Valentines were outgunned.

The 21st Panzer Division battered away at the defences throughout the day and into the next, but was unable to make the breakthrough that Rommel was impatient to have. The field marshal came forward to watch the crucial stages of the battle and reluctantly formed the opinion that the route through Sbiba was not going to be opened without a prolonged struggle. Time was something he did not have, for it was important that the drive be completed before Montgomery arrived on the Mareth Line in his rear. Rommel turned around and went back to Kasserine deciding that the road up through the pass would now be his main attack. Once through the gap, his panzers could sweep all before them and reach a final conclusion to the operation.

On 18 February, 26th Armoured Brigade, less 16th/5th Lancers, was ordered south with all speed. The transport drove non-stop through the night and into the day. It was a forced march along twisting hill roads in complete darkness; no lights could be shown. Drivers had to be helped from their compartments at the end, stiff and weak after eighteen or twenty hours 'behind the sticks'.[1] They arrived in Thala with the news that the enemy was only 20 miles away, just beyond the Kasserine Pass.

The southern approaches and the pass itself were held by around 2,000 men of the US 26th Regimental Combat Team under the command of Col Alexander Stark. It comprised 1st/26th Infantry Regiment, 19th Engineer Combat Regiment, 33rd Field Artillery Battalion, 805th Tank Destroyer Battalion and a battery of French 75mm guns. They faced an onerous task, for they had to hold 3 miles of difficult country stretching out on each side of the pass: boulder-strewn and broken ground through which the enemy could easily infiltrate.

Early on 19 February Rommel had ordered his Deutsches Afrika Korps Assault Group (DAK), commanded by GenMaj Buelowius, to capture the pass at Kasserine. Buelowius decided to try to surprise the American defenders by a sudden attack with his 33rd Reconnaissance Unit. It was not successful, for by then Col Stark's force was in position and able to deal with such an attack by light forces. Buelowius increased the strength of the attack and committed two battalions of Panzergrenadier Regiment Africa against the Americans, one moving along the eastern flanking hill while the other stuck to the floor of the pass. Defensive artillery fire from the French 75mm guns slowed them down and the attack made little headway, but enemy pressure at Kasserine was causing concern back in Thala. If the Germans broke over the pass there was little to hinder them from driving through scattered forces to Le Kef and beyond.

In the late afternoon Brig Dunphie went forward to Stark's HQ 3 miles north-west of the gap to see how the American defence was holding. Col Stark assured him that the battle was 'well in hand'.[2] There were slight difficulties in communications but his forces would hold. Dunphie felt otherwise and ventured forward in his jeep to see how things were for himself, only to be sent reeling back after 400 yards in a hail of enemy bullets. The Germans were further into the pass than Stark had realised.

It was clear to Dunphie that the Kasserine Pass had to be held at all costs. A breakthrough there would leave the scratch force he was assembling in Thala vulnerable. It was also clear that Stark Force was beginning to disintegrate. Until the whole of 26th Armoured Brigade Group had come up to join him, a sustainable defence at Thala could not be organised, nor could the brigade be committed without orders from Lt Gen Anderson's HQ, for the brigade was First Army's only armoured reserve. Dunphie was permitted, however, to organise a small force from those units that had already arrived and send it out along the road to Kasserine to help prevent a German breakthrough at the pass.

Brig Dunphie duly assembled this force from C Company of 10th Rifle Brigade, C Squadron of Lothians and Border Horse, a troop of self-propelled antitank guns from 93rd Antitank Regiment RA and F Battery of 12th RHA, all under the command of the CO of 10th Rifle Brigade, Lt Col Adrian Gore. This small fighting group, given the name 'Gore Force', set out during the afternoon of 19 February along the road to Kasserine to join up with the Americans. Going the other way, intent on putting some distance between themselves and the rumble of German gunfire, were streams of fleeing American lorries and jeeps.

Gore Force came forward to a position well short of the pass and, as darkness fell, the lieutenant colonel formed the group into a leaguer. Fighting was continuing on the other side of the high pass as the Germans put in attacks along the road on the floor of the valley. The Americans seemed to be holding their ground, but in the hills on either side, the men on the flanks were gradually falling back in the face of advancing *panzergrenadiers*.

Throughout the night of 19/20 February the Germans continued to press the Americans, sending more groups of infantry across the slopes of the high ground on to the east of the pass and pressing slowly forward along the road beneath them. Enemy artillery fire increased in strength as the night wore on, rising in intensity even further as dawn approached.

Making its debut on the battlefield that night was a new German weapon. This was the 'Nebelwerfer', a multi-barrelled mortar firing six 80lb rocket-propelled bombs in concert, each of which emitted a screeching wail as it passed through the air to arrive on target with terrific explosive power up to four miles away. These were often too much for many of the American infantry and engineers; as the enemy pressed through the rocky outcrops in the dark, they melted away to the rear.

During the early morning more and more Americans came struggling back through Gore Force shouting, 'It's all over up there.' It was obvious something bad was happening at the pass and so Lt Col Gore moved his small battlegroup forward into more defensible positions guarding the exit from the Kasserine. 'On our way up to the gap,' wrote John Ogilvie of C Squadron of the Lothians later, 'we saw guns dug in and thought good, not all the Americans have run, however, as we got closer we saw only the guns, mortars and machine guns set up ready for action. Their crews had fled leaving everything in working order.'[3]

Gore halted his men just short of the northern corner of the gap and established his left flank against the steep mountainside, with his antitank guns sited to cover the road and his riflemen dug in around them. C Squadron of the Lothians was ordered further forward with its seven Valentines and four Crusaders to hull-down positions on a small hill to the right of the road.

Up ahead of Gore Force, Col Stark's defenders were continuing to crumble. The steady pressure being exerted by the Afrika Korps was working, for it was breaking down the American resistance and the GIs felt very exposed and vulnerable, strung out as they were along the mountains on either side of the gap. Down below on the road, Rommel was very disappointed with GenMaj Buelowius's progress and upset that he had not broken through the pass. He called up 10th Panzer Division to help get the battle moving at the pace he thought necessary. Rommel felt that his enemy was sure to be bringing up major reinforcements. Unless he broke through the pass soon, he would lose the initiative.

At 0700 hr on 20 February the field marshal drove up towards HQ Afrika Korps in Kasserine village to meet with Buelowius and with GenMaj Friedrich von Broich, who now commanded 10th Panzer Division after the death of GenMaj Fischer; but first he went forward to see progress for himself. Two miles in front of the entrance to the pass he met *Oberst* Menton, commander of Panzergrenadier Regiment Afrika. He found Menton directing the battle from the rear and told him to climb into his car with him. Rommel drove the startled *oberst* right into the pass and ordered him to set up his headquarters there. Von Broich came forward to join them at about 1000 hr and the field marshal learned that he had only part of his 10th Panzer Division with him. Rommel was furious, telling Broich to get a battalion of motorcycle troops up immediately and send them along the hill route taken by Menton's *panzergrenadiers* over Djebel Semmama to the right of the road. When Broich explained that he was waiting for the infantry battalion to arrive first, Rommel lost his temper and told von Broich to go back, get the motorcyclists and lead them into battle himself. Kasserine Pass was to be taken that day or else![4] By 1300 hr the panzer attack against Stark Force was in full spate.

On the other side of the pass that morning, Col Stark was now assuring Gore that his troops were in position holding the gap, but the British lieutenant colonel had his doubts. Half-tracks were coming back down the road empty at speed and individual US soldiers were scrambling northwards through the pass on foot. In the afternoon a battalion of American troops came up to join Gore Force as reinforcements. Gore tried with some difficulty to get them to deploy on his left flank as he had been ordered to push his force on into the pass. Maj Tony Beilby moved his C Squadron of the Lothians forward into the gap itself and took up a position ready to repel any of the enemy that tried to advance through the narrow feature along the road. As the day progressed, Gore Force came under increasing shellfire which gradually became more accurate towards late afternoon. The Germans were getting closer and closer. Maj Beilby refused to withdraw and said that he would hold on until darkness.

Up ahead of the British positions the battle raged through the morning. Messages were coming through to Col Stark telling him of the inexorable German advance into his thinly held line. Enemy infantry and tanks were forcing their way up the dirt road into the pass, while *panzergrenadiers* overran artillery observation posts and gun positions on the hills on either side. The American forces resisting them were falling back with some rapidity. High on the hills overlooking the pass the Germans were closing on the French artillery. Without transport the guns were impossible to move so the order was given to abandon the ancient weapons. The French gunners spiked their 75mms with tears in their eyes and then slipped away northwards across the barren hillside.

One American officer described the whole scene around the pass as an 'uncoordinated withdrawal', but in reality it was a rout. Each man on the mountains eventually realised that he had to become master of his own fate. Three options presented themselves: death, captivity or flight. Most made for the relative safety that awaited them across the hills. On the valley floor the defences buckled under the weight of the Panzer Korps. At Stark's command post the air was thick with the crack of bullets. By around 1700 hr the enemy was so close to Stark's HQ that they were attacking it with grenades. Stark knew that it was time to go and set off overland towards Thala with those of his staff who were able, crawling across open patches of ground and trying to evade German soldiers throughout the night.

By around 1600 hr the Germans had brushed aside the main part of Col Stark's forces holding the gap and their tanks were moving over the summit of the pass. Soon enemy tanks were lumbering along the road towards Gore Force. As they came into view they were immediately engaged by the tanks of the Lothians and the antitank guns dug in close by. At the same time, from high ground on the far side of the Kasserine road a group of around fifteen enemy self-propelled guns opened fire on C Squadron. Screened by this barrage of high explosive, thirty Panzer IVs broke through the gap and moved closer down the road. More and more tanks seemed to rise into view and these were frantically engaged by the guns of Gore Force. The 2- and 6-pounder guns of the Valentines and Crusaders could do little in reply and they began to withdraw from their exposed location on a small hillock, but the antitank guns and field artillery resolutely took on the advancing enemy armour.

In Maj Beilby's tank was his wireless operator, John Ogilvie. 'My immediate reaction', he later wrote, 'was even if we had good tanks and guns, we would not get out of this situation alive. All we could do was wait and hope that the tanks would come close enough for our shells to do some damage, at the moment they were just bouncing off without doing the slightest harm. We moved our position as and when possible.'[5]

The German tanks continued to grind forward through the close-range storm of shell and shot and came onto the reverse slope of the slight hill in front of Gore Force. From hull-down positions they then began to pick off the Valentines one by one, sweeping the hillside with armour-piercing fire. Maj Beilby's tank was hit and he was wounded, but he continued to hold his squadron together, walking from tank to tank in the open, giving encouragement and directing their fire. His bravery was an inspiration to his crews and they fought doggedly on, trying to get a lucky shot into the more vulnerable parts of the German panzers. Again and again the Lothians were forced back to a new ridge or a new hillock, making a brief stand and then withdrawing, each move made with fewer and fewer tanks as the numbers dwindled in the face of enemy fire. Just as darkness was falling, Maj Beilby was killed, his tank hit again by an armour-piercing shot.

John Ogilvie later recalled the incident: 'Maj Beilby had just passed his flask round the crew when we received a direct hit. Major Beilby was killed instantly and I was wounded. I remember the way the Major's arm had fallen with his watch showing and I thought I should take it for his wife, though the tank was burning. My first attempt to bail out failed as I was still wearing my headphones.'[6] By then just one other Valentine tank was mobile and as it tried to make its escape after knocking out one of the Panzer IVs, it too finally succumbed to enemy fire.

Some of the Lothians' crews were able to evacuate their tanks and make for the rear, trying to keep ahead of the advancing Germans out on the barren hillsides; some rejoined the regiment that night, while others filtered back into the Allied lines during the following days. Lt Col Gore succeeded in extricating some of his force out from under the enemy and back towards Thala, but many were left scattered over the battlefield, their broken bodies lit by the glow of burning tanks and guns. The force had lost all the tanks and one antitank gun. It now moved back 4 miles down the road and organised an antitank defence. In this position it was joined by four American Grant tanks. By 0200 hr the Germans had closed the gap and Gore Force went into action once again. To begin with, the enemy fired tracer in the direction of the Grants, but as soon as the Americans opened fire in reply with their 75mm guns, German tanks knocked them out. Then the enemy came on to engage the British antitank guns, their task made easier by the light of the burning Grants. Once again, after delaying the enemy advance for more precious minutes Gore Force pulled back, this time travelling the full distance back to the defence line outside Thala.

F Battery from 12th RHA also withdrew in bounds, with the enemy seeming to appear on all sides. 'I don't know how many times that night the plans were changed, but I do know how many times we turned the guns around,' wrote Capt J. Pirie after the action. 'The road was rather narrow with a ditch on each side and it was very dark and wet. Three times we turned ourselves about.'[7]

The resistance put up by Gore Force, and especially that by C Squadron of the Lothians, had held up Rommel's advance and gained time for the remainder of 26th Armoured Brigade to continue with its preparations to defend Thala. The only infantry available were 10th Rifle Brigade, less its antitank platoon, which was away receiving its new 6-pounder guns, but more help was on the way in the shape of 2nd/5th Leicestershires, who were being diverted to Thala from 46th Division.

Rommel had witnessed the action for the pass from Kasserine and in the late afternoon was driven up to the gap to watch 'the exciting spectacle of the tank battle north of the pass as dusk fell that evening'.[8] The stand made by Gore Force had interfered with his plans for the continuation of the advance. The resistance shown by the British had convinced him that Allied reinforcements were moving into the area and that a counterattack would almost certainly be mounted against him the next day. He decided to hold the Afrika Korps's column and assemble the whole of 10th Panzer Division at Kasserine to enable him to take effective measures against whatever the Allies decided to pitch against him.

Out on the mountains, George Turnball from C Squadron of the Lothians was attempting to get back to Thala. His tank had been knocked out, his driver killed and he was trying to get away from the shelling:

I met with others of the squadron including three wounded, who could only walk with assistance and were in great pain. We walked for most of the night until we came to an Arab village where we hid during the day. The head man gave us shelter and food. That evening he directed us on to his brother's village. After much stumbling through wadis and cactus groves we arrived at this village and found the brother, but he was not friendly disposed, no food or drink was on offer so we decided to keep going. The next day the wounded were asked to try for the German lines which were thought to be closer. We continued to try to find the British lines, should there be any. After staggering along a few more miles we were surprised to see a company of Americans, complete with vehicles and a plentiful supply of food and water, hidden in a wooded area. This company had run from the Germans without firing a single shot and appeared quite happy to wait out the war in comfort. They gave us food, which was eaten with a certain degree of disgust. We decided to try to find our own people.[9]

The night of 20 February was a difficult one for the Allied commanders in the area. Most of their units had been split up to patch over pressure points in the line. Stark Force had been so completely routed that its survivors were spread across miles of open mountainside. Gen Fredendall, commander of the US II Corps, believed that Rommel's forces had broken through towards Tebessa and that all that was in front of them were the remnants of Stark Force. He ordered Brig Gen Paul Robinett of Combat Command B from the US 1st Armored Division, to move his battlegroup south onto the high ground around Djebel el Hamra, gather those stragglers of Stark Force that he could find and block the track that led from Kasserine to Tebessa. The remainder of 1st Armored Division was to position itself further to the west, overlooking the Gafsa–Tebessa road. Brig Dunphie was to hold the Kasserine–Thala road with his 26th Armoured Brigade and take overall command of both his and Robinett's forces.

When news of events reached Lt Gen Anderson at First Army, he became alarmed by the whole situation. Dunphie could not fight his brigade and control the Americans to the west of him, without the support of the staff or signals to do so. Anderson decided that the force needed a coordinated command and ordered 6th Armoured Division's second in command, Brig Cameron Nicholson, across to take over the whole Allied force north-west of the Kasserine Pass under the name of 'Nick Force'. Nicholson left immediately, but had to drive through the night to get to Thala, arriving shortly before daybreak. Lt Gen Anderson rang and spoke to him personally, stressing the severity of the crisis and the need to stand firm and at the same time try to save the armour from destruction; Robinett's and Dunphie's tanks were all that First Army had left to prevent Tunisia falling.[10]

At first light the two available regiments of 26th Armoured Brigade advanced from Thala to take up positions across the road up which 10th Panzer Division was bound to advance. Fifteen miles south of the town the Lothians and Border Horse moved out to cover the left of the road, while 17th/21st Lancers spread out across the hills on the right. Around them stretched open country, crossed from east to west by low ridges a mile or so apart. The ground on which they were to make their stand was the best that could be chosen in the circumstances. Brig Dunphie was up with these tanks controlling their movement from his command vehicle. He had ordered his two armoured regiments to hold the enemy as long as possible, at least until 1500 hr, so that the rear defence line could be further established.

Up towards the position of the tanks, but emplaced a few miles behind them, were just two troops of 25-pounder artillery: one from 450th Battery of 71st Field Regiment RA and F Battery of 6th Armoured Division's own 12th RHA. The remainder of this field regiment was dug in back along the main defence line 12 miles to the rear with a newly arrived infantry battalion, 2nd/5th Leicesters. It was here, 3 miles to the south of Thala, that Nick Force was to make its stand. If the enemy broke through this rear line, there was nothing behind it and the road was open for Rommel to advance all the way to Le Kef and beyond.

The previous night 2nd/5th Leicesters had arrived from 46th Division. The battalion had only recently landed in Algeria and was on its way up the line to join its parent division when it was diverted across to Thala. The Leicesters were told to dig in along a ridge to form a final line of defence across the road should 26th Armoured Brigade fail to stop the enemy's drive. It was their first action and they were waiting to be attacked by a panzer division.

That morning, a few miles along the road in front of 26th Armoured Brigade, GenFM Rommel was visiting his forward troops. He believed that because the Allies had not yet counterattacked him after he had broken through the pass above Kasserine, they had chosen to stay on the defensive. He was now sure that the Anglo-American forces would fight a defensive battle rather than come at him. Rommel decided to go back on the attack. Earlier he had ordered the Afrika Korps's Assault Group (DAK) along the road to Tebessa against the American Combat Command B, who he knew were holding the pass in front of El Hamra. His main attack would be towards Thala with 10th Panzer Division. By advancing simultaneously along two separate roads he hoped to split the Allied forces more than his own. He also counted on von Arnim to continue with his attacks in the north to prevent the Allies switching troops to reinforce the Thala position.[11]

Waiting for the enemy advance were Brig Dunphie's two armoured regiments with their tanks lined up in hull-down positions covering the open ground before them. 'Here we waited,' recalls the Lothians' history, 'hour after hour, for the advance of Rommel's veterans. Out-gunned, out of position, and with no reserves, we had little reason for optimism. The whole morning was passed in this suspense.'[12]

The Germans were coming, but they were taking their time about it. True to form, Rommel was up at the front urging them on, as he later described in his memoirs: 'I had gone forward to the 10th Panzer Division with Bayerlain and Horster about midday. The division was not getting forward fast enough, and I had to be continually at them to keep the speed up; they did not seem to realise that they were in a race with the Allied reserves.'[13]

It was early afternoon before GenMaj von Broich finally brought his division forward in contact with the British. Watching the arrival of 10th Panzer Division from his Crusader tank was Lt Allan Waterston of the Lothians: 'From our ridge we had a grandstand view south towards the pass and watched the enemy debouch on to the more open country in front of us. An impressive sight as they seemed to pay little attention to what we might do but formed up with their vehicles as if for an inspection. For our part we moved about a bit and fired off a few ineffective rounds but the enemy did not deign to make any reply.'[14]

At around 1600 hr the enemy advance began. The regimental history of 17th/21st Lancers described the initial contact: 'In the lead were three eight-wheeled armoured cars, in line ahead on the road. They opened fire at long range with their short 75mm howitzers firing HE. A Squadron returned their fire without success and suddenly, under cover of this attack, armour piercing shots came from a longer range; six A Squadron tanks were knocked out in a few minutes.'[15]

The tank battle was one-sided. All the German tanks had guns which out-ranged the British and the Lancers and Lothians could do no more than manoeuvre, try to get a lucky shot onto the advancing enemy and then withdraw to the next hill or the next ridge. The enemy also had superior numbers and the advantage of attack, able to sweep around to get at the flanks while others kept the British looking to their front. The few field guns that were forward with 26th Armoured Brigade tried to seek out individual targets, but it was ineffective to try to destroy tanks by indirect fire; they could do no more than bombard the advancing lines with high-explosive shells and hope to catch the supporting *panzergrenadiers* with the blast.

The battle fought by 26th Armoured Brigade was no more than a holding action. Its tanks could only damage the enemy armour with a lucky shot at quarters closer than they would care to choose. In contrast, the enemy kept the British at arm's length and picked them off one by one. Smoke shells were fired to obscure the ground and give some cover to the British withdrawals, but order soon became lost and individual tank actions, ambushes and narrow escapes took place all down the road to Thala and across the hills and ridges on either side.

Sgt D.G. Antonio of the Lothians' RHQ had lost his tank with a broken track and he and his crew had hitched a ride on the outside of his colonel's mount. He later described the action:

> The retreat had begun. From one ridge after another we were forced back, and, on every ridge we left, a few more of our tanks remained behind, derelict, perhaps burning. The enemy tanks, careful to keep outside our range, were methodically destroying our little force. We put up smoke. From our position on the outside of the CO's tank there was little to be seen of our tanks until the smoke thinned. Then one had the discouraging view of a long wavering line of tanks, their guns flashing, speeding north to cover the next ridge. In the sky, white streamers traced the parabolic course of our smoke bombs. On the ridge we had vacated would appear the van of our pursuit. In between the two forces the air was laced with red and white tracer shot.[16]

Brig Dunphie controlled the battle as best he could from his scout car on the road, calmly directing each of his two regiments to new positions as they fell back. The CO of 17th/21st Lancers, Lt Col Hamilton-Russell, had two tanks destroyed under him and each time had to leap out from one Valentine to commandeer another from which to continue directing his battalion.

Sgt David Antonio was finding the action a little too hot on the outside of his colonel's tank and so he and his crew took cover in a culvert under the road, hoping that some transport might take them back to Thala. Their hopes were raised a short while later when a carrier came speeding down the road, accompanied by a Crusader tank and a scout car. They tumbled into the back of the carrier and raised the number of men on board to thirteen. It was then that the sargeant realised that the scout car contained the brigadier. 'From time to time our little party of three vehicles would halt and the brigadier, microphone to his lips, would direct the final stages of the battle. And all this time bursts of machine-gun fire could be seen snaking up the road straight for us, sometimes over, sometimes short.'[17]

Lt Allan Waterston of the Lothians had become separated from the main body and was feeling a little lost, as he later recalled.

> After a while feeling somewhat lonely we found a Lothians tank which turned out to be that of the Second in Command of the Regiment. During training at home he had the reputation of being somewhat eccentric and even taking off his beret and jumping on it at times of stress! However, on this occasion he could not have been more cool and

collected giving us every encouragement, telling us to carry on as we had been doing and wishing us the best of luck. Very shortly after this encounter his tank was knocked out and he was wounded and taken prisoner. He did in fact lose an arm and for years after the war exchanged gloves with Sergeant Cadger who had lost the other arm. We did see one or two Lancer tanks but otherwise continued on our own until it was almost dark when we joined the road and passed through a rocky defile the sides of which were held by infantry whom we were very glad to see.[18]

Chasing the British back, moving in bounds just one ridge or one hill behind them, was GenFM Rommel. He was pleased with the quantity of burning British armour that gave witness to the success of 10th Panzer Division's advance. He counted seventeen destroyed tanks in front of him and he was interested to see that some had what he thought were 75mm guns. Rommel believed that the Crusader had been up-gunned with a very powerful weapon. He was in fact wrong, for he mistook the Crusader's 6-pounder gun (57mm) for something of a much larger calibre. Up until then, Rommel had only seen the earlier Crusaders of Montgomery's Eighth Army, which were armed with the 2-pounder gun. Also on the battlefield were some Crusaders with 3in (76mm) howitzers which fired HE for close support; perhaps it was these which convinced him that the Crusader was more powerful than it was.

Rommel and his aide Bayerlein twice had to seek cover from artillery fire, once in a cactus grove and once in an Arab village. On his way forward to speak to von Broich he passed the bodies of several British soldiers lying dead beside their antitank gun. He was shocked to find them naked: 'Arabs had plundered the bodies and robbed them of their clothing. There was nothing to be seen of these ghouls, which was fortunate for them, for they would otherwise have had something to remember us by.'[19] When he reached the commander of 10th Panzer Division he called for the advance to be speeded up, ordering von Broich to lorry his *panzergrenadiers* forward close behind the tanks. There would be time enough to dismount, he reasoned, when they came up against solid enemy positions.

By the late afternoon it was clear that the enemy was advancing with greater force than expected and the depleted numbers of tanks and antitank guns were not capable of holding them. Brig Dunphie decided to pull what remained of his tanks and guns behind the main defence line just south of Thala. His battlegroup had delayed the enemy for as long as they were able; it was now down to the infantry line to hold them back.

Capt J. Pirie later recalled F Battery's retreat: 'At about five o'clock, orders came to withdraw behind the infantry battalion position. As the guns limbered up, the infantry carriers swept through the position towards the road and once on the road the whole column closed up. It was a sorry sight and I have never been so glad that the Germans failed to use aircraft against us. Behind lumbered what was left of our Valentine and Crusader tanks. The Lothians had lost all but a few and the Lancers were little better off.'[20] An hour later the guns were pulled into a little hollow about half a mile behind the Leicestershires, with the remaining tanks going into harbour a short distance away.

This then was Nick Force's final defence line. In addition to 6th Armoured Division's units and the infantry of 2nd/5th Leicesters, the line was strengthened by a few scratch units from elsewhere. The 86th Chemical Warfare Company RE brought its heavy 4.2in mortars into positions alongside the infantry. More field guns were provided by 90th/100th Field Battery of 23rd Army Field Regiment RA and antitank weapons were dug in along the road from 229th Antitank Battery of 58th Antitank Regiment RA. A little later, six American 37mm antitank guns came into the area under command of Nick Force. Brig Nicholson was also told that further American support was on its way: artillery from the US 9th Division was driving from Tlemcen in Morocco, a distance of over 800 miles.[21] Closer to hand, the stabilised situation at Sbiba meant that 1st Guards Brigade could be switched across to the Thala sector. Also coming were 16th/5th Lancers, with some of their brand new Sherman tanks. All this was promised to Nicholson, but would the line hold long enough for them to arrive, or would they be welcomed by another Allied rout?

By the time 26th Armoured Brigade had pulled back into these positions, darkness had begun to fall. 'It was just light enough to choose gun platforms and slit trenches,' wrote Capt Pirie of 12th RHA's F Battery. 'About 100 yards in front of us was a tank leaguer and to our right were two 25-pounder batteries from other regiments. The state of confusion and the lack of orders was pretty bad. We laid our guns partly in antitank positions and partly for their normal field role. One troop on the right covered the road; the other the valley in front of the infantry position.'[22]

The pitiful remnants of Brig Dunphie's two armoured regiments struggled through the gap in the minefield which had been laid by the infantry and headed to their harbour for the night. Fuel and ammunition lorries were waiting for them to resupply their needs. Exhausted and slightly demoralised by their losses, the crews knew that before very long they would have to go back into battle with the enemy. The Lothians and the Lancers were each down to about a dozen serviceable tanks. It was now quite dark. The fighting had died down and men stood in groups, smoking cigarettes and talking over the action they had just survived. In just a short while, the sound of firing came from the infantry line behind them and tracer fire passed low above their heads.

The enemy were attacking the infantry just a mile up the road from the tanks and field gun positions. Von Broich's men had continued with their advance in the darkness and were now engaging Nick Force's stop-line. Taking the brunt of this attack were the 'green' troops of 2nd/5th Leicesters and they were shocked by the ferocity of the German attack.

The Germans had used great subtlety to approach the Leicesters' line undetected. Leading their advance was a Valentine tank which had been captured from A Squadron of 17th/21st Lancers during the action with Blade Force back in November. Riding on the outside were a number of *panzergrenadiers*. The British infantry and antitank guns covering the gap in the minefield allowed what they thought was a straggler to come through unmolested. Following closely behind the captured Valentine were more tanks and more *panzergrenadiers*.

Suddenly the men jumped down from the tank, crying: 'Hands up – come out, surrender to the panzers', and began shooting up the Leicesters' positions, while the German armour opened fire on the antitank guns. The Panzer IIIs and IVs slewed across the British infantry in their trenches, crushing many of them under their tracks, then sprayed the fleeing men with machine-gun fire and tracer. Within minutes the enemy force was inside the line and fanning out on either side of the road, some dealing with the Leicesters and others pressing on for Thala. The attack had caught Nick Force completely by surprise.

The roar of the fire welling up around the Leicesters' line spread over down the road, and tank and mortar fire began raking the field guns of 12th RHA. Capt Pirie described the scene: 'The gun detachments were crouching in their half-dug slit trenches while assorted shelling and machine-gun fire swept the position. I don't know whether it was fire from the mortars or from the tanks, but it was very unpleasant. Burning vehicles from the tank leaguer cast an eerie and uncertain light and through this murk, figures could be seen running towards us. Silhouetted high on the ridge on our left were men doubling past our flank. The enemy fire eased up; the men running towards us were the infantry from the ridge in front. They said their position had been overrun by tanks and that the Germans were only 300 yards away.'[23]

A short way off in the Lothians' positions the enemy was attacking with tanks. 'A flare shot up in the air,' wrote Sgt David Antonio later, 'and as it drifted earthwards its cold light lit up the scene. Six German tanks were right upon us, greenish yellow flame flickering from their machine-gun muzzles. Our tanks, caught in the midst of refuelling, were at a disadvantage; many of them were unable to traverse their turrets. Two of our tanks and the ammunition lorry burst into flames.'[24] The light from the burning ammunition lorry illuminated the enemy column for 17th/21st Lancers. One of its tanks managed to get a group of shots off in quick succession and knocked out three of the enemy's tanks.

The German armour continued through the mêlée towards the field guns of F Battery from 12th RHA, spreading alarm and confusion. At first an order was given by the Gun Position Officer to limber up the guns and withdraw, but this directive was quickly reversed by the Battery Commander, Maj Cecil Middleton. He knew that the guns had an important role that was vital to the survival of Nick Force. He ordered that they stand and fight. The guns that were leaving were hurriedly turned around and their detachments ordered into action. Several men were missing, affected by the Leicesters falling back through their positions and the initial order to withdraw. Some had only gone back as far as the road and quickly returned; a few were not seen for several days.

The German tanks were now only 50 yards away. In the gloom, Capt Pirie could not make out the targets so he devised a plan to illuminate them. He crept forward with a few men and fired a Very light, having first given orders for the battery to open fire once a target could be identified. Pirie's first attempt was botched, but his second flare lit up two Panzer IIIs and other enemy vehicles. The tanks were immediately engaged by a 25-pounders at almost point-blank range. One was destroyed and the other limped away into the night, damaged. The German vehicles accompanying them were set on fire. Other gunners peering through the dark night saw the shapes of three further tanks moving around their flank. Sgt Lawrie's detachment was manning the most exposed of the field guns and they trained their weapon on the first of the Panzer IVs as its long barrel swept round towards them. The 25-pounder got off the first shot and smashed one of the enemy tank's tracks. While Lawrie's men were reloading, two other guns opened fire. The first panzer was destroyed and the others reversed into the night.

The first surprise over, antitank guns, tanks and field guns began to organise themselves to hit back at the enemy. B and C Companies of 10th Rifle Brigade were also dug in among the tank positions and stiffened the resolve to stand fast. The panzers had penetrated the British positions as planned, but the point of their attack could not break through the defence line into Thala to get clear of the British guns. Their supporting *panzergrenadiers* were tied down dealing with the infantry and guns that were spread among the scrub land and fields on either side of the road around the tanks. This left the German panzers vulnerable to armour-piercing rounds at very close quarters. It was now the British turn to wreak havoc on the enemy's tanks.

GenMaj von Broich's panzers were now being stalked by individual tanks and guns, located and illuminated by flares fired to light up the battlefield. Enemy infantry were engaged and attacked in the same way, as the British began to get the upper hand. Allan Waterston recalls how his tank from the Lothians was incorporated into the defences: 'When we had collected our wits we found that somebody had formed a sort of hollow square out of all sorts of bits and pieces including tanks, guns, lorries and all sorts of men on foot. I was asked to join in on the north-east corner and keep a good lookout. The scrimmage down on the road gradually died away and in the ensuing quiet a lonely figure approached my position and was challenged by me. I received no reply and was quite entitled to shoot but there was something familiar in the outline of the figure so I held my fire a moment longer which is just as well as it was the colonel looking for his regiment. He did not thank me for not shooting him but passed on at a steady pace into the centre of the "square" without a word.'[25]

The attack had been blunted and the enemy knew it. The defence put up by Nick Force succeeded in halting 10th Panzer Division's thrust for Thala and turning Rommel's force back to the ridge on which the Leicesters' had their original position, leaving many burning hulks along the road. Gradually the firing died down and the scene of the action fell relatively silent. All units in Nick Force remained on high alert, expecting the attack to resume at any moment. Brig Nicholson gave orders that no one would withdraw, and every man capable of fighting as infantry was collected and put into the line somewhere. Cooks, drivers, armourers, engineers, clerks and a whole host of individuals now became fighting men.

Sometime later, the quiet of the night was disturbed by other units tidying up the battlefield as Capt Pirie of 12th RHA later described: 'Somewhere about 3 a.m. some Royal Engineers came and blew up the German tanks. With an almighty roar the cupola, turret doors and tracks flew apart, one door landing in a slit trench, much to the detachment's annoyance. For about an hour afterwards exploding shells and bullets gave an impromptu fireworks display; it is these demolition parties who provide the smashed tanks the news photographer loves, not the antitank guns.'[26]

Just as the battle was raging south of Thala with all available forces, Nick Force was at that moment almost doubling in strength. Arriving in the town was Brig Gen Stafford Le Roy Irwin, the artillery commander of the US 9th Infantry Division. With him were forty-eight guns – twelve 155mm howitzers, twenty-four 105mm howitzers and twelve 75mm howitzers – together with 2,500 men to support Brig Nicholson's defence of the town. The guns went straight into position as they arrived and by dawn Irwin had created a 3-mile arc of artillery around the southern edge of the town.

The enemy had withdrawn, but he was still close by, manning the Leicesters' ridge – too close for comfort and able to dominate the British tank and gun areas once daylight had come. Brig Nicholson knew that they had to be removed, but what with? The only tanks available to Nick Force were the tired and depleted Valentines of the Lothians and the Lancers. At around midnight a few replacement tanks had arrived for the Lothians, brought forward by the Delivery Squadron, and battle-weary crews who had already been knocked out once were asked to man them.

This bolstered the Lothians' numbers somewhat, but the battalion was still in a sorry state. Nonetheless, Nicholson ordered Lt Col Desmond ffrench Blake to attack the enemy at 0500 hr with those tanks that were available and force them off the Leicesters' ridge.

The attack had no prospect of success. The Germans still had seventy tanks available and had lined the ridge with guns. The colonel gathered together the meagre handful of tanks that was left of his regiment – ten in all – and addressed his men, knowing that he was sending them to their doom. He was so convinced that they would all be destroyed that he decided to lead the attack himself. He told his crews of his orders, then said: 'I'm sorry, but we've got to go out on a forlorn hope. I doubt whether any of us will come back.' The battalion history described the action quite simply: 'Moving forward in darkness, without even hope to sustain them, they attacked, and in a short sharp action seven of the ten tanks were lost.' Just a handful of men survived to return to friendly lines.[27]

Morning brought little respite for Nick Force. The enemy remained on the ridge with their observers watching for any sign of life and carrying out counter-battery fire on the British gun positions. With 12th RHA in the front line with nothing before them was Capt Pirie: 'It was one of the longest days I can remember. The previous night there had been moments of pure exhilaration but not so this morning. I remember the gun crew of A Subsection crouching in their slit trenches, each man with his head on the behind of the man in front and four out of five fast asleep as shells landed 25 yards away. Breakfast was cold, straight out of the tin. We could not make tea as the Germans had 88mm guns firing at us over open sights from the ridge. Normally, when a shell arrives the noise gives 15–20 seconds' time in which to take cover, but not so with the 88mm; the shell arrives before the whine, no time to jump.'[28] However, the enemy was not having it all his own way, for Brig Gen Irwin's American artillery were returning fire, shell for shell, from their gun positions just outside Thala.

Everyone in Nick Force now braced himself for the next German attack, but the earlier forlorn attack by the Lothians had unexpectedly brought some respite. Their bold but futile charge against 10th Panzer Division had sent a ripple up its chain of command. Coming so soon after the repulse of the night before, it showed great fortitude and an aggressive spirit by the British. Von Broich believed that the enemy he was facing in front of Thala had been reinforced to the extent that it was moving over to the offensive. Artillery fire against him had increased dramatically overnight and he was not sure that he could now halt a determined move against his division. He was low on ammunition and his stocks of fuel and rations could only last for four more days. Resupply was proving difficult. Von Broich telephoned Rommel and expressed his misgivings, explaining that the planned attack for that morning had been delayed because of heavy Allied artillery concentrations.

Things were also not going well for GenMaj Buelowius and his Afrika Korps Assault Group. Rommel had sent them down the road from Kasserine Pass towards Tebessa with orders to capture Djebel el Hamra and to remove the Americans from the high ground overlooking the route. These were Brig Gen Robinett's Combat Command B and they put up a fierce resistance to the German move. This American battlegroup had been placed under Brig Nicholson and were part of Nick Force, but the high ground separating the formation from the British forces at Thala excluded them being mutually supporting. Robinett's men were virtually on their own. They gave a good account of themselves, dug in as they were in an excellent position, able to dominate the road and the hills around Djebel el Hamra. The Afrika Korps Assault Group were not able to shift them, nor to outflank their defences. Buelowius reported back to Rommel that he was unable to make any headway towards Tebessa.

The German field marshal came forward to meet von Broich and Buelowius to see the situation for himself. A reconnaissance of the ground and information received from the Luftwaffe and from Arab spies indicated that there were Allied reinforcements headed for the Thala area. Later that morning Rommel met with GenFM Kesselring who had flown into Kasserine in his light Storch aircraft to discuss the situation with him. Rommel decided that the offensive had overreached itself and that the Allies were gathering enough force in front of him to stop any further advance. Kesselring was all for going on, believing that the Allies were still reeling in the face of superior German troops. He had scant regard for the Americans and felt that the British could not hold one more determined push which would break through the final defences at Thala and open the way to Le Kef and western Tunisia. Rommel disagreed and the two were locked in argument for a full hour. Eventually, the Desert Fox got his way: the attack would be called off and a general withdrawal would begin. Rommel now had his mind fixed on the other side of the Tunisian front. He needed to hold Montgomery's Eighth Army on the Mareth Line near the coast. Quite rightly, he knew that the attack in the west, successful as it had been in the early stages, was not now going anywhere. The stand made by Nick Force had led him into a strategic backwater.

All day long Nick Force waited for the German attack. As each hour passed Brig Nicholson's battlegroup became stronger. The 1st Guards Brigade and 16th/5th Lancers were being diverted to Thala. Each side spent the time shelling the other, but as the day passed, enemy artillery fire lessened; his ammunition stocks were becoming dangerously low. A calm was beginning to fall over the battlefield.

The next day, 23 February, it was gradually becoming clear to Brig Nicholson that the enemy was withdrawing. Brig Dunphie's brigade was now complete with the arrival of 16th/5th Lancers, and Nick Force had been strengthened by 1st Guards Brigade. In the early morning,

B Squadron of 16th/5th Lancers moved up to the most southern positions of the line and sent its carrier troop further forward on to Leicester Ridge, with A Squadron carrying on to the next ridge along, Djebel el Zuag. Both reached their destinations without meeting the enemy. It was clear that 10th Panzer Division had gone.

On 24 February, 16th/5th Lancers and 1st Guards Brigade, supported by two troops of the Derbyshire Yeomanry, C Company of 10th Rifle Brigade and F Battery of 12th RHA, were ordered to advance to the high ground just short of the Kasserine Pass. Almost before the advance had started, the Lancers lost their Intelligence Officer's tank on a mine. Further losses followed in quick succession, for the enemy had liberally sown hundreds of mines all along the road and verges as he retreated. Parties of sappers from the division were brought up to the leading troops to deal with these mines. That day, in a 6½-hour period, one subsection of 229th Field Company Royal Engineers cleared 100 Tellermines and a number of booby traps of various kinds from a 2-mile section of road. As the advance proceeded, the work was taken over by two troops of 8th Field Squadron RE, who picked up 350 mines in ten miles, three-quarters of which were booby trapped with pull mechanisms.[29]

By 1600 hr the force had reached its objective and was still to find any of the enemy. Half an hour later Maj Gen Keightley came up to 16th/5th Lancers' advance HQ and spoke with the CO. It seemed that the enemy had withdrawn into the pass, but it was not known whether or not he was defending it. Keightley ordered the Lancers to find out. Once again the carrier section went forward under the command of Lt Watson. Shortly after moving off, the leading carrier hit a mine, but the others pressed on and reached the entrance to the pass without further incident. Lt Watson then led his men right through the gap to the other end and reported back that the pass was clear except for large numbers of burned-out vehicles at its southern end. Keightley then sent the Grenadiers and Coldstreamers through the pass and down to Kasserine village. Both were empty; the enemy had flown.

Chapter Five

FONDOUK

During March 1943, Eighth Army continued its long march from Egypt, pushing back Rommel's forces along the coast. Two Allied armies now began to converge in Tunisia. At this point changes in command were made and Gen Alexander was placed at the head of a new Eighteenth Army Group, which combined First and Eighth Armies. Eisenhower was still supreme commander of all Allied forces, but Alexander was now his deputy with responsibility for the overall strategy of the campaign.

Changes had also been made to the German command. Gen Giovanni Messe had taken over Rommel's Italian–German Army and relabelled it First Italian Army – or AOK1 (*Armee-Oberkommando*) for short. Rommel was then made Army Group Commander Afrika with overall command of AOK1 and Fifth Panzer Army. This set-up changed again on 9 March when Rommel left Africa for good. Von Arnim assumed the roll vacated by Rommel, with Gen von Vaerst taking over the command of Fifth Panzer Army.

While the bulk of 6th Armoured Division had moved south to counter Rommel's westward progress, the Irish Brigade had remained in position around Bou Arada. The troops left there being rather thin on the ground, an ad hoc formation was formed to man the line, called Y Division. The 38th Brigade formed the basis of the temporary division and was joined by the Parachute Brigade and a battalion of French infantry, together with artillery support from 152nd Field Regiment RA. This scratch division then fought several spirited actions in the Bou Arada sector over the next month. When it was disbanded, the Irish Brigade did not return to 6th Armoured Division, but went to 78th Division instead. As a replacement, Keightley received 1st Guards Brigade, which had already fought with his forces at Sbiba and in some subsequent smaller actions after Kasserine.

The 1st Guards Brigade had originally contained 3rd Grenadier Guards, 2nd Coldstream Guards and 2nd Hampshires and had seen action as part of the BEF in France in 1940. The 2nd Hampshires was the first of the brigade to arrive in Tunisia with 78th Division and was sent straight into the line at Tebourba in December 1942. During that battle the battalion was decimated

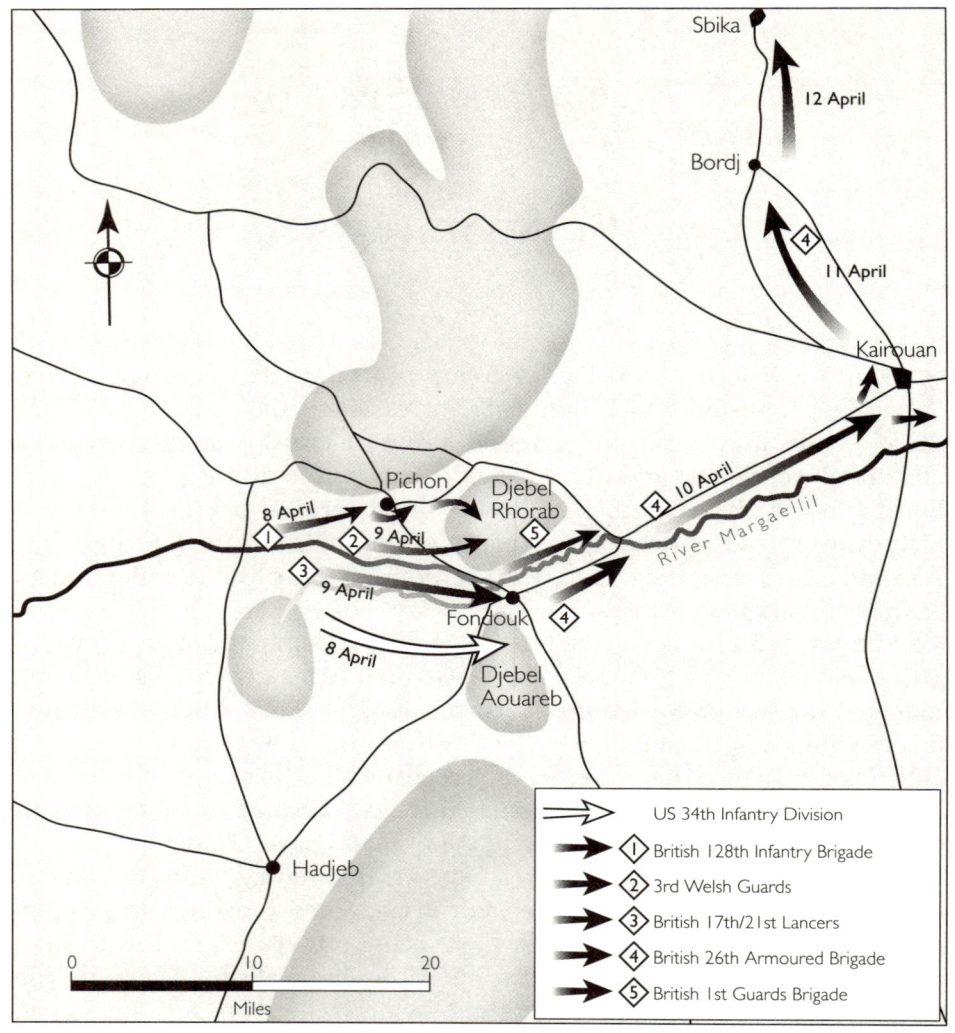

Map 5. The Battle of Fondouk and Kairouan

and never truly recovered. The Hampshires were therefore replaced by 3rd Welsh Guards at the beginning of March 1943, just before the Guards Brigade was permanently assigned to 6th Armoured Division.

About this time the whole of 26th Armoured Brigade was re-equipped with Sherman tanks. It was a great change for tank commanders, for the brigade had, at last, been given a tank that could take on German armour with something like equality. 'Great, snorting, roaring things they seemed to us, churning the earth up and crushing stalwart young trees absent-mindedly in their stride.'[1]

The battalion history of 17th/21st Lancers described the feeling in the regiment about the arrival of the Shermans: 'The best feature of the change to the Sherman was the 75mm gun. At last, here was the answer to the deadly 88mm antitank gun. By shooting into a suspected area with several tanks at once, the blast could strip the camouflage from the big 88s; and if these were of the antiaircraft type with no shield, the crew might be killed before they had fired a shot. Once the antitank gun had fired and had been spotted it was finished; it could be destroyed from three thousand yards or more without revealing more than the tank turret – or not even that if time allowed indirect fire methods to be used.'[2]

Other changes were taking place in the division, one of the most significant being the move of Brig Dunphie to act as an adviser to the Americans. He was replaced as commander of 26th Armoured Brigade by Brig G.P.B. 'Pip' Roberts, a young cavalry officer from Eighth Army with a growing reputation as an armoured commander.

At that time, Lt James Wilson was in command of the antitank platoon of 10th Rifle Brigade. After the armoured brigade had been equipped with Sherman tanks the role of these 6-pounder guns changed. The Shermans were a more effective antitank weapon with their 75mm armament than the smaller-calibre towed guns. As a result, the antitank platoon often lacked a role in mobile action and was relegated to following behind the rest of the battalion. Wilson was told by his CO, Lt Col Adrian Gore, to place himself a tactical bound to the rear of the motor battalion. From this position, travelling just behind the action, the lieutenant was able to watch the direction and control of the fighting. He was a great admirer of Brig 'Pip' Roberts and later explained in his memoirs what it was like to follow the brigadier in battle:

> Pip Roberts was a natural commander of armour and a master tactician. All day he operated from the turret of his command Sherman, the Brigade Major, Tony Kershaw, below, operating the radios and feeding his commander tea and bully beef sandwiches. Pip watched the battle through field glasses, coming on the air occasionally to adjust the position of his regiments. Behind him, part of his small Tactical HQ, were his gunner, John Barstow, CO 12 RHA, and our own Adrian Gore, his motor battalion commander, in case the battle developed an infantry bias. Pip Roberts was indefatigable and unruffled; he was always in the right place and one jump ahead of the opposition. From my Dingo scout car I watched the battle develop and tried to anticipate possible tasks for my 6-pounder antitank guns. I need not have worried; Pip Roberts, like some armoured team manager, organised things so well that infantry were seldom needed till last light when they would be called forward to protect the armoured leaguers. As soon as that moment came, Pip Roberts felt able to switch off. Up would come the main part of his Brigade HQ, with a 3 ton lorry carrying a piano. Sometimes the piano would be unloaded and Pip would relax over its keys – he was a jazz

pianist with a delicate touch – till he was needed for a decision or, as often happened, Charles Keightley called for advice on what he should do next day.[3]

Throughout March the armoured regiments continued to be involved in taking delivery and training with the new Shermans. Various programmes were implemented to allow the crews to become familiar with their new mounts and new weapons. Morale was high as they at last felt that they were no longer outgunned by their opponents. While its armour perfected their new techniques, 6th Armoured Division fulfilled a role as First Army's reserve in the newly raised British IX Corps, which was commanded by the division's erstwhile leader Lt Gen John Crocker.

On 20 March, Eighth Army began its attacks to break through the Mareth Line against Messe's First Italian Army. Fighting was prolonged and difficult, but the entrenched fortifications were eventually breached and Montgomery was able to advance to the next enemy halt-line along the coast at Wadi Akarit. The Americans were also active in the east and were beginning to push back the enemy in their sector. Axis forces in Tunisia were gradually being corralled into an area in the north of the country around Tunis. Allied units were still far from the capital, but their growing strength, coupled with improving weather, would soon enable Eisenhower to contemplate switching First Army over to the offensive.

Providing Montgomery could defeat the enemy at Wadi Akarit and get behind his defensive line, AOK1 would be forced to withdraw further northwards along the coastal plain. This would expose a long flank to Anderson's forces gathered on the western side of the hills of the Eastern Dorsal and present a tempting target for an attack along the Axis line of retreat. Gen Alexander therefore warned Anderson to alert First Army's reserve, Lt Gen Crocker's British IX Corps, to be ready to intercept Messe's army as it retreated across the plain through Kairouan. On 4 April, anticipating victory at Wadi Akarit, he ordered Crocker to organise an operation to get 6th Armoured Division to strike at AOK1's lines of communication as it fled northwards.

As a precursor to this strike, Crocker's corps first had to fight its way through the hilly region of the Eastern Dorsal at Fondouk to get onto the plain in front of Kairouan. Timing was very important. Once Eighth Army had broken Messe's forces at Akarit, the Italian/German withdrawal would be sure to begin. British 6th Armoured Division had to hit them as they came through Kairouan. Too soon, and the division would itself be struck by the massed stampede of enemy divisions that included 10th and 21st Panzer Divisions. Too late, and the enemy would have flown.

The Mailed Fist Division was training and refitting around Sbiba some 60 miles from Kairouan, but still close enough to move into the area to the west of Fondouk in time to make its attack. For the operation IX Corps had been reinforced by Maj Gen Ryder's US 34th Division from the US II Corps, together with 128th Infantry Brigade from the British 46th Division. These two formations were to break through the enemy line before Fondouk and allow 6th Armoured Division to make the main thrust for Kairouan. Further support was available for the operation from the heavy Churchill tanks of 51st Royal Tank Regiment, 5.5in guns from 51st Medium Regiment and sappers from 586th and 751st Field Companies RE.

The strike through Kairouan, if successful, could lead to a further impressive victory. If Messe's force was disorganised there, the Italian general would find it extremely difficult to reorganise his army and prepare further defences before it was overwhelmed by Montgomery's forces driving up from the south. The action could, with boldness on the part of all Alexander's forces, lead to a complete enemy collapse in Tunisia.

Such prospects did not please everybody in the Allied camp. One particular general, George Patton Jr, was livid with rage. At that stage in the campaign he, and many other senior American officers, were very unhappy with the conduct of the fighting in Tunisia. They were still smarting from the Kasserine debacle and from British arrogance. They felt that the British were acting in a condescending manner with regard to the performance of American troops and were trying to take all the credit for any victory. The general feeling in First Army was that the American way was not the British way and was therefore inferior. Patton did have a good point, for throughout the British Army in Tunisia, from privates to generals, there was much bickering and sniping. This was aimed at not only the Americans, but also the French. Neither were the French themselves immune from such attitudes, for their units also contained a large Anglophobic body of opinion.

Patton was also unhappy with Eisenhower, who seemed to be constantly giving in to British pressure regarding strategy. The American lack of success in their actions so far led to a feeling that they were doing all the hard fighting while the British reaped the accolades. Alexander's proposals for the Fondouk operation, with a British corps being introduced between existing French and American corps, would mean that Patton's US II Corps would be pinched out of the fighting and therefore not be present in the final battle to take Tunis. Patton took this plan quite personally and recorded in his diary: 'I hope the Boches beat the complete life out of 128th Brigade and 6th Armoured Division. I am fed up with being treated like a moron by the British.'[4] It is extraordinary that one Allied general should wish for the complete destruction of an Allied division prior to such a decisive battle, but then national pride was sometimes more important than Allied victories. In the event, Patton was to get his wish, or partially so, and the recriminations as to who was to blame continued to be debated among historians and participants along nationalistic lines for decades.

To achieve surprise, the move of IX Corps to the area in front of Fondouk had to remain secret from the enemy. The line through Fondouk marked the junction of American and French forces, so the enemy had to be kept ignorant of the new armoured division's arrival. Movement towards the forming-up area was done at night and dummy tanks were left at the training area to mislead enemy air reconnaissance and Arab spies into believing that 6th Armoured was still in place at Sbiba. Such actions, however, did not fool the enemy, for the whole of the Allied force had to deploy on the flat ground in front of Fondouk prior to the attack and not even a jeep could move without churning up a cloud of soft dust. A German prisoner later described how they were amazed at the incredible array of tanks assembling to attack them.[5]

Kairouan lies in the plain between the Eastern Dorsal – high ground running north–south – and the eastern coastline of Tunisia. The IX Corps's attack had first to break through a narrow pass across this high ground in front of Fondouk before its armour could be let loose against the western flank of Messe's fleeing army. The problem was that the pass and the high ground on either side were all held by the enemy. The gap itself was about two miles wide, overlooked to the north by Djebels Houfia and Cherichira and to the south by Djebel Aouareb. A further rocky outcrop bulging from Houfia was called Djebel Rhorab; it sat menacingly above the gap looking down on the route through the pass and across to the slopes of Djebel Aouareb.

The enemy holding the area had been in residence for over three months, kept in check by both the Americans and the French. Gen Welvert's Division of the French IXX Corps held the ground to the north of the pass across to Pichon, and Maj Gen Ryder's 34th Division of the US II Corps occupied the ground to the south. The US 34th Division had been in the area since 27 March, when Ryder had been ordered to seize the high ground to the south of Fondouk and make a threatening move towards Kairouan. 'Make a lot of noise, but don't capture anything,' Patton told Ryder. The attack was a diversion for American operations further south between Gafsa and Gabes – a display of strength in the rear of the enemy holding Akarit, but one designed to cause consternation rather than to gain territory.

The attack on the Djebel Aouareb feature by 34th Division was not a success. Ryder's division had still not recovered from the effects of its action at Sidi Bou Zid during the German Kasserine offensive. It arrived at the forming-up point for the assault after a long approach on 26 March and was launched straight into the attack at first light on the 27th. Moving forward on a 3,000-yard front, the infantry were expected to advance across open ground in full view of the enemy and then uphill over a distance of ten miles. Not unexpectedly, the leading battalions went to ground after just a few miles of trudging across heavy ground under enemy artillery bombardment. The enemy on Djebel Rhorab had perfect observation over 34th Division's line of attack and could see them coming for miles.

Each time the attack faltered it had to be got moving again by junior officers passing among the troops urging them on. The hesitant moves took all day to reach the enemy hillside and it was not until nightfall that the Americans got among the German positions. They gained little more ground before they were gradually driven back in the face of close-quarters small-arms fire. The struggle continued to and fro as each side skirmished over the next few days; some brave sallies were made against the enemy, but the Germans were content to stay deep within their prepared trench system, picking off the Americans as they showed themselves. Eventually, after three days, the attack was broken off, Maj Gen Ryder having felt that his show of strength towards Kairouan had alarmed the enemy sufficiently. He had captured nothing, but he had complied with the orders given to him by Patton. The cost – 527 casualties.[6]

Crocker's plan for the Fondouk operation was first to employ the infantry to seize the high ground on either side of the pass, then send 26th Armoured Brigade through the gap to drive on Kairouan and catch Messe's forces in the flank. The news of victory at Wadi Akarit and of the northwards withdrawal of AOK1 resulted in Crocker deciding to open the battle on the night of 7/8 April, with 128th Hampshire Brigade attacking the northern hills to take Pichon and Djebel Houfia before swinging southwards to take Djebel Rhorab. In concert with these moves, Ryder's US 34th Division would advance over the same flat land south of the pass that it had crossed ten days previously and attack Djebel Aouareb again. With both sides of the Fondouk gap in Allied hands, the tanks would start their drive eastwards some time after 1300 hr on 8 April. The timetable was tight, for it was imperative that Keightley's armour hit the enemy while they were passing through Kairouan.

When Maj Gen Ryder heard of the plan, he was not pleased. His attempt to take the Aouareb feature in March had taught him that his advance would remain very difficult while his division was overlooked from the north by an enemy-held Djebel Rhorab. As this hill was not the primary objective of the Hampshire Brigade, it would still be in German hands when his 34th Division made its attack. He was convinced that the outcome would be the same as before: casualties during the long approach to the djebel would almost certainly disorganise his assault.

Lt Gen Crocker came up to see Ryder at his HQ on 6 April to hear the American's misgivings about the attack. Maj Gen Ryder pointed out how experience had shown that an attack on Aouareb was not a sound proposition until Rhorab had been captured. The Hampshire Brigade would not be moving against Rhorab until it had first captured Pichon and the hills to south of the town. All this while, the Americans would be vulnerable from fire from their front and flank as they went in. Ryder suggested that Rhorab should be attacked before, or in concert with, his assault on the heights of Aouareb.

Crocker would have none of it. He insisted that Rhorab was only weakly held by second-rate troops and that their observation of the American advance would be screened by smoke. Crocker also knew that the bulk of the enemy was pulling back towards the north. He was sure that they would not reinforce the Fondouk position. 'If he is strongly attacked, he will go,' was Crocker's response. Ryder accepted the orders from his superior, but remained very unhappy. Gen Louis Koeltz, commander of the French XIX Corps, was also at the command post and he added his misgivings to Ryder's. Koeltz explained that it was his men who had lost the Fondouk area to the enemy back in January and that he knew the ground very well. The American approaches were completely flat with no cover. The enemy was dug in on Rhorab in strength; a frontal attack on Aouareb would fail. Crocker listened with growing discomfort, but refused to change his plan.

Crocker was wrong about the effectiveness of enemy troops in the Fondouk area. His intelligence informed him that the German infantry holding the heights were inferior. They came from 961st Regiment of 999th Light Afrika Division, commanded by GenMaj Kurt Thomas. The division was a penal unit, comprising of battalions of men who had run foul of the authorities, most of whom were political prisoners or convicted criminals. Many were court-martialled soldiers who had regained their freedom by volunteering for the front. Others were black marketeers, demoted officers, thieves, rapists and thugs, none of whom was expected to be filled with blind obedience to the Third Reich. British intelligence assumed that most would be looking for a way to desert to the Allies at the earliest opportunity. Reality proved somewhat different, for the division had a stiff backbone of regular officers and NCOs and, to everyone's surprise, it fought remarkably well, most especially its artillery regiment. Desertions during the division's whole existence amounted to only 10 per cent.

With Ryder now resigned to the attack, the American general looked for ways to lessen the impact that the enemy-held Djebel Rhorab would have on his men. He decided that, with luck, he might be able to get his men past the feature if he began his assault under cover of darkness. He requested Crocker to allow his move to begin two hours earlier than the planned start time of 0530 hr; Crocker agreed.

The attack made on Fondouk was the first action to be fought by 6th Armoured Division as a whole. Prior to this, its engagements in

Tunisia had been piecemeal, with units, brigades, armoured regiments and infantry battalions split up to hold the line or to plug gaps in the front. Here at Fondouk, Maj Gen Keightley could fight his division as a division. His armoured brigade would force an opening through the gap and his infantry brigade would consolidate. Then his infantry brigade would advance to form a base west of Kairouan while the armoured brigade sallied forth to attack the enemy columns. That was the plan; good, solid armoured tactics.

By 7 April, the day after the Akarit battle, air reconnaissance confirmed that Messe's men had withdrawn and were streaming back towards Kairouan. Early the next morning, Crocker launched his attack eastwards to intercept them. There were immediate problems. Maj Gen Ryder had gained permission to bring forward his start time, but the changes in timing had not been agreed by the air forces. The air strikes that were to take place at 0530 hr were therefore cancelled for fear of hitting the Americans. Worse was to follow, for when the division moved out at 0230 hr to cross the open ground to the start line, one battalion of 135th Regiment got lost, moved too far to the left and got itself tangled up in a wadi. The remainder of the two assaulting regiments struggled forward in the darkness on a front of two miles. Progress was slow and disorganised so that it was not until the original start time of 0530 hr that the assault actually got started. Daylight found the Americans spread out across open ground under intense fire from both front and flank just as Ryder had predicted. Again, the Americans went to ground in the open and suffered accordingly.

Artillery, mortar and machine-gun fire raked their vulnerable positions. Orders were given to pull back 2,000 yards to await a bombing raid on Djebel Aouareb. Ryder's men did so and waited, but the raid never took place. When the troops finally moved forward again, the enemy had their range and direction pinpointed to perfection. Once again the shattering explosions and fountains of dirt that were thrown up all around them forced the infantry to ground and the attack halted 700 yards short of the hill. Throughout the day Ryder's men dug deeper and deeper into the rocky soil, seeking some respite from the enemy fire. In the early afternoon American tanks came up to join them as Ryder tried to get the attack going again. Little happened, for the armour attracted even more fire. One by one they fell victim to the fast flat trajectory of antitank shot and burst into flames or scuttled away from the battlefield.

When at 1500 hr Ryder ordered the attack to resume, nobody moved. Again at 1700 hr another resumption of the assault was ordered and more tanks from the US 751st Tank Battalion came forward; but no infantry would get out of their slit trenches to follow them. Enemy fire continued; six tanks exploded into flame and the remainder withdrew. The US 34th Division was stuck fast.

To the north, the attack by 128th Hampshire Brigade started as planned. The brigade had made the 140-mile move from the area near Beja over two tortuous days, bumping its way along twisting roads in trucks, arriving just before daylight on 7 April. Just a short rest and then the two assaulting battalions undertook the long six-mile advance on foot to get to the assembly area for the 0530 hr start. Leading 128th Brigade was 1st/4th Hampshires, supported by a squadron of Churchill infantry tanks from 51st Royal Tank Regiment. Pichon was soon captured as were the heights to the north of the town, both with few casualties. The 2nd/4th Hampshires then took up the advance with another squadron of Churchills and swept southwards across Djebel Houfia towards Rhorab, again with light casualties. The brigade then launched 5th Hampshires against Djebel Rhorab. Here the going got tough and the enemy penal battalion holding the heights made full use of its commanding position and well-established defences to bring the advance by the Hampshire Brigade to an abrupt halt. Heavy mortar fire forced 5th Battalion back on to a reverse slope where it dug in behind the commanding feature.

Crocker was not pleased with how the day had progressed. The Americans had not seized the high ground to the south of the gap and 128th Brigade had not taken the important height of Rhorab to the north. The gap was still closed to armour. The need for speed dominated Crocker's thinking; Messe's army was in retreat and beginning to pass through Kairouan, its passage clearly marked by great clouds of dust billowing up into the sky on the horizon.

The corps commander was now beginning to fret and the army group commander was starting to apply pressure for results. Alexander told Crocker to launch 6th Armoured Division through the pass the next morning whether or not the hills on either side had been taken, whatever the cost. Crocker in turn ordered Keightley to commit the whole of his division into the attack. His 1st Guards Brigade would seize Rhorab with an attack from the west, straight at the heights from the valley floor without tank support. The 26th Armoured Brigade was to force its way through the Fondouk Pass. Messe's army was escaping and high command was becoming exasperated.

Two miles short of the gap, Brig 'Pip' Roberts had brought his tactical HQ forward to see the area over which his armoured brigade would have to attack. He was certain that the gap was mined and asked Lt Col Gore of 10th Rifle Brigade if his riflemen could ascertain if this was so. Gore agreed to send out a patrol that night to reconnoitre the pass. In the meantime, Gore's battalion came forward to guard the approach during the hours of darkness. Behind it, Robert's three armoured regiments leaguered for the night, with the guns of 12th RHA dug in close behind.

On 9 April, the attacks on the two important heights resumed. To the north, 3rd Welsh Guards, with little artillery support and no air support, advanced along the valley floor against the strongly held Djebel Rhorab. To the south, Ryder's reluctant infantry were urged from their foxholes and sent forward again against Aouareb behind more American tanks of 751st Tank Battalion. In the centre, the lead regiment of Roberts' Armoured Brigade, 17th/21st Lancers, sent a reconnaissance group forward to probe the gap. The patrol made by the Rifle Brigade during the night had found little to report; it had not got to the area of the suspected minefield so the Lancers would have to find out for themselves. The Shermans swung southwards to reconnoitre an entry point to the pass, but got themselves tangled up with, and thoroughly annoyed, the Americans. They cautiously pushed towards the gap trying to determine whether or not it was mined, then lost four tanks one after another to high-velocity antitank fire. The route to Fondouk and Kairouan was still most definitely closed and well guarded, but was there a minefield?

Brig Roberts was also concerned that the US 34th Division's infantry were still on the valley floor. He had expected that by this time they would be scrambling over the heights of Djebel Aouareb, clearing out the enemy. Ryder's men were still finding it hard to make any progress up the hill. They had been subjected to artillery and mortar fire throughout the night as they sheltered in their narrow slit trenches out on the open ground. This started to ease as the Welsh Guards made their attack on Rhorab and occupied the attention of those of the enemy who were giving the Americans so much trouble. Tanks then came forward to renew Ryder's attack. Junior leaders urged their men on and the advance resumed, only to hesitate and fall back once the leading troops started to take casualties. Some tanks actually made it on to the top of the hill, but few infantry followed them up the slopes. Hopelessly exposed, the armour was quickly eliminated.

On Djebel Rhorab, 3rd Welsh Guards were putting in their first major attack of the war. The battalion had replaced the all but destroyed 2nd Hampshires in 1st Guards Brigade and now began their initiation into action. Their assault began at 0630 hr just as daylight began. As with the Americans, the initial stages of the attack were across several miles of open ground in full view of the enemy. Artillery and mortar fire fell among them during the whole of the advance. Return fire from 12th RHA helped limit some of the enemy concentration, but casualties began to mount. By 0930 hr all four of the rifle companies had made it to the base of the hill and some guardsmen had started to move up its rocky slopes. Here the volume of enemy fire increased, artillery shells having been replaced by mortar bombs and machine-gun bullets.

The advance was beginning to take its toll on the battalion. Several section and platoon leaders lay dead or wounded and the assault began to slacken. Wireless contact between the companies and battalion HQ was becoming difficult. Men were going to ground, seeking shelter where they could among the boulders and scrub that covered the hillside. The 3rd Welsh Guards were beginning to run out of determination.

While the attacks on Djebels Rhorab and Aouareb were under way, Brig Roberts was still trying to decide how he would tackle the pass. Was it mined or not? At about 0900 hr he received a surprising visitor at his tactical HQ: Lt Gen Crocker had come forward to see Keightley and to urge for more progress. Roberts jumped down from his tank and met Crocker storming towards him across the broken ground. 'Where is your divisional commander?' he shouted, obviously in a bad mood. Roberts replied that he had not seen Gen Keightley and suggested that he was likely to be over with 1st Guards Brigade. Crocker then asked the brigadier what he was doing. Roberts explained that he was using 17th/21st Lancers to probe forward towards the Fondouk Pass, trying to determine the location and extent of the minefield, motioning towards his tanks in the distance with shells falling among them.

This information was not well received by Crocker, as Brig Roberts later explained in his memoirs. 'Don't you realise', said the general, 'that the Germans and Italians are now streaming back from Eighth Army and we have to attack them and cut them off? You should be doing more than you are.' Roberts was slightly bemused and replied, 'Of course we could attack now sir, but it would be expensive, and the plan was that we should attack the pass as soon as the hills on either side have been captured or neutralised.' 'Attack now,' said the corps commander and stormed off to find Keightley to relay the order to him.[7]

Brig Roberts was left in an unpleasant situation: he now had to throw caution aside and send his armoured brigade through the gap at a charge. If the gap was mined it would be a disaster. There was not time to confirm the location or extent of the German-made obstacle; the corps commander had made it quite clear that he had to act immediately. He called up the commanding officer of 17th/21st Lancers, Lt Col Hamilton-Russell, to give him his orders. Roberts told Hamilton-Russell of the situation and of the pressing need for speed. Orders were quite simple: 12th RHA would put down an artillery concentration on the far side of the gap and on a small hill on the right just beyond the pass, which they called the 'Pimple'. The Lancers would then attack under cover of this barrage with two squadrons up. Once they were through the gap, artillery fire would be by direct observation as needed. Roberts finished by wishing the Lancers officer good luck.[8]

When the squadron commanders of 17th/21st Lancers were hurriedly called to an orders group by their CO they knew that something was up. The regiment was already under shellfire and the officers would have expected to receive their orders over the radio. They drove back to regimental HQ in their scout cars to hear the news; to their dismay they were told that the regiment had been ordered to force the gap using speed and weight of numbers. They were to charge through the valley as their forebears in the old 17th Lancers had done at Balaclava in the Crimea in 1854, with 'cannon to the right of them and cannon to the left'. None of these officers were in any doubt as to the enormity of what lay ahead. Maj Nix turned to his friend Maj Maxwell and said, 'Goodbye – I shall never see you again. We shall all be killed.'[9]

The squadron leaders returned to their tanks and organised the attack. Within a short space of time all was ready and the field guns of the Royal Horse Artillery opened up on the enemy positions with as heavy a barrage as they were capable of firing. Then smoke was put down to help shield the advancing Sherman tanks of 17th/21st Lancers. Their battalion history describes the opening moves of the charge: 'After going forward a few hundred yards B Squadron ran into the edge of the minefield. Immediately tanks began to blow up on the mines, though some got through, only to be knocked out by antitank guns beyond. As the crews baled out they were met by an inferno of mortar bombs and machine-gun bullets from the high ground, and accurate sniping by infantry close to the tanks and well camouflaged. Beyond lay a further belt of mines.'[10]

One troop was successfully led by Lt Micholls through the second belt and reached the base of the 'Pimple', in the plain beyond the pass. They were through the mines, but now lay exposed on the valley floor at the mercy of the German guns. Within minutes, the enemy antitank weapons all trained on this leading group with a fury of solid shot. Unable to find cover the tanks stood their ground and returned fire in an act of defiance. All of them were gradually knocked out one by one and their gallant leader, Lt Micholls, killed.

The remainder of B Squadron struggled on through the mines, losing more and more tanks as they went. Maj Nix conducted the attack from the open hatch of his turret, urging his squadron on, before he too succumbed to enemy fire, killed by a bullet in the head, his dire prophecy realised. Eventually the squadron was down to just two tanks. The task now seemed hopeless and a radio message was sent to call them back.

C Squadron followed behind B Squadron, but moved more to the right. In the first few minutes of the advance all of the tanks of the two leading troops were blown up on mines. The squadron commander, Maj Maxwell, could see that it was pointless to continue and requested permission to withdraw. Brig Roberts had seen enough; he agreed to halt the carnage and told Hamilton-Russell to pull back his tanks, requesting covering fire from the artillery to hide the move. The remainder of C Squadron now reversed out of the minefield, backing carefully over their own tracks.

After the appalling losses to B and C Squadrons, A Squadron had the unenviable task of going next, knowing the fate that probably awaited them. However, word had come into the Lancers HQ that there appeared to be a possible route forward near the wadi on the left. Orders were given to A Squadron to try this route alongside the bank of the River Margaellil. It was hoped that the river bed might give some cover for the advance. With some trepidation, A Squadron tried the latest plan. It began well and in the initial stages the main obstacles to be met were antitank guns rather than mines. Two of these guns were knocked out by the leading troops and a third was dispatched after it had actually been passed by the forward tanks. When the leading armour got to the river bed they found that the drop down the bank was too steep for tanks. Entry into the wadi would have to be made further back.

Pressing on alongside the wadi, A Squadron now found that enemy antitank fire was lessening. The attack by the two previous squadrons had actually knocked out many of these guns. The enemy was also feeling the effects of artillery fire and the presence of the Welsh Guards on Djebel Rhorab. The defence by the penal battalion of 961st Regiment was starting to crumble. The tanks pressed on through another minefield and a few more became victims of shattering explosions; but by 1130 hr enough progress had been made to justify launching the rest of the brigade through the pass in support. The boldness of the assault was beginning to win dividends.

Brig Roberts now brought 16th/5th Lancers into the attack, sending their tanks along the wadi. To assist them in clearing out the enemy defences, a company of 10th Rifle Brigade went forward in support. Classic tank/infantry tactics won the day, for 16th/5th drove up the wadi with the loss of just one tank. No antitank mines were found in the bed, but there were many antipersonnel mines. Heavy casualties were inflicted on German infantry while passing up the wadi; accurate return fire was directed at every antitank gun that opened up on the advancing armour. The riflemen in carriers followed closely behind, ready to debus and attack any of the German infantry that refused to give up. Tanks shooting high explosive and infantry firing light machine guns swept the Germans from their posts. The Lancers then swung their tanks round to the right out of the wadi to try get behind the 'Pimple' and put the enemy defenders to flight. Two more tanks were damaged in the process, and one knocked out, but the Shermans and their supporting riflemen eventually won through. By mid-afternoon, the advance was over a mile east of Fondouk; the gap had been breached.

In one of the knocked-out Shermans belonging to 16th/5th Lancers was Lt J. Metcalfe. Three of his crew were killed and he and his lance-corporal were badly burned. He later described his experience in the tank for the regimental history: 'We were the first to be hit. It seemed within two seconds the whole of the squadron let fly with everything, including smoke. The support gunnery was first class. It was appalling to think that after so much training I had "bought" it. I was virtually blown out of the turret by the exploding of the ammunition. I ran over to take command of Corporal Skelton's tank, but there I realised I was beginning not to see.'[11]

Following behind 16th/5th Lancers were the Lothians and Border Horse. Their passage through the gap was virtually uneventful, for most of the antitank guns had by then been eliminated. There were, however, the minefields to be negotiated, a worrying task even though there were safe tracks marked by the tanks who had been before. Sgt David Antonio crossed these minefields with the Lothians and later described seeing all the knocked-out tanks of the first waves that had succumbed to the buried explosives: 'On either hand derelict tanks lay awry, their broken tracks hanging limply over the top rollers, bogies and suspension units blown off. It was strange to think that the innocent seeming ground over which we were travelling might at any moment erupt in a shattering explosion beneath our tracks.'[12]

All over the battlefield that day, forlorn tank crews made their way back to the rear, taking care to walk along the track marks made by their tanks. Much of the armour that hit mines merely had its tracks blown off and was able to be put back into service quite quickly by REME units. The crews of these Shermans for the most part escaped uninjured. At the height of the battle there was great danger for the crews when they did bale out, for the enemy tried to knock off the tank men with small arms and mortars. Both sides did this, even though they thought it unchivalrous. The reason was obvious: tanks could easily be replaced from the production line, tank crews took months to train.

One observer watched as the crew from a disabled tank was making its way to the rear. Among the dejected group was a tanker holding a tin aloft which the observer took to be a tin of marmalade pudding. Marmalade and treacle puddings were the most highly prized articles among the rations and were not to be abandoned lightly. A surprisingly high number were salvaged under the most difficult and dangerous circumstances during the campaign.[13]

The presence of tanks behind Djebel Aouareb lessened the enemy's grip on the hill and permitted the US 34th Division finally to take it. This allowed sappers to come forward to begin clearing the minefields so that transport could pass through the gap. By around 1600 hr tracked vehicles were moving past Fondouk, but wheeled vehicles were still stuck in the rear. This meant that the armoured brigade would have to move on without the support of the field guns of 12th RHA.

The tanks through the gap now began to probe further forward towards Kairouan, but the shock of breaking through the enemy defences and surviving seemed to be enough success for one day. The pursuit now started to lack the urgency earlier instilled by the corps commander. The enemy response to the loss of the pass was to dispatch armour westwards to check the advance. It was a half-hearted attempt and amounted to just half a dozen Panzer IVs, with allegedly one or two Tigers. The Shermans of

16th/5th Lancers engaged them at once and set two of the Panzer IVs on fire; the other enemy tanks withdrew. The appearance of tanks in front of 26th Armoured Brigade caused further hesitation in the advance. Was the enemy armour proof that one of the panzer divisions was about to launch a counterattack against 6th Armoured Division, or were the tanks just a flank guard to hold back and threaten the British, but not to engage? Reports coming into corps HQ suggested that both 10th and 21st Panzer Divisions were near Kairouan. The questions remained unanswered, for a gathering dust storm worsened visibility, and failing light caused the brigade to think about leaguering for the night. Brig Roberts allowed his armoured battalions to halt their advance and reorganise, restocking supplies of fuel and ammunition and receiving replacement tanks for some of those which had been knocked out. Meanwhile, a few miles ahead, the rear of Messe's army was slipping by Kairouan.

Maj Gen Keightley's division had performed reasonably well that day. The 1st Guards Brigade had taken the important heights of Djebel Rhorab and had later pushed on along the high ground to the north of the gap to be in a position to get forward when the advance resumed. His armoured brigade had forced its way through a heavily defended pass with a mixture of supreme bravery and dash. The Fondouk position had been broken, albeit a day later than planned and with the aid of some forceful urging by the corps commander.

It was now a time to bury the dead. A reporter from Kemsley Newspapers, John D'Arcy-Dawson, described the scene after the battle for his readers: 'Coming back along a winding track, I passed a tank. On the back under a ground sheet lay the commander, shot dead as he tried to guide his tank forward, his head out of the turret. Now he was borne back on his tank as a knight of old would have been carried from the battlefield on his charger.'[14] The 17th/21st Lancers lost thirteen men killed and thirty-two wounded during the charge. Thirty-two of its tanks had been knocked out. The other two armoured regiments lost seven tanks between them.

The next day, 10 April, the pursuit continued. Just after first light, a replenished 26th Armoured Brigade advanced across flat countryside perfect for tanks. The Shermans bowled along through stretches of high crops and masses of wild flowers. Very soon they came upon the remnants of the penal battalions. They were trudging eastwards on foot; their transport had escaped the previous day with the regular officers and NCOs of the regiment. These tired, disillusioned foot-soldiers were only too happy to surrender to the British. As the tanks overtook them, they were waved back towards the rear where they were met with some fascination by the infantry. It was the first time that a large number of prisoners of war had been taken. The Coldstream Guards' history describes these German captives: 'The battalion was to have its fill of German prisoners before the month was out, but now they were something strange and new: the unseen menace of a death among the hills resolved itself into these ordinary, shabby, tired men who lifted incurious eyes to look at the guardsmen and dropped them again to the wide dusty road which led to their captivity.'[15]

For the first time, the tanks of 6th Armoured Division found ideal conditions, perfect for exploitation: firm ground, a wide-open plain, fine weather and a clear run. The regimental history of the Ayrshire Yeomanry described the advance: 'It was an exciting time. There can be few sights more exhilarating than that of an armoured division in pursuit, and after the cold, mud and rain of the winter and the boredom and tension of static positions, the Yeomen now found themselves chasing the enemy, with yellow mustard brightening the plain, and wild flowers, marigolds, daisies, sweet-peas and poppies among the wheat. Spring and success were in the air.'[16]

The open ground was well suited for an armoured advance and the division moved forward in box formation for the first and only time during the war. Tanks moved on the outside of the box with lorries and infantry in the centre. The 16th/5th Lancers led the division, with 17th/21st Lancers on the right and the Lothians and Border Horse on the left. The 10th Rifle Brigade and the unarmoured vehicles were in the centre as were the guns of 12th RHA. It was mechanised warfare in its purest form; something that could only be undertaken in ideal conditions with plenty of room to manoeuvre.

When Kairouan came into sight, it was clear that the enemy had escaped. The great dust clouds thrown up by his passing could be seen away to the north. Messe's army had beaten the trap. The armoured brigade now moved across to cut the road leading into Kairouan from the south – the escape route up which the Germans and Italians had passed – to try to cut off any stragglers.

At around 1500 hr as 16th/5th Lancers approached the road, they saw an armoured column heading north at speed. The enemy were engaged at around 2,000 yards' range and the leading German tank was hit. A one-sided battle followed in which all the enemy's vehicles were knocked out, including a self-propelled gun and three other tanks. The Rifle Brigade's A Company then attacked and killed or captured any of the enemy that they found.

Just after this skirmish, the Lothians were also in action, this time with a more substantial German force of fifteen tanks and self-propelled guns. B Squadron engaged the enemy at once while A Squadron wheeled in a wide turn to attack from the flank, losing one tank in the process. The enemy, however, was determined to fight. C Squadron moved out and joined the battle on the other flank. It was a tank-versus-tank struggle, with the enemy scrambling to achieve a better position from which to counter the Lothians. A few tanks tried to outmanoeuvre B Squadron, but were seen off by A Squadron of 16th/5th Lancers who had moved across to help, just as darkness was falling. The Lancers had come out from behind a cactus grove on the blind side of the enemy and opened fire at about 1,500 yards, knocking out ten of his tanks and SP guns. The regimental history describes the action as a 'manoeuvre carried out in true textbook style'. Such tactics would not have been possible with Valentine tanks, but with the larger-gunned Shermans the armour was able to take effective action at much longer ranges. The tables had at last been turned and it was now the enemy with his smaller guns who had to close on the British tanks to have any chance of success. It also showed, as the Lancers' historian points out, that the tank battles in Tunisia were as much about equipment, as they were of training and tactical skill.[17]

Kairouan was now effectively cut off from the south and any more of the enemy who were still trying to retreat to the north had to sidestep the city and try to cross the flat plain between there and the sea. It was now early evening and Brig Roberts called his armoured brigade in to leaguer for the night, spread out across the undulating semi-desert to the south of Kairouan. The advance eastwards now became pointless since the enemy was to the north, retreating with speed into the defences along the high ground to the west of Enfidaville. The dash forward by the division to hit Messe's flank would now have to be switched to the chase, trying to catch the tail of the fleeing panzer rearguard before it reached the shelter of the hills.

At 1000 hr on 11 April, the advance continued, but not before many of the division's units had been hit by German dive-bombers. Several tanks were knocked out and a surprisingly high number of casualties suffered, including twenty-three by 16th/5th Lancers alone, eight of whom were killed. In bright sunshine 26th Armoured Brigade swung around the city and headed north, while the bulk of the infantry of the division liberated the holy city of Kairouan and ensured that there were no more of the enemy to the south and east. Patrols were sent eastwards towards Sousse and the sea to meet up with Eighth Army, who were advancing up the coastal road.

It soon became clear that the Germans and Italians could not be overtaken, for every time that the lead tanks came close, the enemy's mobile troops would stand firm, fire a few rounds and cause the pursuers to halt and deploy. The advance, although not catching AOK1, was still reaping dividends by cutting off the enemy in the Eastern Dorsal away to the west. The opposition there were being pressed by the French, who were attacking through the hills to the north of Pichon with the aid of British Churchill tanks.

The armoured brigade advanced north of Kairouan parallel to the Kairouan–Sbika road, with the Lothians on the left and 16th/5th Lancers on the right. The tanks and transport bowled along at speed, each tank trailing a wake of dust behind it, with here and there a pennant flying. After an hour or so, they began to pass over rougher ground as the leading battalions neared the foothills of the high ground that reared up out of the plain. The going here was more difficult for the support units as the history of 12th RHA explained: 'Cornfields had given way to heath and bumpy patches of scrub interspersed with innumerable tricky little wadis; and the gunners' quads and trailers, especially the 3-ton ammunition lorries, had increasing difficulty in keeping up with the Shermans, which still made nothing of such obstacles. By the time they could add the weight of their 25-pounders, so much fire was falling on the enemy from the tanks that the batteries had great difficulty in observing their own rounds.'[18]

Late in the morning the Lothians, driving ahead on the right of the armoured brigade, reported that they had come upon a low ridge behind a small river blocking the advance at a place called Bordj. It appeared that the enemy had decided to defend the hills and had at least twenty tanks in position along the undulating ground. Brig Roberts came forward to the Lothians' CO to determine how the enemy might be removed. He decided that the brigade would take the position by a turning movement from the east with 16th/5th Lancers, with 17th/21st Lancers operating wide on the right, on the extreme eastern flank. Roberts was going to launch a massed tank attack against the enemy. As 16th/5th Lancers' historian explained, 'It represented the nearest equivalent to a horsed cavalry charge of which an armoured unit is capable. The old cavalry spirit was given some play.'[19]

The charge took place through a thick heat-haze through which the landscape was distorted by mirage. Without interrupting the forward movement of the Brigade Group, Roberts switched the whole of 17th/21st Lancer Regimental Group at full speed diagonally from left to right through the rest of the formation, in order to bring it into position for a right outflanking movement. The Lancers' historian recognised the manoeuvre as being something special: 'It was a supreme example of the confidence that Roberts gave his troops and expected from them, for such a manoeuvre had never been attempted by the brigade in training. In fact, up to that time, there had been no ground on which it could have been done; yet here it was executed in battle as easily as "forming fours".'[20]

The tanks raced through heavy enemy shelling, attacking enemy antitank guns with high explosive as they opened fire. The 16th/5th Lancers drove straight at the main position and engaged enemy tanks. B and C Squadrons charged directly into the enemy line and scattered the defenders with the shock of the assault. Capt E. Maitland was with B Squadron in the attack: 'The ground, though flat, was very rough, and at the speed we were going the tank rocked like a tug in a high sea. On we went engines revving, Browning rattling, guns crashing, being flung backwards and forwards from side to side, with the wireless blaring and excitement reaching boiling point.'[21] Several Panzer IIIs and Italian

M13/40s were soon hit and burst into flame. Almost at once they began to withdraw, trying to save themselves from the fire put down by 17th/21st Lancers, who hit their flank with some force.

Five of 16th/5th's tanks were hit, including that of Capt Maitland: 'A great clang and the turret was full of flames. It seemed only a fraction of a second that I was struggling to open the lid of the turret, but in that time the gunner had slipped up from his seat in front of me, pushed open the lid and clambered out. With a heave I made it out and jumped from the top of the turret to the ground, rolling over and over to put my clothes out.'[22]

In the haze and the dust it was difficult to see friend from foe. HE and solid shot criss-crossed the hills as the Shermans pressed home their numerical superiority. The tide of the battle was one-sided, and soon all those of the enemy who were able to, took flight, withdrawing northwards through hills and wadis towards the remainder of AOK1.

When silence returned to the battlefield, Roberts and Keightley took stock of the situation. The flat plains across which the division had driven from Kairouan were giving way to the foothills of the high ground before Tunis. The country to the north was going to be difficult for tanks and the task of trying to force a way across the numerous ridges and valleys which crossed the advance was better suited for infantry. Lt Gen Crocker agreed and Maj Gen Keightley's division was pulled out of the line and began the long withdrawal back through the Fondouk Pass to the other side of the Eastern Dorsal. Alexander already had another operation lined up for IX Corps; the final battles for Tunis were starting to get under way.

The action fought at Fondouk was a mixture of indecision, bravery and missed opportunities. Almost immediately after the battle, accusations and recriminations began to circulate through the Allied camp. Crocker had given an interview to a group of war correspondents who wished to know the full story of the battle. Questions were being asked why Messe's army was allowed to retreat northwards without interception. Crocker was frank with the journalists and elaborated on the faults made by both the British and Americans. Included in his comments was some censure regarding the slowness of the US 34th Division in taking Djebel Aouareb. He thought that the division ought to be withdrawn and retrained. The comments did not go down well with anybody. Criticism of an American division by a British division gave rise to sensational headlines on both sides of the Atlantic and made Eisenhower furious. The sentiment was also picked up by everyone in First Army, who continued unfairly to disparage the American contribution to the fighting in Tunisia. Predictably, Gen George Patton gave vent to more of his xenophobic expletives in his diary: 'God damn all British and all so-called Americans who have their legs pulled by them. I would rather be commanded by an Arab. I think less than nothing of Arabs.'[23]

Chapter Six

THE END IN TUNISIA

On 11 April Gen Alexander decided how enemy forces in Tunisia were to be finally eliminated. Anderson's First Army would make the main effort, but first Montgomery's Eighth Army would push northwards near the coast against the Axis positions north-west of Enfidaville to draw off some of the opposition. Facing Eighth Army was a barrier of great natural strength based around Djebel Zaghouan and its surrounding subsidiary peaks. This was definitely not tank country and would require a great infantry effort to capture. Nonetheless, Monty was confident that his men would take the position and be the first into Tunis.

First Army would make its main thrust along the Medjez–Massicault road, the most direct route into Tunis from the south-west, with Gen Allfrey's V Corps. To aid this attack and to tie down some of the enemy's armour, Crocker's IX Corps would attack first in the Pont du Fahs/Goubellat plain area with 6th and 1st Armoured Divisions accompanied by 46th Infantry Division. Eisenhower insisted that American troops be included in these final battles, so the US II Corps was shifted northwards to take over the front north-east of Medjez, with a view to attacking in unison towards Bizerta. Gen Koeltz's French IXX Corps was to continue holding the Eastern Dorsal between IX Corps and Eighth Army, attacking the enemy as circumstances permitted.

Montgomery's operation against the Enfidaville Line got the ball rolling, opening on 19 April, but immediately ran into difficulties. Two of Eighth Army's best divisions, 4th Indian and the New Zealand Division, tried to seize the lesser djebels of Garci and Takrouna, only to be forced back by tenacious German resistance, the enemy's resolve no doubt having been bolstered by von Arnim's decree: 'The enemy is in front of you; the sea is behind you; there can be no retreat.' Twenty-three enemy battalions were in the hills facing Eighth Army. They were clearly not going to give Montgomery an easy ride to Tunis.

Over the following few days the assault area widened, with both the US II and the British V Corps attacking either side of Medjez along the whole of the northern front. The IX Corps's operation was to start on 22 April and Crocker's plan was to lead off with an infantry attack by 46th Division

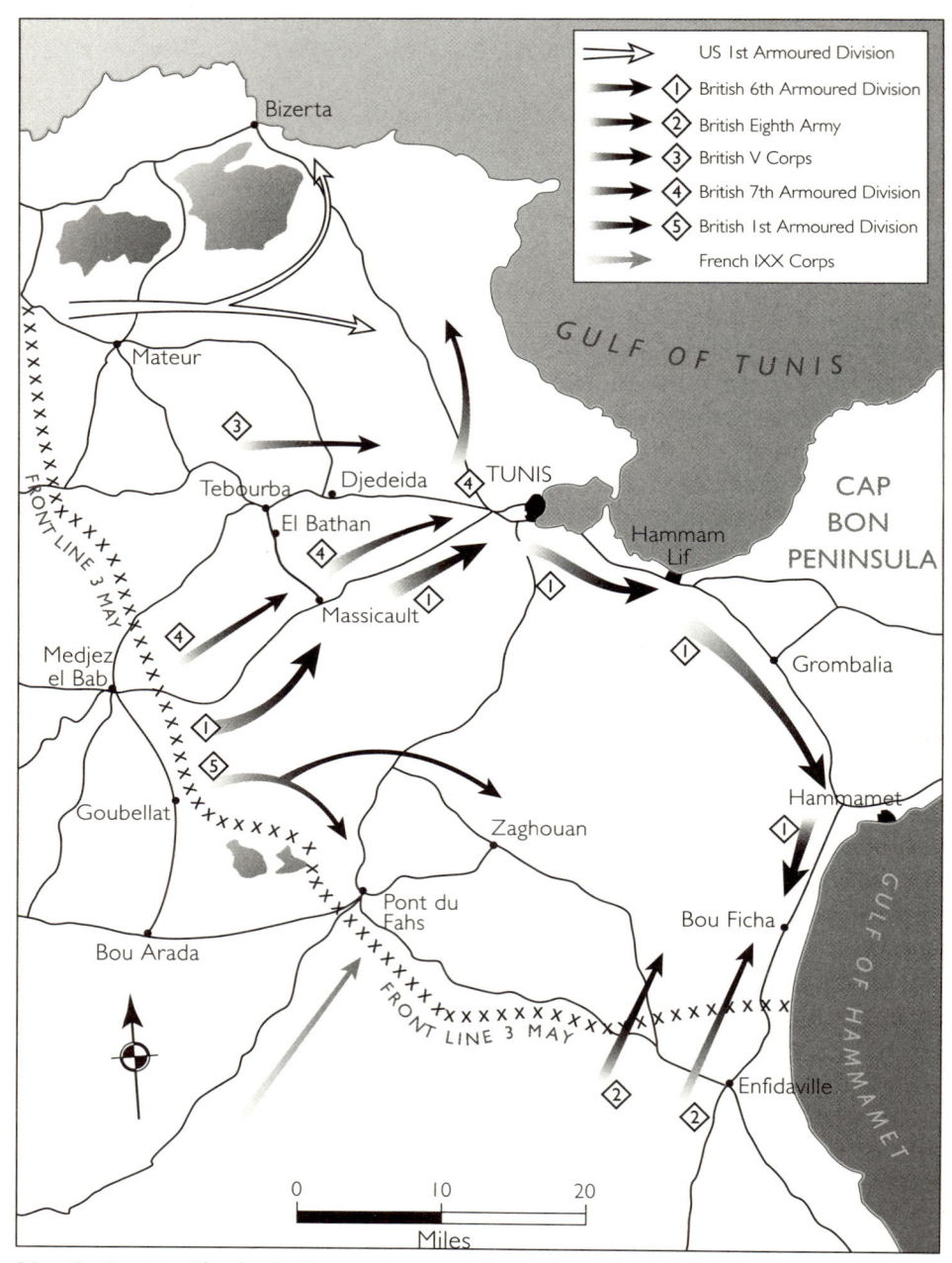

Map 6. Tunisia: The final offensive, May 1943

on the area of Two Tree Hill and the great salt lake of Sebkret el Kourzia. From this base, 6th Armoured Division would break through on to the Goubellat plain, ready to swing north and threaten Massicault, while 1st Armoured Division drove northwards on the western flank of the corps.

Opposing IX Corps were 6th Armoured Division's old adversaries, the Hermann Göring Division and 10th Panzer Division. The Hermann Göring Division had been in the line around Goubellat for the past few months, in positions that had been fortified at leisure since the first battles around Bou Arada back in January. Holding the front a little further south towards Pont du Fahs were a number of second-rate infantry battalions, with 10th Panzer Division held in position behind as an armoured reserve ready to attack any Allied break-in.

By mid-April, Axis forces in Tunisia were gradually being forced into a pocket in the north-eastern part of the country, pushed ever rearwards by the inexorable advance of two Allied armies. It was clear to everyone that the Germans and Italians would eventually be defeated; the question was, how long would it take? Allied supremacy in the air and the virtual closing of the Mediterranean Sea to Axis shipping meant that few supplies and no reinforcements were reaching North Africa. The Führer had dictated that no ground was to be given up and that each man must fight on to the end.

Joining 6th Armoured Division in IX Corps for the battle was 1st Armoured Division from Eighth Army. When it arrived the men of each of these divisions eyed each other with some amazement. Both units had seen a lot of action, but 1st Armoured Division had brought with it a great string of victories from its service in Eighth Army and viewed the Mailed Fist Division as relative newcomers. Its men demonstrated a perceived superiority over those of First Army and exhibited a flamboyant style of clothing and a carefree attitude to regulations. Their vehicles were painted a sand colour from their days in the desert and stood out incongruously against the more sombre greens and browns of 6th Armoured's tanks and trucks. Ribald comments passed between the two divisions and a great deal of banter was tossed to and fro, all of which helped to cement relationships between the two armoured formations.

Also joining the division from Eighth Army to support 26th Armoured Brigade was 11th (HAC) RHA. This artillery regiment had one great advantage over the division's sister regiment from the Honourable Artillery Company, 12th RHA, in that it was equipped with Priest self-propelled guns. The American-built Priests sported a 105mm gun mounted on a Grant chassis and had very good cross-country ability. Unlike the towed 25-pounders used in most field regiments, the Priest had armoured sides and gave some protection from enfilade fire from enemy tanks moving round their flanks. The Priests were also easily able to keep up with armour moving at speed over rough ground.

Lt Gen Crocker's IX Corps attacked at 0200 hr on 22 April with 46th Division. Maj Gen H. Freeman-Atwood's division opened the operation with simultaneous assaults by 128th and 138th Brigades, supported by the tanks of 51st RTR, from a start line which ran roughly along the route of the Goubellat–Bou Arada highway. Up until then, 46th Division had been fighting from relatively static positions in the hills to the north of Medjez, holding the line against German incursions and launching spoiling attacks against the enemy. This was its first full-scale divisional attack.

The struggle to break into the hills north-east of Bou Arada was prolonged and difficult. Five hours was allocated to complete the task; it took thirty-three. This belt of high ground that ran along the southern edge of the Goubellat plain had seen many attacks in the past, and most of its summits had acquired grim reputations. Grandstand Ridge, Two Tree Hill, Point 286 and many more hills and wadis had to be assaulted and taken by force, but unlike the piecemeal attacks of January, this time the enemy positions fortifying them were bombarded by the full weight of the artillery fire of 224 guns from division, corps and army, and had to resist whole brigades of infantry sent against them, including 1st Guards Brigade, which was placed under command for the attack.

In action with 138th Brigade were the guns of the Ayrshire Yeomanry. The regiment supplied seven mobile observation points to help direct the massed guns that were on call to the brigade. During the initial moves across the open ground in front of the hills, the advance was bombarded by heavy shell fire. At a crucial point in the attack one of the OP tanks with Lt Col Bedford's group of the Yeomanry shed a track on the rough ground and some contact was lost with the batteries. To halt in the open invited disaster and it was not long in coming, as Capt Box later explained:

> I heard a high-pitched whistle and flung myself flat on the corn. A 105mm shell had dropped on the track about 20 yards away on my left, and as I scrambled to my feet I saw the Colonel of the King's Own Yorkshire Light Infantry emerge from the smoke with a look of extreme agony on his face and half of his left arm missing. I dashed forward and found the Battery Commander on the spot too. He said, 'The Colonel has been hit,' and I thought for a moment he meant the CO of the KOYLI, but a glance behind our Colonel's carrier showed me that he was mortally wounded and could not live for more than a few minutes. He died without gaining consciousness. Three of his carrier crew were also killed outright, and the CO of the Lincolnshire Regiment was also killed. Truly a disastrous shell.[1]

Throughout the morning the advance pressed forward and was soon among the hills. Each time the infantry faltered in front of some djebel or ragged summit, an artillery concentration was put down, Churchill tanks rolled forward and the attack resumed. Artillery support was prodigious.

Each of the brigades had immediate call on 104 guns. When a heavy fire plan was requested by one of the artillery OPs, each of the guns replied in rapid order and 3,120 shells plunged down on the enemy position within the space of ten minutes. Inexorably, the infantry battle rolled out across the hills, pushing the German defenders aside to allow elbow room for the armoured divisions.

During the afternoon of 22 April, Maj Gen Keightley was ordered to set loose his tanks through the gap gained by 138th Brigade that morning. Although the infantry battle was still in full spate, a route had been opened over the first belt of high ground on the edge of the plain, leading around the north of the salt lake. Brig Roberts led off with two of his armoured regiments: 16th/5th Lancers on the right, the Lothians and Border Horse on the left. The initial advance was to the north-east and the tanks advanced against little opposition, but took casualties in both men and machines from mines. At the same time, further to the north, 1st Armoured Division attacked with its 2nd Armoured Brigade, heading northwards to clear the south-east of the plain below Goubellat.

Once through the hills that 46th Division were still trying to clear, 26th Armoured Brigade swung eastwards along the edge of the marshy ground which lined Sebkret el Kourzia. This brought it across the rear of the high ground north of Two Tree Hill, which 128th Brigade was at that moment attempting to capture. Antitank fire and enemy activity from the area forced 17th/21st Lancers, who had come up behind the leading regiments, to dispatch their C Squadron in that direction to protect the division's flank. During the afternoon, enemy fire increased from positions to the north as 10th Panzer Division started to move south against the offensive. Towards nightfall, 6th Armoured Division was told to establish an all-round defence on the ground it had won and prepare to resume the attack the next day. It had to be ready to take on the German armoured reserves.

Next day, 23 April, the advance continued with the high peak of Djebel Kournine as the division's objective. The mountain barred the way on to the flat plain beyond, on which the armoured division planned to advance towards Massicault. At 0530 hr 2nd Lothians and 17th/21st Lancers headed directly east on a frontal assault. Their move stirred up the enemy and several German tanks opened fired on 17th/21st Lancers from hull-down positions, knocking out three Shermans. The advance was being led by A Squadron, who promptly withdrew to a position where they could return fire. A flanking move to the right was tried, which was soon confronted by eight Panzer IVs and a Tiger guarding a wadi which crossed their path. B Squadron came forward to support and a tank-versus-tank battle ensued in which five of the enemy tanks were knocked out, including the Tiger, for the loss of three of the Lancers' Shermans. Other enemy tanks were seen moving into position and C Squadron came forwards to join in the shoot. Seven more German Panzer IVs were hit before the enemy armour retired. The same opposition was also causing problems for the Lothians. The 16th/5th Lancers then came forward and passed through the Lothians to try to shift the attack round onto the southern slopes of Kournine bordering Sebkret el Kourzia. Some of its tanks actually crossed the dry bed of the lake.

The 16th/5th Lancers sent their A Squadron down the eastern side of the lake, making a sweep of five miles. The move got behind some of the enemy and the tanks overran the HQ of 3rd Battalion of the Jäger Regiment Hermann Göring, capturing much booty and scattering its local defence. The squadron was loose in the rear of the enemy and opened fire at about 1,500 yards' range on artillery emplacements and groups of German vehicles, knocking out ten guns, six half-tracks and a number of trucks, all without any loss to itself. However, this swan to the south did little to loosen the enemy's grip of Djebel Kournine and the squadron rejoined the regiment to continue with its attack.

By this time 17th/21st Lancers had gained the forward slopes of Djebel Kournine, but the way was blocked by a deep wadi which could only be approached from the west. Enemy shelling increased the more the brigade pressed home its attack – the worst experienced by the division during the whole Tunisian campaign. A troop from A Squadron tried a long outflanking movement, but its lead tank was knocked out as it crossed the skyline. Tanks and antitank guns seemed to guard every fold in the ground and began pounding the Lancers with shellfire. The hill was broken by rough ground and deep wadis, impassable even for tracked vehicles, save for the most direct route. For a while there was deadlock. The tanks could not advance directly up Djebel Kournine, nor could they achieve flanking movements against well-fortified positions. A report was sent back to brigade explaining that any further advance up the hill from this side would mean very heavy tank casualties. Brig Roberts accepted the report and ordered the Lancers to hold their position.

The next day, Roberts resumed the attack, this time with the Lothians on the left and 16th/5th on the right, with 17th/21st in reserve. The plan was to aim for the high ground on either side of Djebel Kournine, leaving the Guards Brigade, who were at that moment under command of 46th Division, to take the mountain itself later. It was important to Crocker's timetable that the tanks were passed on to the plain behind Kournine to join up with 1st Armoured Division and advance on Massicault. Roberts personally organised the attacks, controlling his brigade from a vantage point on another hill. He thought it was invaluable for a brigade commander to get into a position where he was able to see battle area. 'That was one of the greatest advantages of fighting in Tunisia,' he later wrote. 'It was almost always possible for an armoured commander to see the whole of a brigade operation.'[2]

The three armoured regiments of 26th Armoured Brigade all put in attacks that day, working their way across a string of small hills and gullies, each natural obstacle containing some sort of hasty German defence or harbouring tanks and antitank guns, all of which were overlooked by the enemy on Djebel Kournine. Even the Luftwaffe put in an appearance and bombed and strafed the attack. Several British tanks were disabled by this air action and more suffered from heavy mortar fire from the flanks. Further problems arose when the massive Panzer VI Tigers of 501st Heavy Tank Battalion were identified in the area.

Some local success was gained when B Squadron of 16th/5th Lancers was relieved from its pole position after it ran low on ammunition. It began to reverse out as C Squadron came up to take over. The enemy saw this as a general withdrawal and moved forward to occupy the positions vacated by B Squadron. The Germans ran headlong into C Squadron as it moved forward, presenting the Shermans with a magnificent target. The tanks ripped the enemy apart, killing or wounding scores of their number, smashing four guns and several vehicles. Those who survived the onslaught turned and fled in disorder.

Entry on to the plain on either side of the mountain involved moving through small passes and German guns engaged the tanks as they approached. Brig Roberts could see that these gaps would need to be taken by infantry before his tanks could get through, but that the riflemen of 10th Rifle Brigade accompanying him were not strong enough for the tasks. It would need a full brigade attack to capture the features and keep them open, but Keightley had already committed the Guards Brigade to capturing the heights of Kournine. Roberts therefore withdrew his armoured brigade and set out the riflemen of 10th Rifle Brigade to protect it as it leaguered for the night.

The Guards Brigade moved up during 24 April ready for the attack on Djebel Kournine. The 2nd Coldstream was to mount the initial assault, backed by the guns of the Ayrshire Yeomanry who had also come forward. Some confusion about when it was to be committed resulted in the Coldstream not advancing to its start line until the next day, with the final assault to be mounted in the early morning on 26 April. During the move up, the Ayrshire Yeomanry watched a German bombing raid on the forward positions of the armoured brigade and a wayward attack on the Germans' own defences. The Yeomanry's historian described the scene: 'One group of Focke-Wulfs put in a determined attack on a squadron of German tanks, as a result of which scores of signal rockets and flares went up in protest from the German lines, giving the Yeomanry OPs a most accurate picture of the enemy dispositions. There were chuckles in the Yeomanry gun-pits at the ineptitude of the German pilots – regretted a few days later when the Yeomen in their turn found themselves under attack from their own planes.'[3]

A close reconnaissance of the ground to be attacked was not completed by the Coldstream before the battalion moved off and the officers had to be content with the view obtained through field glasses. Night fell as the guardsmen set out, following compass bearings to guide them across the rough ground towards their objective. The whole of 2nd Coldstream advanced slowly through the darkness in box formation. Just after midnight a mist descended and made direction-keeping even more difficult. Following behind, the battalion's transport column carrying tools and stores became hopelessly lost.

During the early hours the forward companies reached their positions and began to dig themselves some protection before the start of the main attack on Kournine at 0630 hr. They had only light entrenching tools and it was very hard work to try to scratch a slit trench in the rock-strewn landscape; their picks and shovels were still in the trucks of the wayward transport column. It was almost daylight before the lorries joined the battalion and they were hurriedly dispersed in a hollow behind the main positions. But before the guardsmen could deepen their foxholes with effective tools, the first rays of morning light lit the sky.

The weak point of the whole operation was the enemy's observation over the attack zone. To counter this, 3rd Grenadier Guards were to send a strong patrol up on to Kournine to eliminate a known enemy OP, a task that was to be accomplished in advance of the Coldstream assault. During the night the patrol ran headlong into the enemy and was shot up quite badly. It failed to capture its objective, which turned out to be protected by at least a company of enemy infantry.

The Coldstream at the base of the hill began the final assault by moving No. 1 Company forward to a small ridge. The lead platoon of the company advanced 500 yards and word was sent back for the remainder of the company to follow. Up with this platoon, making a reconnaissance of the ground to be attacked, was the Coldstream CO, Lt Col Stewart-Brown. It was at this moment that the warm sunshine began to burn off the low mist and the positions held by the battalion slowly began to emerge from the fog. Machine-gun bullets cracked through the air and ricocheted off rocks and boulders; mortar rounds crashed down into the exposed guardsmen and enemy shellfire raked the ground all around. Splinters of jagged rock and red-hot shrapnel flew everywhere as the area was riddled with enemy fire.

The whole battalion was trapped in a cauldron of fire. Lt Col Stewart-Brown crawled back to advance HQ and tried to organise a response, but the well-organised German OP on the high ground ahead looked down coldly on the Coldstream and controlled the combined firepower of all the weapons on the adjacent hills. The Ayrshire Yeomanry quickly brought its field guns into action and responded with return fire. Capt Box then relayed target coordinates back to artillery in the rear and all the division's artillery joined in the battle. Observation was poor, however, for the volume of fire aimed against them and the exposed positions of the Ayrshire's own OPs hampered the direction of this supporting fire. Further problems arose when it was realised that the quantity of ammunition at the guns was limited. They were located well forward of supply dumps in the rear and would not permit a prolonged general blasting of the area.

The 25-pounders of the Ayrshire Yeomanry were straddled by this incessant German fire and the experience was described by Capt Box after the battle: 'Antitank quads and infantry 15cwt ammunition trucks were blowing up in all directions, and we were suffering heavy casualties in personnel. To make matters worse, there were several Tiger tanks cruising around near Djebel Kournine, who were shooting us up with their 88mm guns over open sights. Of all the weapons with which one can be shot at, the 88mm is the worst. Its muzzle velocity is so great that the bang of the gun, the noise of the shell and the burst all merge into one, and there is no time to dodge it. We were under terrific fire for nearly two hours, and I knew that it would be a miracle if we got out alive.'[4]

In the meantime the guardsmen kept low in their shallow trenches and tried to return the enemy's small-arms fire. Casualties quickly began to mount. The Coldstream's Medical Officer, Capt Elston Grey-Turner, later told of his experiences at the Regimental Aid Post that day: 'Our little hollow was like an inferno – never have I felt so frightened. Soon the wounded came pouring in and we had to treat them as best we could with mortar bombs dropping all around and machine gun bullets whizzing past the RAP. After a time the companies started withdrawing. Eighteen trucks were blazing. We were advised to clear out and leave our trucks, but I was determined not to lose the kit and ordered the drivers to get the trucks out. This they did, and two ambulances full of wounded, in a hail of shells and bullets.'[5]

The situation had become hopeless and at 1000 hr the order to retire was given. One by one the guardsmen started to pull out of their exposed positions and filter back to the rear. The battalion was compelled to abandon much of its transport and some of its equipment. Some platoons were still pinned down unable to move and it was not until darkness that the last of these were able to extricate themselves from under the German guns. The 2nd Coldstream had lost almost a hundred men that day killed and wounded.

While 6th Armoured was trying to batter its way past Djebel Kournine, 1st Armoured Division had been trying the same against Djebel Srassif in the north. It, too, made little headway. Crocker's offensive was not making the gains he had hoped for. In one desperate last fling, he decided to move 1st Armoured Division back southwards and then swing it through part of 6th Armoured's line so that the two divisions could attack together on a narrower front. The moves changed little: 6th Armoured remained anchored before Djebel Kournine and 1st Armoured hit the same stubborn defence thrown up by the Hermann Göring Division, 10th Panzer Division and elements of 15th Panzer Division which had been drawn into the fighting.

By 26 April it was clear that the enemy was offering a resolute defence on perfect ground of his own choosing. Tanks in hull-down positions, antitank guns in hidden wadis, mortars behind large outcrops and machine guns in every crevice had forced the advance to a slow crawl, with mounting casualties for the two armoured divisions. The Germans were putting up a stubborn defence in the south even though von Arnim feared a breakthrough in any one of the sectors under attack in the north.

Crocker's attack was a failure in that it did not make the penetration that was hoped for, but it did succeed in its secondary objective of bringing onto it the German armoured reserves from the plain around Massicault. Lt Gen Anderson's other forces in the north were making headway, but none had made a breakthrough. Anderson was now thinking of a new plan, which involved drawing IX Corps closer to V Corps and directing them both on Tunis by a more northerly route thus exploiting the gains already being made by Lt Gen Allfrey's corps. On 26 April, 6th Armoured Division broke off its attack and handed over its gains to 1st Armoured Division. Keightley then withdrew his division into Army reserve to replenish its losses, ready to move over to V Corps's sector for what must be the final push for Tunis.

The division was happy to be leaving the area and handed over its sector to 1st Armoured ungrudgingly. The relief was detected by the enemy and the division was shelled viciously on its way out. The Ayrshire Yeomanry seemed to fare worst of all, losing its second commanding officer killed in just a few days. 'Even when relieved, the Regiment was still not left in peace,' explained the unit's history. 'In its rest area, a pleasant spot on the northern slopes of Djebel Rihane, it was attacked by American Mitchell bombers escorted by Spitfires. C Battery lost Gunner Knight killed and a number of men wounded including the BSM Sergeant Simpson. At the time the Yeomanry were at least ten miles behind the front line, and it would be hard to excuse such a gross error on the part of Allied pilots,' complained the historian.[6]

Over on the coast, Eighth Army's attack, trying to force the eastern route towards Tunis, was not making the gains its commander had hoped for. Its attack on the Enfidaville Line was bogged down in the mountains. Troops who had spent months and years in the wide-open spaces of the desert were finding mountain warfare difficult. Monty was confronting the same stubborn enemy defence of the line that was being experienced elsewhere. Eighth Army continued with its attacks through the hills while it planned to make its main assault along the narrow, and heavily fortified, coastal belt. The 56th Division, untried in battle, was brought 3,200 miles from Iraq to take over in the mountains, with little success. Both Monty and Alexander then realised that it would be too costly for Eighth Army to try to force its way along the coastal route to Cap Bon and that it was not now necessary to do so, for First Army was almost at Tunis and the Axis forces were so well stretched that a total collapse in Tunisia had to be imminent. On 30 April, Alexander decided to move some of Eighth Army's strength across to reinforce Anderson's army. He now transferred 7th Armoured and 4th Indian Divisions, together with 201st Guards Brigade in front of Tunis.

In the north the US II Corps was pushing through old battlegrounds and closing on Bizerta, while V Corps tackled the main route towards Tunis in the Medjez–Massicault area. Both were making steady, if not spectacular, progress against stiff enemy opposition. The commander of Eighteenth Army Group, Gen Alexander, now met First Army's commander to finalise a new version of the plan to finish the campaign in Tunisia. Von Arnim's forces were known to be weakening by the hour, with virtually no reinforcement. One more decisive push would be sure to bring about total victory.

During this period, Lt Gen Crocker had been wounded while watching a demonstration of a new infantry antitank weapon, the PIAT (Projector Infantry Anti Tank).[7] To replace Crocker, Lt Gen Brian Horrocks was sent to take command of IX Corps. Horrocks had a great reputation from his handling of X Corps in many of the major battles fought by Eighth Army. He joined First Army at a most opportune time, just as the climax battle for Tunisia was about to be launched. Lt Gen Anderson briefed him on the final plan, Operation 'Strike', and he remembers that the commander of First Army made it quite clear what he was expected to do – simply 'Capture Tunis'. Under its command IX Corps was to have two infantry divisions (4th British and 4th Indian) supported by 160 Churchill tanks, two armoured divisions (6th and 7th), 201st Guards Brigade, a great weight of artillery and the whole of the tactical air force. 'If I failed to break through with this immensely powerful force under command,' Horrocks later wrote, 'I deserved to be shot.'[8]

Holding the area in front of Tunis, facing both the British V and IX Corps were the Hermann Göring Division, 334th Infantry Division and what was left of the once-mighty 15th Panzer Division. All of these units had been severely depleted by the long struggle to hold First Army's inexorable drive towards the capital. Horrocks planned to concentrate his force against them, proposing to attack on a narrow, 3,000-yard front either side of the Medjez–Tunis road. His two infantry divisions would assault the German line after a tremendous artillery barrage. Speed was important and he hoped to be able to release his armoured divisions through the gap seized in the German defences within a few hours of the start, before the enemy could switch forces against him. Then it was all-out for Tunis.

Alexander visited Horrocks before the 'off' and stressed that IX Corps must pass its armoured divisions through on the same day that its infantry attacked, to deny the enemy time to throw out a strong antitank screen; mopping-up could come later. He needed to destroy the enemy in front of Tunis before they could escape to the Cap Bon peninsula. He emphasised that the armoured divisions 'with their power of manoeuvre must get on with it'.[9]

Horrocks's attack was preceded by that of Lt Gen Allfrey's V Corps, which followed along the line of the Medjerda valley to the north-west of IX Corps. By the evening of 5 May, the British 1st Armoured Division had captured Djebel bou Aoukaz and secured the left flank of IX Corps's attack, allowing Horrocks safely to launch his armoured thrust north-eastwards. In the early hours of 6 May, over 600 guns opened fire on the ground in front of IX Corps, a barrage even greater than that before Alamein. Throughout the next twenty-four hours the combined artillery fired an average of 368 rounds per gun, with 16,632 shells falling on the enemy in the first two hours.

Zero hour was at 0300 and by 0730 hr the two attacking infantry divisions had made a breach through the German line wide enough for the armoured divisions to squeeze through. Initially 6th Armoured Division found the going slow, hampered by a scattered minefield and by the numbers of Churchill tanks that were supporting the British 4th Infantry Division; but against little opposition the leading tanks of 26th Armoured Brigade reached the area in front of Furna by 1045. Here they met some resistance from tanks and antitank guns.

The 16th/5th Lancers were advancing on the right, 2nd Lothians and Border Horse on the left, with 17th/21st Lancers in reserve. Facing the brigade were a number of enemy Panzer IIIs and IVs, with two Mark VI Tigers. This battlegroup was also supported by two 88mm guns. The Germans put up a half-hearted attempt to stop the brigade and were soon in action against 16th/5th Lancers in a tank-versus-tank engagement. The two 88mm guns were quickly knocked out, along with the Tigers and few of the other panzers. The sheer weight of numbers of Shermans and the accurate fire of the self-propelled guns of 11th RHA overwhelmed the enemy. The advance resumed with 17th/21st Lancers in the lead.

The drive by the armoured divisions had made five miles by early afternoon and was just over halfway to Massicault. At around that time Horrocks's HQ reported that there was a general impression the enemy was not aware of the direction of the attacks and that he was pulling out as fast as he could. This should have been a signal to press on regardless, but the divisions, in contrast, started to grow cautious. Both of the armoured division commanders were anxious to form firm bases before they continued the advance, wishing to have infantry up with the tanks before they pushed their armour too far ahead.

The 201st Guards Brigade, now attached to the division, came up to join 6th Armoured, while 131st Brigade did the same with 7th Armoured. Both of these moves took some time and it was not until late afternoon that the advance resumed. At around 1700 hr, with two and a quarter hours of daylight left, Brig Roberts' armour settled for the night about two miles east of Massicault, with 7th Armoured Division just north of the town.

There is no mention of any disappointment in the slowness of the advance in Horrocks's memoirs, but the official history of the campaign suggests that the armoured division failed to carry out Alexander's exhortation to 'get on with it'.[10] It was almost as if they couldn't believe that such an advance would not be met with a sudden and severe German counterattack. It was true that there were a lot of enemy about, but many of them were more intent on streaming back towards Tunis than standing to fight. However, the failure of the armoured divisions to go all out for Tunis on the first day of Operation Strike had little consequence, for von Arnim's forces were in a state of almost total collapse.

Army Group Africa's report on 6 May agreed that the Allies had made their decisive breakthrough to Tunis. The Hermann Göring and 334th Divisions had been completely worn down and 15th Panzer Division 'must be deemed to have been destroyed'. The report went on to admit that 'on 7th May the road to Tunis will be open to the enemy and that the fall of Bizerta is only a question of time'.[11] Von Arnim and his senior commanders had lost control on 6 May and all they could now do was order a step-by-step retreat into two areas: those forces in the north-east would withdraw into a fortress area around Bizerta and those in front of Tunis would retire on to the Cap Bon peninsula.

The Mailed Fist Division met only scattered resistance when it resumed its advance on 7 May. In the early afternoon the leading troops had their first sight of Tunis. The 1st Derbyshire Yeomanry had moved on to the plain in front of the city to cut off any enemy troops retreating from the west. It soon became clear that there would be no serious fighting around the capital. At 1515 hr 7th Armoured was ordered to close on the town and at 1630 hr Keightley was told to turn his division to the south-east and to try to stop the enemy taking positions to defend Cap Bon. The day's final objective was the high ground overlooking La Mohammedia. This was reached an hour later.

Meanwhile, the Derbyshire Yeomanry had continued on towards Tunis and two troops of C Squadron actually entered the city at around 1545 hr. Their armoured cars had met others from 7th Armoured Division's reconnaissance regiment, 11th Hussars, and together they motored cautiously into the built-up area. They were confronted with a city going about its daily business, seemingly oblivious to its imminent capture. Groups of German soldiers were marching down the street, mess tins in hand, making for the cookhouse. Two Germans were found having a leisurely shave in a barber's shop and a car full of staff officers was followed for 100 yards before they realised who was behind them. 'This party was stupid enough to try to make a getaway; they suffered the consequences,' related Sergeant 'Doc' Edwards later.[12]

By 8 May, it was clear to everyone, including the enemy, that the Axis forces in Tunisia were in their final death throws: Tunis had fallen, the American II Corps had captured Bizerta and the whole area between the two cities was being swept by numerous Allied divisions. There was little opposition to these moves and enemy troops were surrendering en masse to anyone who would accept them. The only semblance of any German organisation and control was with those enemy units who were withdrawing towards Cap Bon. 'That day the extent of the German disintegration became more obvious,' wrote Lt James Wilson later. 'We passed ration dumps and transport parks, evidently hastily abandoned. There were signs everywhere telling the Germans to make for the Cap Bon peninsula.'[13] This gathering of forces along roads that led only to the sea, left von Arnim and his men with just three choices: escape, death or captivity, and there was very little chance of any of them escaping from those North African shores.

Maj Gen Keightley's division now became the focus of all attention in Tunisia. It was the only division on the road to Cap Bon. Eighth Army had not begun to squeeze past the Enfidaville position, for the enemy there was only just beginning to melt away in front of it. Monty's men were still a few days away from the southern corner of Cap Bon. The 6th Armoured Division now had to take on the task of containing all that was left of German Army Group Africa.

Brig Roberts led his 26th Armoured Brigade eastwards towards the enemy's last foothold in Tunisia early on 8 May. The Cap Bon peninsula juts out into the Mediterranean Sea, with the Gulf of Tunis on its northern side and the Gulf of Hammamet on the southern flank. At the base of the peninsula are two towns: Hammam Lif in the north and Hammamet in the south, linked together by a road which effectively cuts the peninsula off from the mainland of Tunisia. The 6th Armoured Division was now ordered to drive down this road and isolate Cap Bon, thus closing the escape route to those of the enemy who were still at large to the south and west, but first Hammam Lif had to be captured in order to get onto this road.

A quick reconnaissance of Hammam Lif showed that an attack on the town would be an extremely hazardous venture. It was located in a narrow defile, barely 300 yards wide, between the sea and a group of hills which overlooked the town. It was a neat town consisting of rows of whitewashed houses arranged in uniform square blocks on either side of the main road. The slopes of Djebel Rorouf rose straight out of the gardens of these houses, soaring almost vertically for 600 feet before reaching the summit a further 150 feet above. The whole approach from the west was covered in olive groves, making visibility extremely limited. Any attack on Hammam Lif without previously gaining the heights would almost certainly be suicidal. Numerous enemy observation posts on Djebel Rorouf would make it possible for them to direct accurate and heavy shellfire onto troops concentrating for the attack. A frontal assault on the town was certain to be a desperate undertaking, and it was impossible to attack from the right because of the hills and from the left because of the sea.

Holding the town were two and a half battalions of parachutists from the division's old adversaries, the Hermann Göring Division, and from the Ramcke Regiment of 90th Light Division. In short, Hammam Lif was a problem that the division could have well done without, especially as the fighting in Tunisia was now almost over.

There was an outside chance that the enemy might be prepared to surrender, given that victory or escape for them was out of the question. News had been received that the Germans had declared Hammam Lif an 'open city', but this was just a ruse to gain time to arrange its defence. This faint hope was dashed when, in the early afternoon, 2nd Lothians approached the town hoping to rush the defences and were immediately halted by concentrated artillery and antitank fire. There was nothing for it but to withdraw the Lothians and prepare the division for a set-piece attack on the town, its first experience of urban warfare.

Maj Gen Keightley decided that his first move should be to call the Guards Brigade forward and have it sweep the hillside to the south of the town. Then 2nd Lothians and Border Horse would drive down the main road into Hammam Lif, supported by artillery fire and the riflemen of 10th Rifle Brigade to tackle the town defences at close quarters. Even with the enemy off the high ground, the Lothians' task would still be hazardous, for several 88mm guns, minefields and tanks had been located in the town, and to the north, lining the sea, were pillboxes and more minefields.

The 3rd Welsh Guards were three miles short of Hammam Lif when word was received by Lt Col Hodgson at 1330 hr that his battalion would lead the attack on Djebel Rorouf. While the guardsmen were organised into carriers for the move forward, the lieutenant colonel went on ahead to reconnoitre the position. Hodgson was confronted with a formidable objective. The battalion would have to cross 600 yards of open ground and then assault the steep-sided, rocky djebel whose crest was divided into three distinct summits: three hills on top of a hill. Each of these features would have to be captured and the enemy cleared completely before the armoured attack could go in on the town below. Speed was important, for the sealing-off of Cap Bon could not continue until after Hammam Lif was taken. A hurried fire-plan was organised by Brig Lyon Smith, CRA of the division, and the Welsh Guards began assembling for the attack.

Many senior commanders had come up to the front, eager to urge on the division through the bottleneck of Hammam Lif and to be in on the final surrender. The historian of the Ayrshire Yeomanry recalls seeing an impressive group of 'red hats' including Anderson, Horrocks, Keightley and Roberts all assembled, watching events at Hammam Lif, and noticed that their reactions to Nebelwerfer fire were much the same as anyone else's: 'When the woop-woop of the "Minnies" was heard they hastily jumped for cover under the nearest tank without much concern for personal dignity.'[14]

The IX Corps commander, Horrocks, later recalled his drive up to 6th Armoured in his memoirs: 'In my eagerness to get on I didn't pay sufficient attention to where our front line was, but went off with my ADC on a personal reconnaissance. Suddenly eight figures with hands above their heads jumped up almost at our feet. To my disgust I realised that they were very frightened Italians. Had they been stalwart members of the Afrika Corps it would have been different; we could have escorted them back proudly into our new lines. But for the corps commander to return with eight weedy, miserable Italian prisoners in tow would have made me a laughing stock of the entire corps. So, feeling rather ashamed of myself, I handed them over to my ADC and went back alone along another route.'[15]

Just before 1500 hr the Welsh Guards launched their attack. As soon as the guardsmen moved out across the open ground towards the hill the enemy began to rake them with fire. In reply the division's artillery plastered the rocky slopes with shellfire. Tanks were on hand to help cover the ground and the leading two companies of the Welsh Guards made the scrub at the foot of Djebel Rorouf with few casualties. Then began the long haul to the top, with No. 2 Company, commanded by Capt Llewellyn, on the left and No. 3 Company, commanded by Maj Smith, on the right. The slopes were so steep that the troops had almost to crawl their way up, moving from boulder to boulder in bounds, dodging enemy small-arms and mortar fire as they went. Machine guns fired down gullies and bullets ricocheted off the rocks, sending splinters of sharp stone in all directions. As the men neared the top, the artillery stopped their fire and the guardsmen were left with just the support of their own weapons and grenades. The southern end of the hill was reached by Maj Martin and No. 3 Company and the first of the summits along its crest taken. Thirteen of the enemy surrendered. The Welsh Guards were on the top of

Djebel Rorouf, but their struggle to clear the whole feature was only just beginning.

It was now that the strength of the position was realised. The crest was just a few yards wide and curved like a crescent linking the next two hills, both of which were held with excellent fortified weapons pits. Capt Llewellyn's company could not take the second peak along the ridge and No. 3 Company could not hold on to the first in the face of enemy fire, so Maj Smith brought his company back below the crest line to gain the only cover available.

Down below, the CO of the Welsh Guards watched the attack on the hill carefully and received clear reports as to their progress. Lt Col Hodgson now decided to introduce his remaining two companies into the attack. He ordered Capt Gibson-Watt to take No. 4 Company up, pass through Maj Smith's men and attack along the far side of the ridge, with Maj Dimsdale's No. 1 Company attacking simultaneously along the near side. To keep the enemy's heads down, he requested artillery fire on the far end of the ridge.

These two fresh companies moved across the open ground at the foot of the hill in the company of a squadron of tanks and began the climb in the face of less fire than the two previous companies had met. By 1700 hr they were well forward in the ascent and the whole of Djebel Rorouf seemed to be swarming with Welsh Guards. Maj Dimsdale led his men up to No. 3 Company and moved along the ridge just below the crest, clinging to the almost-vertical sides of the rock. Then, having got below the second summit, they went over the top and took it. Meanwhile, No. 4 Company on the rear face had disappeared from view. Gibson-Watt found that this side of the feature was covered with scrub and his men moved carefully along towards the third hill on the crest. Part of the way along, his company came to an abrupt halt when the path was closed by concentrated enemy fire. His men were pinned down on the exposed rear face, it being impossible to move any further along below the summit. Undaunted he sent a platoon down the rear face, along the base and back up the sheer rocks to arrive beyond the pinch-point below the summit. No. 4 Company had outflanked the resistance and the platoon gained the third summit, ejecting the enemy. By this time it was almost dark, but the main ridge of Djebel Rorouf was now in safe hands and the strength of the position was beginning to be broken. It just remained to clear the enemy from the next few hills so as to push him back from any view of Hammam Lif.[16]

The 2nd Coldstream Guards now came up through the Welsh Guards to take the next three features, which were linked to Rorouf. The battalion carried out its attack through the night. In the darkness, one of the Coldstream's companies provided carrying parties as the other three companies bounced the smaller peaks one after the other. Each attack started with a skirmish of intense small-arms fire and the tossing of grenades, followed by a rush of determined guardsmen. In each case the German defenders gave up quite readily. By morning the whole of the high ground overlooking Hammam Lif was held by the division. Just before dawn, the Coldstream sent a patrol, led by Lt Ponsonby, down into the town and found a strong force of enemy tanks in residence. Plans were now made to attack the town.

Patrols by both 2nd Coldstream Guards and B Company of 10th Rifle Brigade showed that the German defences in Hammam Lif were considerable. Tightly packed houses and narrow streets made the town an almost impenetrable warren. The Germans had around twenty antitank guns in the town, hastily sited in the gardens of the houses, with some actually inside the larger buildings whose walls they had had time to breach.

The first attempt at taking Hammam Lif was made by B Company of 10th Rifle Brigade at 0530 hr, but this attack was beaten off by heavy machine-gun fire. At 0830 another attack was put in, this time by C Squadron of 2nd Lothians supported by the greenjackets of both A and B Companies of 10th Rifle Brigade. Artillery fire directed from the heights above the town concentrated on enemy positions identified earlier, but as each of these fell silent, more resistance popped up a few buildings away, or in an adjacent street. The Lothians began to probe cautiously around the western part of the town, exchanging shots with the enemy gunners. Once the Shermans had penetrated into the built-up area along the main road they became vulnerable to enemy infantry, but the supporting riflemen could not get close enough to winkle out these defenders because of intense machine-gun fire. After an hour the attack was broken off with some loss to both riflemen and tanks.

The problem of Hammam Lif was beginning to concern everyone from the army commander downwards. Anderson ordered Horrocks to tell Keightley that his division had to be through the town that day, no matter if he reached the far side with only a score of tanks left. The Hammam Lif gap was now the most important objective of First Army.

At 1100 hr the Commanding Officer of the Lothians, Lt Col R.S.G. Perry, was told that Hammam Lif must be entered at all costs. He would have to attack again, this time with the help of 1st Guards Brigade. He therefore decided to push one troop of B Squadron across the railway to the beach to hold the left flank, while C Squadron made a frontal attack against the gap between the railway and the westerly buildings of the town. The attack started at 1130 with the Lothians' tanks storming across open ground in the face of antitank guns, heading directly for the town. A few Shermans were hit and burst into flame. Caution was thrown aside as the remaining tanks charged down the enemy guns before they could reload. The squadron fought its way into the narrow streets only to get bogged down among the houses where every corner seemed to be guarded by some sort of gun.

Over to the left, 2 Troop of B Squadron, commanded by 2/Lt P.J. Morey, advanced over 800 yards of exposed ground to the railway line with its flanks open to enemy antitank gunfire. There had been no time for reconnaissance of the railway line and it was with some relief that the tracks were found to be free of mines and had not been made into an antitank obstacle. Fortunately, no casualties were sustained and the CO ordered the remainder of B Squadron to follow this troop. Once across, the squadron was ordered to advance and reach the far end of the town regardless of casualties, while C Squadron and 3rd Grenadiers plugged away along the main route.

With B Squadron that morning was Lt Allan Waterston, who commanded 3 Troop. As he had led the advance to Hammam Lif the previous day, his troop was now in the rear of the squadron: 'We were ordered to move over the railway track towards the beach. By then the enemy had begun to react strongly and we found ourselves in some unpleasantness. I had no time to worry about this as in crossing the railway line I got about four strands of telegraph cable round my neck which were steadily throttling me. This prevented me from speaking to the driver on the intercom and telling him to reverse. Fortunately I was wearing leather gloves and with the strength of desperation I managed to push the wires over my head before being catapulted out of the turret, or worse still being decapitated.'[17]

It soon became apparent that both squadrons were meeting very stiff opposition and had very little room to manoeuvre their way past. C Squadron was stalled in the western edge of the town; any attempt to progress through the maze of streets was being forced back by antitank fire. Several tanks were hit and casualties began to mount. Considerable trouble was met from the Gendarmerie, a large white building which dominated the western entrance to the town. C Squadron expended a lot of ammunition engaging the building before a few tanks squeezed a little further into the closely packed streets. Friendly artillery fire was proving to be ineffective, for the OPs in the hills were unable to identify individual targets in the houses.

B Squadron was equally in trouble: its advance on the northerly route was barred by an impassable wadi on the edge of the built-up area. Movement stopped while a way round the obstacle was found, leaving the now-static Shermans of the squadron to endure the increasingly fierce enemy fire. A quick reconnaissance showed that there was no easy way forward round the wadi; the only possible route left was to follow the watercourse down to the beach and try to establish whether progress was possible along the sea front. No. 3 Troop was called forward and given the task, led by Lt Allan Waterston in his Sherman:

It became apparent that the squadron had got a bit stuck and I was asked to find a way along a wadi in the direction of the sea. This I was able to do and as the troop turned to run along the beach in line ahead things really got exciting. We were fired on heavily by a number of 88mm guns in a long clump of dark scrub across the crescent of the bay. All we could do was speed up and move into the sea to try and get some 'hull down' cover. As the enemy projectiles hit the sea all round us it was like a naval battle with plumes of white spray rising twenty feet into the air. Indeed the only thing that I heard on the radio that I recall clearly was somebody reporting that he was being shelled by an enemy submarine. I must admit that on the flat shore line the belt of scrub did look rather like the silhouette of a submarine with its guns in action. At this point I realised that I was the front tank of the front troop of the front squadron of the whole 1st Army. What is more there was no sign of any other tank behind me. I therefore made urgent representations in strong language over the radio to my other two tanks and after a short pause Sgt Askew reported that L/Sgt. Haston's tank had struck a mine and was out of action. (It was only afterwards that I learned that the driver, Trooper 'Freddie' Barwell, had been killed and the other members of the crew either wounded or badly shaken.) Sgt Askew caught up and we turned sharp right off the beach into the town and I remember running over the trail of an antitank gun to make sure it could not be used again but I saw no sign of the gun crew. We then turned left down a tree lined avenue of houses with a lot of cattle wandering about or lying injured. The avenue was not wide enough for any tactical advance so we kept going fast with one tank on each side of the road until we came to a narrow part with a left turn back towards the beach. I could not get round in one and remember clearly having to jam the right sprocket of my Sherman into a doorway flattening the door into the hallway. I was greeted by the sight of about a dozen screaming Arabs of both sexes stacked up the staircase in a considerable state of alarm![18]

Lt Griffiths now followed along the beach with No. 4 Troop, with the rest of the squadron frantically trying to catch up. The Shermans swept along the sand in single file, throwing up sheets of spray, with enemy fire coming at them from the front and from the guns on the sea wall to their right. The 88mm gun across the bay kept up its fire and was joined by more guns at the end of the promenade. The speed of advance along the firm sand meant that in a short while the tanks had almost reached the other end of the town. One by one the tanks turned down side streets to get clear of the enemy fire along the sea front.

The Lothians' Adjutant, Capt Gordon Goodrich, takes up the story: 'It was not long before the complete squadron was in the middle of the town and manoeuvre and control became more difficult. Troops and even tanks found themselves acting as separate units and had to use their own initiative. The enemy guns redoubled their shelling and when the squadron had fought its way through the streets to the east end of the main part of the town into the open, this shelling became even more intense.'[19]

The spectacular outflanking manoeuvre through the sea by B Squadron had cracked open the enemy defence. The Lothians now had tanks behind those German defenders facing C Squadron in the west of the town. The enemy garrison was in a hopeless position, made worse by the arrival of 17th/21st Lancers at around 1300 hr. The whole regiment took the sea-front route which was still under enemy fire. However, by driving at full speed in the sea and letting off smoke, the Lancers gained the eastern edge of the town with only two losses.

Ahead of the Lancers, B Squadron of the Lothians were continuing eastwards to clear the town. Allan Waterston was still in the lead:

We moved on steadily towards the far end of the town where we took up positions behind the last few outbuildings and walls. We hoped that we would not be called upon to cross the open ground to our front and it was with considerable relief that we heard that the Lancers were to pass through us and keep up the momentum. I then became aware of a large concrete bunker about a hundred and fifty yards to my front with a sinister black hole facing me which appeared to be a gun slit. I fired a solid-shot armour-piercing round from my 75mm gun which went straight through the hole. Almost at once a figure appeared waving vigorously and running towards us. This turned out to be a very brave gendarme who told me that over a hundred people had taken shelter in the bunker and please would we cease firing. There could have been a complete disaster as my usual troop drill was for me to keep a high explosive round 'up the spout' during action and the others in the troop to load armour-piercing shot in theirs. The citizens were lucky as the scenes of carnage inside the confines of the bunker would have been horrendous if I had fired an HE round.[20]

The enemy now realised that Hammam Lif was no longer tenable and the men of the garrison began either to give themselves up, or to try to melt away to the east. The Lothians' A Squadron joined C Squadron in the town and advanced along the main route, flushing out German guns, while 3rd Grenadier Guards eliminated snipers and anyone else who looked aggressive. House by house and block by block, the guardsmen swept through the town, finding that there were few Germans left who were unwilling to surrender without further argument.

By late afternoon Hammam Lif was deemed to be clear of the enemy. It was discovered that there had been at least twelve 88mm guns, six 50mm and sixteen dual-purpose 20mm guns used in the defence. The 88mm weapons were antiaircraft guns manned by Luftwaffe troops. Had they been the antitank type manned by experienced antitank gunners, the capture of Hammam Lif might have taken twice as long. The Lothians had lost two officers and seven men killed in the action, as well as twelve tanks. GenMaj Broich, commander of 10th Armoured Division, later acknowledged that the forcing of the gap through the town was a great feat of arms: 'I did not think it was possible to get armour through the defile at Hammam Lif,' he confessed. Such sentiments were also felt by the rest of the division. The Grenadier Guards's historian thought that B Squadron's dash along the beach through the sea was 'a scene without parallel in the history of armoured warfare'.[21]

The road to Hammamet was now open. Brig Roberts sent his brigade forward, urging it on from the open turret of his tank. The drive was led by the tanks and armoured cars, with the two guards brigades held back clear of the roads to mop up areas bypassed by the Shermans. The 16th/5th Lancers advanced on the right of the road with 17th/21st Lancers sweeping along on the left, nearest the sea. The next objective for 26th Armoured Brigade was the town of Soliman which guarded one of the Axis escape routes on to the Cap Bon peninsula.

Lt James Wilson was told to take his antitank platoon and the scout platoon of 10th Rifle Brigade and establish a defensive flank in the hills to the right of the road so as to prevent any enemy coming back into Hammam Lif and cutting the road behind the advancing armour. Wilson felt this was an easy task and it provided him with a fascinating view of the Guards Brigade clearing the hills ahead of him and of the road below him, jam-packed with the traffic of 6th Armoured Division. He later described his role:

> All day, as we sat sweltering above Hammam Lif, a steady trickle of prisoners came to surrender. They were not, unusually, the weaker brethren who had somehow become detached from their units. By contrast, these prisoners came from some of the best-known German units in Tunisia – the Hermann Göring Division, Colonel Koch's paratroopers, and some from the famous 90th Light Division. We felt no animosity, rather admiration, towards these splendid soldiers, who, whatever the abysmal quality of the Nazi regime, had fought bravely and correctly. One particular officer came in about the proper time for afternoon tea. He was a kindred spirit, replying in perfect English to my welcome in Wiccamical German, 'Well done, lads, you took your time, but better late than never.' He gave me his field glasses – I have them still, and find them perfectly suited to watching cricket at Lord's and Trent Bridge.[22]

The Guards had a number of important tasks to perform during the advance, such as marshalling prisoners, patrolling the byroads and searching the hills that lined the route which the tanks could not penetrate. There were Germans everywhere and it was difficult at first sight to know if they had given up the fight or were struggling to form a new rearguard to buy time for other units to escape.

Just outside Hammam Lif, overlooking the road to Hammamet, were the Poninville Hills. The 10th Rifle Brigade had found that these hills were occupied by the enemy in some force, so 201st Guards Brigade, still under the command of 6th Armoured Division, were sent up to clear them. At 0500 hr on 10 May 2nd Coldstream Guards also moved on to the hills and swept along their undulating heights, silencing the guns on the top and capturing great numbers of the half-hearted defenders. By 0800 hr 3 Company had taken twelve guns and over 1,000 prisoners, while 4 Company had bagged four guns and 4,000 captives, with just one guardsman slightly wounded. Because of the danger that retreating Germans who had not yet been overrun on the plains might still burst across the road and attempt to get on to the peninsula, both guards brigades were strung out facing west in order to block all possible routes towards Cap Bon.

Back in Hammam Lif, 3rd Grenadier Guards were given a special task to perform. Word had come through that one of the armoured units had captured the Bey of Tunis and that he was being held prisoner in his palace along with his bodyguard. The Bey was no friend of the Allies and had thrown in his lot with the occupying Axis forces. The Grenadiers' Intelligence Officer, Lt Lambert, was told to go and investigate. Lt Lambert and a small escort made their way through streets of cheering civilians to the palace gates and forced an entry. He was shown up to the shell-damaged throne-room, where he found the entire Tunisian Cabinet waiting among the shattered glass and smashed gilt furniture. Lambert demanded to see the Bey in person. Almost immediately the one-time ruler of the province came out from a side room with his attendant bodyguard, resplendent in their uniforms of scarlet, black and gold. Through an interpreter the Bey asked graciously after the health of Their Majesties The King and Queen and offered to invest the British divisional commander with a high Tunisian order. This offer was declined with equal grace and the Bey was removed to Army HQ amid much wailing from the harem.[23]

With the Poninville Hills free of the enemy, 26th Brigade drove on and through Soliman on 10 May. The advance continued over roads devoid of Axis troops, but still susceptible to being cut by the Germans and Italians fleeing northwards. Every time the armour was held up by 88mm guns, 12th RHA quickly came up and shelled the enemy positions unmercifully. Large numbers of prisoners were continually being passed back by the guards brigades. They began running a shuttle service for this purpose, using their own lorries and captured German trucks.

Still the armour was urged on; senior commanders would not be satisfied until the Cap Bon peninsula had been severed. The 17th/21st Lancers were told to move at all possible speed for Hammamet, accompanied by some of the lorried infantry of 1st Guards Brigade. The 16th/5th Lancers were meanwhile sent south-west to seize a large body of the enemy who were reported moving northwards. No opposition was met and over 4,000 prisoners were taken.

Roaming a little further west in their armoured cars were 1st Derbyshire Yeomanry, trying to intercept and clear out the enemy. Lt Vin Moore later wrote an account of one such sweep out into the vast area of scrub, where the almost silent approach of the wheeled vehicles took a group of enemy by surprise:

> Topping a small rise we came upon the perfect view of an antitank gun – the back view. About a dozen men were sitting or walking about, and others could be seen in a depression on the right of the gun. Metcalfe drove the car to within twenty yards of the position. I covered the gun crew with our machine gun and fired a burst over their heads. There was no time to start a fight; panic might cause some of them to shoot back. Men poured out of holes everywhere. One man, out in the open, looked at us, and then slowly put his hands up. He was an officer. At this, one of the men threw down his helmet and jumped on it – for joy at being captured unharmed, evidently! Then Metcalfe yelled, 'Look out!' and pointed. Fifty yards away on the left was another antitank gun. The gun crew was trying to manhandle it round. A burst of fire over their heads brought them clambering out of the gun pit with their hands up. Eighty-odd Italians, including a captain of infantry and a gunner lieutenant gave themselves up to us.[24]

Hammamet was taken by 17th/21st Lancers early on 11 May; no more escaping Germans or Italians could now get onto the long peninsula that led up to Cap Bon. Those of the enemy that were already there had been sealed into a pocket. All danger now lay in the south-east, where the German divisions in front of Eighth Army were retreating northwards. The armoured brigade moved on down the road to Enfidaville towards the town of Bou Ficha, meeting groups of dejected enemy soldiers trudging towards it. Bou Ficha fell the next morning. Now all that was left of enemy territory was a long line of hills and the final stretch of road that led to Enfidaville, up which Eighth Army were advancing. More and more of the enemy were retreating before them, driven northwards by the fighting in the south, all thinking that they were making for Cap Bon and escape. The appearance of 26th Armoured

Brigade in front of them convinced them that there was no escape and they surrendered en masse.

On 13 May, Maj John Davie of the Derbyshire Yeomanry was sitting in his scout car directing mopping-up operations just outside Bou Ficha. To his surprise, he heard a foreign voice on his radio: 'Hullo, British Eighth Army – Hullo British Eighth Army, this is Italian First Army calling.' Davie thought this was strange, but continued with his tasks. The call was repeated a short while later, and, as no one else was answering the signal, he went on the radio himself to respond. He told the caller that he was British First Army. It transpired that the person on the radio was at Gen Messe's HQ and his commander wished to surrender and asked what the terms would be. 'Unconditional,' replied Maj Davie, conscious of the decisions reached between Allied leaders at the Casablanca conference. The voice replied that he would have to consult with his general. He was back after a short while saying that the general insisted on the full honours of war. Maj Davie replied that he was not sure what this involved and would get someone more senior to speak to him.

Maj Davie referred the matter to his colonel, who in turn spoke to Maj Gen Keightley. Word then came back to Davie that 'full honours of war' would mean the Italians surrendering with colours flying, drums beating and bayonets fixed. Keightley said that that was completely out of the question and the Italians had to surrender 'unconditionally'. The news was passed on to Messe's representative who went away in some disgust.

An hour later the Italian came back on Maj Davie's radio, still the only means of communication between the British and Italian armies. Messe would agree to 'unconditional surrender'. The major replied that the Italian Army was to lay down its arms at once and its commander was to drive to Bou Ficha that evening in a car flying a large white flag, to surrender in person.[25]

Also near Bou Ficha that day was Brig Roberts. He was forward with his leading tanks, watching an attack on the enemy-held hills which crossed the route to Enfidaville. Three German divisions were known to be in the area, including parts of the famous 90th Light Division. Through his field glasses he could see enemy artillery ahead, but they were firing to the south, away from the brigade. They were in fact taking on the advancing Eighth Army. Just then Roberts had a call on his radio and recognised the voice of Maj Gen Graham, commander of 56th Division. His division was being held up by the very guns that Roberts could see in front of 26th Armoured Brigade. Graham asked if Roberts could act as an observer for his guns. Roberts readily agreed and was soon acting as OP for 56th Division's artillery, observing the fall of shot and correcting their aim. First and Eighth Army had at last met.[26]

The commander of 90th Light Division, GenMaj Graf von Sponek, for a while refused to surrender and had to be blasted out of his command post in the hills. Eventually he came down from his mountain retreat and gave up his division to Maj Gen Keightley, who, out of courtesy, sent him on to Lt Gen Sir Bernard Freyberg, VC, whose New Zealanders had so often been confronted by von Sponek's crack division.[27] Von Arnim had surrendered the previous day, captured by an officer of 4th Indian Division. The fighting in Tunisia was at last over and 250,000 Axis troops were taken out of the war in a defeat that rivalled Stalingrad.

Chapter Seven

ITALY: THE FIRST WINTER

After the fighting in Tunisia had ended, 6th Armoured Division spent a long period in North Africa reorganising, replenishing its losses, training and putting itself in order. It was not recalled to battle for many months so it had ample time to assimilate new personnel into the unit, consider new ideas, familiarise itself with new weapons and practise the art of armoured warfare, employing many of the lessons it had learned in action.

In August, 12th RHA received replacements for its old, vulnerable 25-pounder field guns. The regiment was rearmed with American Priest 105mm self-propelled guns and the forward OPs were provided with Sherman tanks for protection. This was all part of making 6th Armoured Division a totally mechanised force, capable of moving at speed with all of its component arms. The Ayrshire Yeomanry, who normally supported 1st Guards Brigade, kept their 25-pounders, but their OPs were also provided with Sherman tanks. During this period it was also decided that armoured cars would no longer be practical once the division had moved on to the continent of Europe, and therefore the Derbyshire Yeomanry would be re-equipped with armour. It was now to become an armoured reconnaissance regiment with Sherman tanks, which meant that it had to lose its D Squadron. The changeover necessitated a considerable amount of new training and squadron exercises for the crews, to allow them to familiarise themselves with their new role in battle.

Meanwhile the hostilities rolled on, with the invasion of first Sicily then Italy by the Allies, drawn into waging war in Italy through the urgings of the British Prime Minister, Winston Churchill. The Americans were set against it, for they saw a campaign up the long Italian peninsula as being a sideshow. The most direct route into the interior of Nazi Germany was through France and the Low Countries. Any further campaigns in the Mediterranean would be sure to draw off forces that could be used to better effect in north-west Europe. Churchill demurred, reasoning that as the cross-Channel attack could not be mounted until the spring of 1944, they had to attack the Germans somewhere in order to tie down German divisions that might be used against Russia. Stalin was pressing for the opening of a 'second front' to ease the pressure being suffered by his armies in the east. He felt that of all the Allies, it was the Russians that were having to bear the brunt of the fighting.

Churchill appealed to President Roosevelt and eventually got his way for Italy to become the Allies' next battleground. The initial chain of command remained the same as in North Africa: Gen Eisenhower was Supreme Commander, with Gen Alexander as Commander Fifteenth Army Group consisting of the British Eighth and US Fifth Armies.

Italy was invaded by Gen Montgomery's Eighth Army on 3 September. Five days later, Italy left the Axis and surrendered to the Allies. The Germans reacted quickly to this act of treachery by their ally. Within just a few days, they had disarmed all Italian troops, taken over all the important military installations and imposed military government on the country. Then they rushed divisions southwards to counter Montgomery's invasion.

On 9 September, Lt Gen Mark Clark invaded the west coast of Italy at Salerno with his US Fifth Army. GenFM Albert Kesselring, Commander-in-Chief (South), quickly committed GenObst Heinrich von Vietinghoff's Tenth Army against the landings and almost succeeded in throwing the US Fifth Army back into the sea. The Germans then fought hard to contain the lodgement and challenged the Americans along every yard of the road northwards. It soon became clear that the fighting in Italy would be as complex and intense as it had been in North Africa. Hitler had again decreed that no ground was to be given up without a fight.

In choosing to continue the fight in Italy, the Allies found themselves struggling to overcome not only the enemy but the terrain as well. Italy is not a country any student of military history would willingly choose in which to wage war. Indeed many military strategists have called such a decision 'technically absurd'. Much of the country is suited for defensive warfare. The Apennine mountain range running down the length of Italy acts like a spine, splitting the country in two. On either side of these mountains, narrow coastal plains, often only tens of miles wide, form the only effective ground on which to move forces up and down the long peninsula. These plains are themselves bisected by a series of rivers flowing down from the Apennines to the sea and by spurs of high ground running east to west. Each of them forms a natural defence line which the enemy was more than capable of exploiting. With the Allies landing in the south of Italy, their advance northwards was confronted by one after another of these natural obstacles crossing their path, each of which had a German defensive line strung out along it and had to be taken by planned assault. No sooner had the Allies overcome one of them than another would rear up and bar their way.

By early 1944 it was evident that the fighting in Italy was going to be a long slog. The country was perfect for defence and the great master of the defensive battle, GenFM Kesselring, was controlling the show. As German

Commander in chief responsible for the defence of Italy, he made the campaign a gruelling one for the Allies. The autumn of 1943 set the pattern for the rest of the campaign. The advance north by Clark and Montgomery's forces was fiercely contested: on the west coast the US Fifth Army was held on the River Volturno, then in the mountains by the Bernhardt Line, while on the eastern side of the country Monty's army had to assault the Biferno, the Trigno and the Sangro river lines. Every one of Alexander's plans, every attack, and every switching of his forces to gain the edge was frustrated by a German defence line. Kesselring's astute generalship in handling his meagre forces to stall any Allied breakthrough was masterly. His performance during the Italian campaign is recognised as being among the best of any German commander during the war.

By the beginning of 1944, Alexander's armies were stalled on another German line of defence called the Gustav Line. It ran right across the middle of Italy, about sixty miles south of Rome. While the Allies had been bludgeoning their way across lesser lines of defence further south, Kesselring had been organising the construction of a 'winter line' of fortifications further to the north on which he planned to hold Alexander until at least the spring. The line was based on the mountains which backed the Garigliano/Rapido rivers in the west and the River Sangro in the east. Along these rivers the Germans constructed concrete fortifications and gun positions, linking them with minefields and machine-gun posts. Overlooking the River Rapido and dominating the entry into the strategically important Liri valley was Monte Cassino, the most heavily fortified section of the line. In between the two flanking river sections were the massive barren heights of the Apennines. Even there, among the snow-covered peaks of the central highlands, where one man and a machine gun could hold up the advance of a whole division, the Germans had more concrete pillboxes and minefields.

The three months of fighting that had led the Allies to the Gustav Line had been hard and the US Fifth Army had suffered most of all. The western route to Rome was always going to be the most promising for the Allies and Kesselring had located the bulk of his forces there to defend it. The route taken by Montgomery's Eighth Army along the Adriatic coast was less attractive. The coastal plain there was quite narrow and the succession of rivers and mountain ranges dissecting it were more formidable. This route left virtually no room for manoeuvre and certainly no ground on which to deploy armour. Monty's battle to take the line along the Sangro in late November successfully crossed the river, but became hopelessly bogged down in the hills and mountains on the other side. With the onset of winter, the only realistic way forward for Alexander's forces across the Gustav Line was in the west, across the Garigliano and Rapido rivers. However, by the time the Allies had reached the German fortifications their forces were tired, depleted and in need of rest. It was winter and, as luck would have it, the weather was the worst and wettest on record. The final few miles to the River Garigliano had been across the most inhospitable mountain terrain against a determined and unpleasant enemy; Clark's forces were almost on their knees.

The war in Italy had gone hopelessly wrong. One of the original reasons to launch a campaign in Italy was to tie down German divisions that could be used elsewhere. The fact that the campaign also tied down even more Allied divisions that could be used elsewhere seemed to have been overlooked. With the onset of 1944, the need to assemble divisions for the invasion of France had become a pressing one. Some of Alexander's best units were now removed from the Mediterranean to serve in north-west Europe. Also going back to England were the Supreme Commander and the commander of the British Eighth Army. Italy was rapidly becoming the sideshow predicted by the Americans.

The fighting in Italy was mostly an infantryman's war, with few open plains on which to deploy armour. Tanks were used as infantry support, mobile pillboxes to attack fixed defences. Their deployment was mostly of troop strength in local company actions, with occasionally squadrons and battalions employed during a larger attack, again directly in support of the infantry. Once the fighting had reached the mountains, tanks became redundant and tracked vehicles often got no further forward than a few miles behind the front. Warfare regressed almost to the Middle Ages, where manpower and pack horse became the transport, tracks and exposed footpaths became supply arteries, the fighting degenerated almost to hand-to-hand combat, and soldiers of both sides saw their enemy as individuals as they killed each other.

This type of warfare had little place for numbers of mobile armoured divisions. The Mailed Fist Division was not needed in Italy, nor was it required for the Normandy invasion, for 7th Armoured had been returned to England for that role and the untried 11th Armoured Division – now under the command of Maj Gen 'Pip' Roberts – was planned to follow it over, with the Guards Armoured Division joining them later. So 6th Armoured Division was left in North Africa, training and exercising, and exercising and training, waiting for the call that would summon it back to war.

In December 1943 there was a change in the command of the division. Maj Gen Charles Keightley was replaced by Maj Gen Vivian Evelegh. The move was a double swap; Keightley left 6th Armoured for 78th Division, Evelegh gave up 78th Division for 6th Armoured. Both of these generals had forged good reputations with their formations in Tunisia. Evelegh's division had performed well in the mountains in front of Tunis and was recognised as being the best infantry division in First Army. Both generals were now being considered for further promotion to corps command.

Vivian Evelegh was an infantryman and had commanded 78th Infantry Division since it was formed in June 1942, after a spell in command of

The sleek design of the Crusader gave it the image of a very modern fighting machine, but its performance failed to live up to expectations, although its 6-pounder gun was an improvement on the 2-pounder 'pea shooter' which armed the Valentine. (*IWM NA323*)

Crusader tank crew of the 17th/21st Lancers receiving mail from home. The spotless tank has yet to see action. (*IWM NA286*)

The tank crew of a battered Valentine relax with a bottle of Johnny Walker after action. Picture taken in January 1943 to the north of Bou Arada. (*IWM NA508*)

Gen Anderson, Commander First Army, presenting a DSO to Col Dick Hull of 17th/21st Lancers, who commanded Blade Force during the early battles for Tunis. (*IWM NA491*)

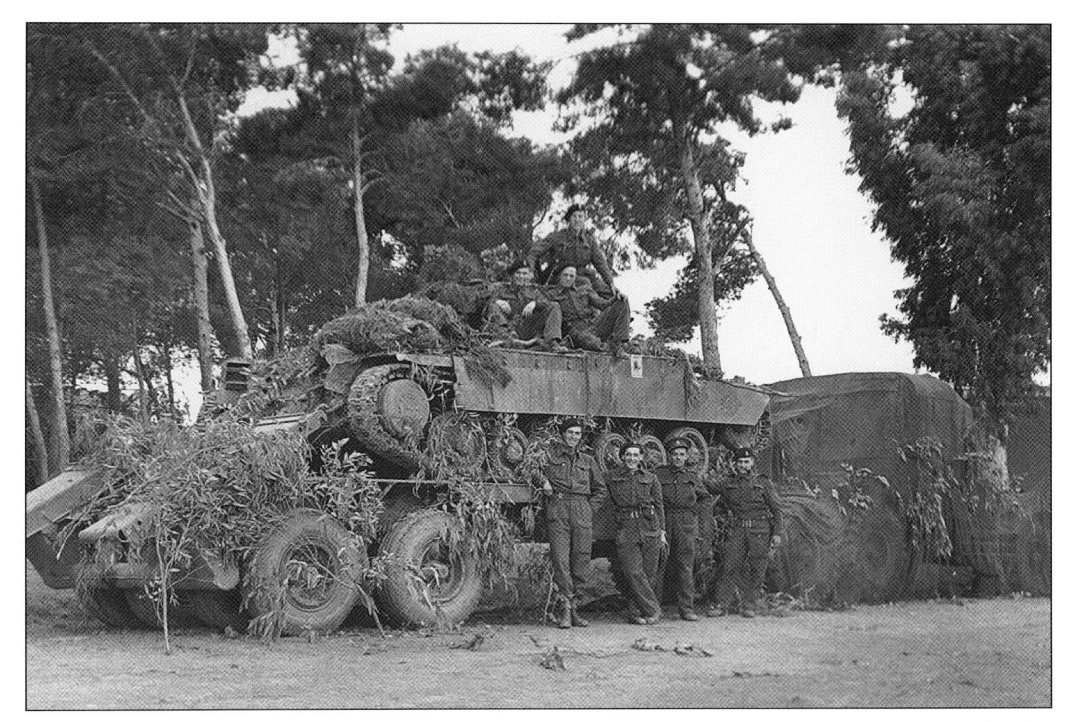

A heavily camouflaged Valentine of 17th/21st Lancers is brought back to a REME repair facility by a heavy tank transporter. Many of the early tank losses in Tunisia were due to mechanical failures rather than enemy action. These were recovered from the battlefield for repair wherever possible. (*IWM NA282*)

Infantry of 10th Rifle Brigade on the outskirts of Bou Arada. The picture was taken on 18 January 1943 during the attack on the town by 10th Panzer Division. (*IWM NA460*)

An attack on Two Tree Hill during January 1943. The 6th Inniskilling Fusiliers have failed in their attempt to take the summit and are pulling back under a smoke screen laid by the artillery. Tanks of 17th/21st Lancers can be seen on the right, covering the withdrawal. *(IWM NA505)*

The Valentine tank from A Squadron of 17th/21st Lancers captured by the Germans in November 1942 from Blade Force. It was painted in panzer colours and used as a 'Trojan Horse' to gain passage through the British line in front of Thala during the Kasserine battle. (*IWM NA844*)

A newly delivered Sherman tank of 16th/5th Lancers passes by a knocked-out Panzer III after the battle of Thala in February 1943. The German tank has been totally destroyed by explosives placed by Royal Engineers to prevent the enemy retrieving it for repair. (*IWM NA838*)

Valentine tanks, thought to be C Squadron of 2nd Lothians and Border Horse, moving up from Thala to the pass at Kasserine. The town of Thala can just be discerned 3 miles away in the right-hand middle distance. The photograph was taken on the ridge where 2nd/5th Leicesters manned their final stop-line. (IWM NA826)

Sappers of the division's 8th Field Squadron RE along the road from Thala up to the Kasserine Pass, probing for antitank mines with their bayonets. (*IWM NA856*)

Maj Gen Charles Keightly (centre), Commander 6th Armoured Division, talks with Lt Gen John Crocker (right), Commander IX Corps, before the Fondouk battle. (*IWM NA1593*)

Infantry carriers of 3rd Welsh Guards moving through hilly countryside just before the start of the operation to take Kairouan in April 1943. The Welsh Guards joined 1st Guards Brigade in March to replace 2nd Hampshires, who were decimated at Tebourba during the early battles to take Tunis. (*IWM NA1717*)

Sherman tank of 26th Armoured Brigade moving up towards Fondouk at the start of the battle. The high ground attacked by US 34th Division is in the left background. (*IWM NA1899*)

Brig 'Pip' Roberts, Commander 26th Armoured Brigade, talks to Maj Gen Keightley after the Kairouan battle. (*IWM NA2210*)

Gun detachment from 152nd (Ayrshire Yeomanry) Field Regiment RA manning a 25-pounder field gun in support of the attack across the River Rapido in May 1944. (*IWM NA14781*)

A 6-pounder antitank gun manned by guardsmen of 1st Guards Brigade in a ruined house overlooking a road near Cassino. (*IWM NA14848*)

Tanks of 26th Armoured Brigade in the Liri valley during Operation Diadem. (*IWM NA14891*)

The graves of the crew of a Sherman from 1st Derbyshire Yeomanry buried in front of their tank close by Aquino airfield. The Sherman has been knocked out while trying to penetrate the Hitler Line defences. Seven direct hits can be seen around the turret area. (*IWM NA15844*)

Guardsmen from 3rd Welsh Guards are passed by one of 26th Armoured Brigade's Shermans during their attack on Monte Piccolo outside Arce. (*IWM NA15664*)

Maj Gen Vivian Evelegh (left), Commander 6th Armoured Division, talking to Lt Gen John Harding (right), Gen Alexander's Chief of Staff, with an unnamed officer. (*IWM NA14669*)

Guardsmen from 1st Guards Brigade pause during the fighting in the hills to the north of Arezzo. (*IWM NA16966*)

Crew of a Priest 105mm self-propelled gun from 12th (HAC) RHA taking on board ammunition before the start of the drive to Perugia. (*IWM NA17769*)

A patrol from C Company of 10th Rifle Brigade moving along the Arno valley near Arezzo in July 1944. (*IWM NA16879*)

Maj Gen 'Nap' Murray (left), Commander 6th Armoured Division, confers with Brig Adrian Gore (centre), Commander 61st Infantry Brigade, while his ADC (right) holds the map. (*IWM NA24400*)

Transport from 6th Armoured Division lined up along a road leading into the northern Apennines. It was in this type of difficult terrain that the division spent its second winter in Italy. (*IWM NA19036*)

Maj Gen Murray visiting some of his forward troops in the mountains in late 1944. The men are from 72nd Antitank Regiment, who had been assigned to help the Royal Engineers in the task of keeping open roads and tracks during the appalling winter weather. (IWM NA21681)

An officer of 3rd Grenadier Guards uses skis to visit one of his guardsmen in a forward position near Monte Penzola during 1st Guards Brigade's stay in the mountains. (IWM NA21690)

A carrier platoon of the Support Company of 3rd Grenadier Guards reaches the River Po near the end of the war. The two carriers in the foreground are Wasp flame throwers, with their large tanks of napalm prominent at the rear. (*IWM NA24509*)

Brig N.M. Mitchell at the division's tactical HQ during the final battle. To his rear is Lt Col Johnny Barstow, who commanded 12th Field Regiment RHA during the whole of the regiment's fighting war. The side arm worn by Brig Mitchell was actually used in action by him, when one of his Orders Groups was raked with fire from a German machine gun. While all Mitchell's colonels scattered and sought some hiding place, the brigadier remained standing, engaging the enemy with his revolver. (*IWM NA24401*)

11th Infantry Brigade. In contrast, Keightley was a cavalryman who had experience of handling only armoured formations. The two generals now had to prove themselves fit for higher command by working with an arm in which they had not previously served. Keightley joined 78th Division on 13 December 1943, just after the division had completed its successful attack across the River Sangro. He was able gradually to acquaint himself with his new role over the next few months when the division was used in static positions, holding first the mountain line in the east of Italy in front of Eighth Army, and then the heights above Cassino with the US Fifth Army. His first battle with 78th Division was in May 1944 during Alexander's major offensive through the Liri valley to get behind Monte Cassino. The division again performed well both there and during the march up Italy. This performance eventually led to Keightley's getting his corps command when he took over V Corps from his previous boss, Lt Gen Allfrey, in August 1944. Keightley's career continued to prosper after 1945, as he gained further promotion in the postwar years.

Maj Gen Evelegh was not left for long in North Africa with his new division, for his administrative talents were soon needed elsewhere. In January 1945 Clark's Fifth Army tried to outflank the Gustav Line by carrying out an amphibious landing fifty miles to the north at Anzio. The plan was to land an American corps behind the German defence line to threaten Rome, forcing the enemy either to withdraw from Cassino and the Garigliano positions, or to switch some of his strength from that sector to counter the landings at Anzio. Kesselring did neither; he quickly found formations from other areas outside Italy and formed new scratch units to frustrate the US VI Corps at Anzio and confine the lodgement to an area of territory just a few miles deep. On the Gustav Line little changed. Fifth Army remained stalled and frustrated. Maj Gen Evelegh was sent into the Anzio beachhead to perform liaison duties as deputy to the US VI Corps's commander, Maj Gen Lucas.

January 1944 was a most depressing month for the Allies in Italy. The Gustav Line had halted their advance completely. Static lines had forced the return of trench warfare, with both sides facing each other across just yards of no man's land. Winter rains had washed away the means to deploy large numbers of troops and reduced the battlefields to the consistency of liquid mud reminiscent of the worst days of the First World War. The landings at Anzio had failed miserably, unable to cause the enemy more than a few days of unpleasantness and concern. Churchill was very disappointed, claiming that he thought the Allies were landing a 'wild cat' behind German lines, but all that came ashore was a 'stranded whale'.

Serving with Alexander's forces in Italy was 23rd Armoured Brigade, which had seen action with X Corps at Salerno, Naples and on the River Volturno. Its armoured regiments were tired out and needed rest and retraining. This was best done in North Africa, so each regiment in turn was sent back across the Mediterranean to carry out a programme of renewal and to sharpen its cutting edge. To fill in while they were away, 6th Armoured Division was asked to supply 16th/5th Lancers to 23rd Armoured Brigade.

The Lancers left North Africa on 6 January 1944 and arrived with their new brigade just in time to take part in an attack across the Garigliano against the Gustav Line. The attack by the US Fifth Army consisted of an infantry assault across the Garigliano by the British X Corps and an assault across its subsidiary, the River Rapido, and the heights above the town of Cassino by the US II Corps. The first gained the Garigliano and got troops into the mountains on the far side; the second was repulsed on the Rapido, but did succeed in getting men on to the high ground above the town of Cassino. These American troops were strung out along a line of ridges dominated by the heights of Monte Cassino, with its formidable monastery overlooking the whole of the battlefield. Enemy resistance everywhere was ferocious. In effect, Gen Mark Clark had men in the mountains of the Gustav Line, but they were not going anywhere. Once the attacks had petered out, the Germans were then content to leave the Allied troops where they were and let their artillery and mortars and the atrocious winter weather drain away their strength.

The 16th/5th Lancers' part in the Garigliano battle was in support of the British 5th Division, but they were not sent into the battle until after the bridgehead on the other side had been established. The plan was for the armour then to begin a drive northwards to link up with VI Corps at Anzio, culminating in the capture of Rome. Unfortunately enemy resistance ensured that nothing so grand was accomplished and the Lancers were only called upon to help the infantry to hold on to its meagre gains close to the river at Minturno. A second attack was planned to resume the offensive, but this, too, petered out without any further gains. For the whole of January and February, 16th/5th Lancers' role was to stiffen a defensive line within 5th Division's lodgement over the Garigliano.

The bulk of the US 5th Army was in the mountains, holding an undulating line on the most inhospitable of terrain. This type of warfare requires men, lots of them, just to preserve the status quo. The soldiers in the line have to be assisted and supplied by other soldiers simply for them to remain there. For every infantryman in the line, five more are behind him, giving him sustenance and support. Even more men have to be held in reserve to relieve those in the trenches after their spell at the front is over, and still more men are needed to look after him out of the line. Casualties, sickness, desertions and sheer exhaustion all whittled away at their numbers and appalling weather lowered their resolve. January 1944 was a bad month for the US Fifth Army and the call went out for more men to be brought across the Mediterranean to join in the struggle.

Towards the end of that miserable January, 6th Armoured Division was among the first of the divisions in North Africa to be ordered to provide fresh troops for the Italian campaign. Alexander did not want more of its tanks, he wanted its guardsmen and their supporting artillery. On 1 February, the 1st Guards Brigade under its new commander Brig Haydon was transferred to Allied Forces Mediterranean HQ, prior to a move to Italy to join US Fifth Army. Between 3 and 5 February the brigade arrived in Naples and was sent north to join 46th Division to become part of Lt Gen McCreery's British X Corps. On 20 February, 152nd Field Regiment, the Ayrshire Yeomanry, followed them across the Mediterranean.

The British 46th Division, commanded by Maj Gen Hawkesworth, was holding a small three-mile-deep salient in the Arunci Mountains north of the River Garigliano, which it had carved out in an attack on 21 January, but then became too weak to exploit. The assault had been halted by the German 94th Infantry Division after just a few days and the enemy knew that this local penetration of its defensive line was of little strategic consequence. Both sides then went onto the defensive, leaving their front-line troops to harass and worry their opponents by fighting patrols, small skirmishes and sporadic gunfire. Hawkesworth's men were becoming very tired and needed relief, and it was this task that was now given to 1st Guards Brigade in preparation for a new assault on the nearby peak of Monte Faito, which, if successful, would outflank the enemy in the eastern part of the Arunci Mountains and force him to withdraw his line. The guards had not been trained in mountain warfare, but they were about to become experts at it the hard way.

The proposed attack on Monte Faito was in fact postponed, and 2nd Coldstream and 3rd Welsh Guards were sent into the line to relieve the troops on Monte Ornito and Monte Furlito, with 3rd Grenadiers in reserve. The move on to the mountains was arduous. There were insufficient porters and mules to convey equipment, ammunition and supplies up to the forward positions, so the guardsmen had to carry it all themselves. Each man was laden with his own rifle, full equipment, greatcoat, blankets, rations and spare ammunition and had to make his way up narrow paths, across craggy mountainsides and through rock-strewn gullies, in torrential rain, to reach waterlogged slit trenches and mud-splattered holes in the rock. Worse was to come for the Welsh Guards, for the next day they were ordered even further along the mountain line to take over the positions of 5th Hampshires on the most-forward apex of 46th Division's salient on Monte Cerasola. The Hampshires had fought off numerous attacks by the enemy on their positions and the battalion was down to less than half of its fighting strength.

The relief of 5th Hampshires had to take place in darkness, for the forward positions on Cerasola were overlooked by the Germans. There was no time for a proper reconnaissance. The CO of the Welsh Guards,

Lt Col Sir William Makins, took his company commanders forward with him to organise the changeover with the Hampshires' CO. The adjutant was to bring up the battalion during the night. Lt Col Makins and his party moved from Monte Furlito, across Monte Fuga and were just winding their way round the back of the Coldstream-held Monte Ornito to pass over on to Cerasola, when they were startled to find themselves in the middle of a battle. The enemy were putting in an attack on Monte Cerasola and the action was spilling over onto Ornito as well. Mortar and shell fire fell all around them as they pressed on to find the Hampshires' HQ. It was a bad time to make a recce of their new positions, but daylight was fading and they needed to get their bearings.

They found the Hampshires' HQ on the rear face of Cerasola just below the crest, but not before they had stumbled into a party of Germans trying to infiltrate up the slopes of the mountain and had put them to flight with rifle and pistol fire, killing the leading German and scattering the others. Fortunately the fighting was beginning to die down and the company commanders were able to identify their new positions and to decide where machine guns and mortars should be placed before the light had completely faded. A few hours later the guardsmen came up to effect the relief in the dark, buffeted by rain, sleet and flurries of snow. It was a nightmare.

The Welsh Guards' companies on Monte Cerasola were adjacent to German positions just below the crest line. The two sides were only a couple of hundred yards apart. Overlooking all of this were the main German lines on Monte Faito and Girofano. Enemy OPs looked down on Cerasola and were able to direct shell and mortar fire on any movement. The guardsmen knew that the enemy was close by, but did not know just how close until, just before dawn, another German assault took place.

The attack came at the Guards before daylight had given them the opportunity to see the ground around their positions and to familiarise themselves with the layout of the battalion. Before they could organise a concerted response the enemy was among them. The German assault hit the Welsh Guards in the centre of their line, with No. 2 Company taking the main shock of the attack. Enemy soldiers quickly pushed across the ground separating the two sides and began scrambling up the rocks to the crest of Cerasola as mortar and machine-gun fire raked the Guards' positions. Rifle fire and grenades from the guardsmen in their sangars slowed down the attack, but the enemy managed to establish themselves in positions along the edge of the crest, just below No. 2 Company. They were too close to be effectively shelled or mortared, so Capt Elliot, the company commander, ordered a bayonet charge to remove them.

The captain and a group of his men sallied out from their line of sangars and dashed at the enemy, killed and captured many of them and drove the others back across the boulder-strewn moonscape to their lines. A gallant act, but one that cost the life of the company commander: Capt Elliot was killed at the head of his men. Lt Barbour, the battalion's Intelligence Officer, then came forward to take over the company. He settled No. 2 Company down again and arranged for the wounded to be evacuated, only for the desperate situation to repeat itself a short while later. Another enemy attack came in and again established itself near the crest. Rifle and grenades could not shift them; they had to be removed once more at the point of the bayonet in a charge led by the new company commander. Sadly, history repeated itself and Lt Barbour was killed leading his men forward.

Twenty-two Welsh Guardsmen lost their lives in these two attacks, with forty-nine others wounded; No. 2 Company was left with just thirty-eight men. The battalion had held its positions, but the losses in just one morning's defensive fighting were very sobering. Getting the wounded off the heights was a monumental task. With just one rough track leading back across the hills, each casualty had to be carried out by stretcher-bearers. One of the first to be removed was a young lieutenant who had been wounded in the attack. It took thirty-six hours for six men to get the officer down the mountainside to the Regimental Aid Post on the rear of Monte Ornito and then on to the nearest supply dump, where a jeep could take him the distance to a Casualty Clearing Station. Sappers worked hard to improve and widen the track and the time taken to get casualties out was reduced later; but it never took less than twelve hours.

The attack experienced by the Welsh Guards was repeated that afternoon against 2nd Coldstream on Monte Ornito. The assault across to the Coldstream positions happened so quickly that the enemy was almost among the guardsmen before the whole of the battalion could be warned. Rifle-fire and grenades failed to halt the Germans, so Maj Green requested artillery fire support. The danger was that incoming friendly fire was at such a shallow angle that it often did not clear the crest and fell among the British positions. Nonetheless, the situation was so critical that this support was requested urgently. The gunners back in the valleys responded with alacrity and shells soon crashed down among the Coldstream and the enemy. Its effect was devastating; fortunately most of it fell on the exposed attackers rather than the sheltered defenders and the assault was broken up. Small-arms fire sent the remainder packing and the few resilient Germans who stayed behind were flushed out at the point of a bayonet.

Once again an enemy attack had whittled away at 1st Guards Brigade; the Coldstream lost six men killed and forty-five wounded. Total casualties to the brigade during one day's holding of the line were 122. More were to follow over the ten days that the Garigliano salient was held by the Guards. Many casualties were as a result of conditions in the mountains. Frostbite and exhaustion contributed to the numbers evacuated, as did injuries caused by shelling and mortaring, as well as those suffered by contact with the enemy on the numerous patrols that were mounted to deny the Germans the occupation of no man's land.

After the attacks of 10 February, the Germans opposite the brigade remained fairly quiet, but niggled away at the British with sniper and mortar fire, occasionally supplementing this with violent bouts of shellfire. The 3rd Grenadier Guards later moved up into positions further along the line on Monte Tuga, overlooking the German-held village of Castleforte. Here the Grenadiers suffered more from shellfire than from direct attack, although their well-constructed sangars and holes in the rocks often gave them good cover. On one particular occasion 142 shells fell on No. 1 Company during a single night, none of which caused any casualties; one fell just 6 feet away from their sleeping Commanding Officer but left him unharmed.

Life in the line for 1st Guards Brigade in the Garigliano salient was one of endurance. For most of the time the guardsmen were crouched in their stone sangars, unable to move, watching for any enemy activity. Long, flat periods of calm were suddenly shattered by bouts of shelling which might herald the start of another rushed German attack. Short snatches of sleep were grabbed whenever possible, although the freezing cold weather and bouts of rain, sleet and snow, made this almost impossible. During the day everything was wet; during the night everything froze. Each and every single item needed by the battalion, from water to ammunition, had to be portered up the mountains along narrow goat tracks from bases down in the valley. When extra carrying parties were needed to bring supplies forward, it was the guardsmen who had to provide them. They toiled through the night to get the rations up to the summit before daylight left them exposed on the open mountainsides.

On 19 February, an hour before dawn, the enemy made a last, determined effort out of the darkness to surround and capture Cerasola. The main German force moved around the northern slopes of the mountain to get behind the Welsh Guards. Once again artillery and mortar fire, directed from OPs on Monte Faito, pounded the British. The Germans managed to get to the rear of the Guards to engage many of their companies' positions from behind and attack the battalion HQ.

Fierce fighting, including hand-to-hand skirmishing, broke out all along the summit. The battalion's mortar line was fired on from the rear while the weapons were directed to the front, dealing with the main part of the attack. Sgt Mairs kept his mortars firing as he and a few men counterattacked the enemy behind him. Mairs was killed, but the Germans were beaten off, then either killed or captured. By this time the enemy was among the Guards' positions, rushing isolated sangars and trying to pick off the Welshmen from the front, side and rear. Fighting continued without the Germans taking any of the company positions. Daylight turned the battle by exposing the enemy in the midst of the Guards. It was now the Germans' turn to be overlooked on three sides and the besieged guardsmen caught them in the open. The companies were now freely able to seek out enemy individuals and dispatch them with expert marksmanship. Few Germans got away; most were killed or captured. In total, 112 prisoners were taken that morning. They were marched away over ground littered with their dead.[1]

A similar attack was also launched at the same time on Monte Ornito. This fared much worse for the enemy and it was stopped dead on the ground in front of the Coldstream's positions. This time the killing began well short of the battalion's line and the surrenders swiftly followed. Sixty-five prisoners were taken, with almost the same number left dead on the mountainside. The attacks were the enemy's last attempt at eliminating the salient. The front here remained static for the next three months until the French launched themselves out of the line as part of Alexander's great spring offensive.

The Guards Brigade was relieved from its spell on the mountains on 20 February. It had been in the hills for just ten days, but had suffered over 400 casualties. Once off the hillsides the three battalions were lorried back to the rear for a rest and became the corps reserve for a time. All three were to return to the mountains again in early March, but their stay lasted only eight days. They did not suffer any further enemy attacks while there, but the cold, the rain, the snow and the shellfire were just the same.

Even though a bridgehead had been carved out across the River Garigliano, and Fifth Army had troops on the hills behind Cassino town, the Gustav Line remained intact. The only practical route to Rome capable of carrying an army lay along Highway 6 and this road passed through the Liri valley. But the entrance into this valley was barred by the Gustav Line defences and was dominated by Monte Cassino. The Allies knew that the line had to be broken there for the advance to continue, but while Monte Cassino and its monastery remained in German hands, no one was going up the Liri valley.

By the middle of March 1944 there had been three separate battles to take Monte Cassino. The first, by the US II Corps, petered out in snow storms just yards from the monastery when Clark's two attacking divisions ran out of steam. The second, by the New Zealand II Corps, failed through a combination of a lack of urgency and fierce resistance by the German 1st Parachute Division. The attack was at the expense of the medieval monastery on the summit of the mountain, which was bombed to oblivion. The third battle, again by the New Zealand corps, destroyed the town of Cassino at the foot of the mountain and cost thousands of casualties, but gained only part of the ruined town and the destroyed castle. The New Zealanders did not get one yard nearer to the monastery.

The loss of life and sheer frustration suffered during these three battles prompted Alexander to find another way to get into the Liri valley: he decided on overwhelming brute force. The army group commander chose to reinforce the front with all available units. Leaving a small force holding Eighth Army's line on the Adriatic coast, he brought the remainder of the army, now commanded by Gen Oliver Leese, over to the west. A new plan was developed that would see a massive attack on the Gustav Line by American, British, Canadian, French and Polish corps, along with a coordinated breakout from the Anzio beachhead. Alexander planned to use infantry to bludgeon his way into the valley and then exploit the breakthrough with armour, and for this massive offensive he needed 6th Armoured Division. A call now went out to North Africa to summon the Mailed Fist Division back to war.

During the second week in March, 26th Armoured Brigade and the artillery and support regiments of 6th Armoured Division made their way across the Mediterranean to join Eighth Army. On 18 March the divisional HQ became active in an operational theatre once again and the next day Maj Gen Evelegh rejoined the division as its commander after his tour of duty with the US VI Corps at Anzio. On the 27th, 1st Guards Brigade moved back to its parent unit in the divisional concentration area north of Capua. The division was once again complete.

After the third attempt to take Cassino had failed, the two divisions involved in the main attack, 4th Indian and 2nd New Zealand Divisions, withdrew from the battlefield. The third division in Gen Freyberg's New Zealand Corps, Maj Gen Keightley's 78th Division, was then sent up into the hills behind Cassino to hold the line. The division was strung out along the peaks overlooked by Monte Cassino, among the debris of the castle and in Cassino itself, disputing the ruins there with the enemy. It was a long line for one division to hold, so 1st Guards Brigade was sent across to help. Brig Haydon was now ordered to move his brigade into Cassino and occupy the rubble which constituted the western area of the obliterated town.

The Guards arrived in what was left of Cassino on 5 April. Their occupation of the town was shared with German paratroopers. The western side, below the monastery, was enemy territory; the eastern part, fed by Highway 6 leading into Cassino along the 'Straight Mile', had been captured by the New Zealanders during the third battle and was deemed to be worth holding on to. Both sides had observation over almost every inch of the rubble that was once orderly rows of streets and houses. Every single building had been destroyed by bomb and shell. What was left was a moonscape of rubble: blocked streets, jagged masonry, and demolished stone walls. A watercourse, the River Gari, choked with debris, spilled through the ruins trying to find its way to its confluence with the Rapido, filling bomb craters with stagnant water and creating cesspits of dead bodies, filth and decay. Each night a mist would rise from the water and cover the town with an eerie grey blanket from which the massive heights of Monastery Hill towered above everything.

Those troops who occupied this devastation lived a subterranean life, cowering in cellars and crypts by day, moving cautiously through darkened shadows by night. There was no movement at all in Cassino in daylight. The Guards entered the town in complete darkness, led into their positions by guides who pointed out the traps and dangers that lurked around every corner. The Welsh Guards held the northern side below Castle Hill, with the Coldstream in the centre opposite the notorious Hotel Continental and the Grenadiers in the southern edge by the railway station.

The Welsh Guards established their battalion HQ in the cellars of the town gaol, the only building on their side of the town that had any overhead cover. The battalion history said that it resembled the Black Hole of Calcutta. There were no air outlets; the one small window had been blocked by rubble and closed by a blanket to prevent light shining out at night. At one time or another, there were up to twenty people sharing the room, organising and supporting the two companies that were holding the Welsh Guards' sector.[2] The other two guards battalions had equally cramped accommodation. They each kept two companies in the town, with the other companies held just outside in reserve. The 2nd Coldstream and 3rd Grenadiers combined their battalion HQs in the same crypt beneath the ruins of a church. The entrance to the crypt was through a small hole tunnelled through the rubble. Entry and egress was made on hands and knees. Inside the underground HQ were two commanding officers, two adjutants, a Regimental Aid Post, a gunner officer, signallers, intelligence staff and cooks. Thirty men shared the smoke-filled room, each trying to make the most of the cramped squalor.

For the men holding the town, life was even more arduous. The platoons were spread among the ruins, carving out shelter where they could. Their positions were no more than 150 yards from the enemy, often in a bombed-out house with no roof and few walls. They held their posts for ten days at a time, sleeping, reading and keeping watch, unable to move and only able to be resupplied during the night. Rations were brought to them by portering parties who carried the stores; vehicles could get no closer than a few miles to the town, for the sound of engines brought down salvoes of enemy shells. With all resupply being done at night, the German paratroopers were aware that the men portering these supplies into the town were above ground and vulnerable. They might not be able to see the carrying parties, but they knew the routes that the porters were taking. The Germans fired machine guns along fixed lines covering entry points into Cassino and brought shellfire down on the 'Straight Mile' leading into the town. Every night, scores of men had to run the gauntlet of this fire, and every night there were casualties. Random death and injury came to men who were caught in the wrong place at the wrong time. Most of the casualties suffered by the Guards Brigade in holding the town were men hit while in the open during this nightly routine.

The enemy in Cassino were from the German 1st Parachute Division, a veteran unit which had fought in Crete and Sicily. They were very tough opponents. The division had been in Cassino since the second battle and had survived the dreadful bombing of the town with great resolution. It was commanded by GenMaj Richard Heidrich, a leader beloved by his men and one who had extreme confidence in his division. He believed that his men would do anything he asked of them, taking the fight to the last round and the last man; and he was right – they would.

The paras became openly active after dusk, patrolling and laying booby traps in buildings known to be patrolled by the Guards, admitting later that they did so to retain self-respect. They preferred fighting to waiting and lost no chance of relieving the monotony of static warfare by getting at their enemy. They shelled and mortared every slightest movement by the British and fired on all approaches and known routes during the night, trying in every way to interfere with the relief and resupply of the Guards Brigade. And when there was nothing else to do, they chatted and taunted in English on the Guards' radio network. The Coldstream Guards had only been in the line for one day when a German voice came over their net saying: 'You are all brave – you are all gentlemen.'[3] The Welsh Guards took to speaking in their native tongue while in radio contact to confuse the enemy, imitating the New Zealanders who had often spoken in Maori on their net. The Germans replied by firing propaganda leaflets written in Urdu.

The Guards Brigade remained in possession of Cassino from 7 until 23 April, then after a spell at rest, they returned to the ruins once again on 4 May. On this occasion, the brigade took over responsibility for the castle, perched high on a conical hill that rose straight up out of Cassino town. It was probably the most exposed position of all, looked down on by Monastery Hill and the numerous other enemy-held positions on three sides. Access to the castle was up one steep path which passed within 50 yards of the enemy. It was a hard twenty-five-minute climb, possible in some points only with the aid of ropes. The castle could only be held by one company at a time, and for two days at a time. Most of this period was spent by the men sheltering in the crypt of the castle, while lookouts kept a round-the-clock watch for the enemy.

As April turned into May, this period of watch by the Guards Brigade, so reminiscent of the worst days of the First World War, was coming to an end. Alexander's massive spring offensive was taking shape, and it was obvious to both sides that the day for its launch was drawing near.

Chapter Eight

THE LIRI VALLEY

The taking of Monte Cassino to open the way into the Liri valley along Highway 6 had frustrated Gen Alexander and Gen Mark Clark for almost four months. Three separate battles by the US Fifth Army had achieved little. Troops were on the hills behind Cassino, almost touching Monastery Hill, and part of the town was in Allied hands, but the way into the valley was still closed to the Allies. What little gains that had been made were achieved at great cost to both men and morale. The troops who had battered away at the great bastion were tired, very tired.

During the last attempt to gain Monte Cassino, by Lt Gen Freyberg's New Zealand Corps, even while men were immolating themselves in the ruins of the town, Lt Gen John Harding, Chief of Staff to Alexander, was putting together a new approach to the problem of Monte Cassino. There had to be another way rather than continuing to send troops to batter themselves to a standstill against the strongest point of the German defences. Harding's new plan, Operation 'Diadem', called for the bulk of all Allied forces in Italy to be brought together in front of the Gustav Line and then to launch an offensive of such great strength as to be irresistible.

Gen Mark Clark was to be relieved of the problem of Cassino. His troops would concentrate on the coastal sector opposite the River Garigliano. He would attack there with two divisions of the US II Corps and four divisions of the French Expeditionary Corps, striking up the coastal road and across the Arunci mountains. The British Eighth Army would leave holding divisions in the east to keep the enemy in that sector occupied while it shifted its remaining divisions across the Apennines to come before the entrance to the Liri valley and Cassino. The British XIII Corps was to make the main attack over the River Rapido into the Liri valley with three infantry and two armoured divisions. The Polish II Corps was to take Monte Cassino with its two divisions. Freyberg's New Zealand Corps was to hold the line to the north of Cassino vacated by the French. That was the plan and the start date was set for 11 May.

Maj Gen Evelegh's Mailed Fist Division was not to fight in the initial stages of the attack as a division, but was to be spread over the battlefield, providing armour and infantry where it was needed. The 6th Armoured

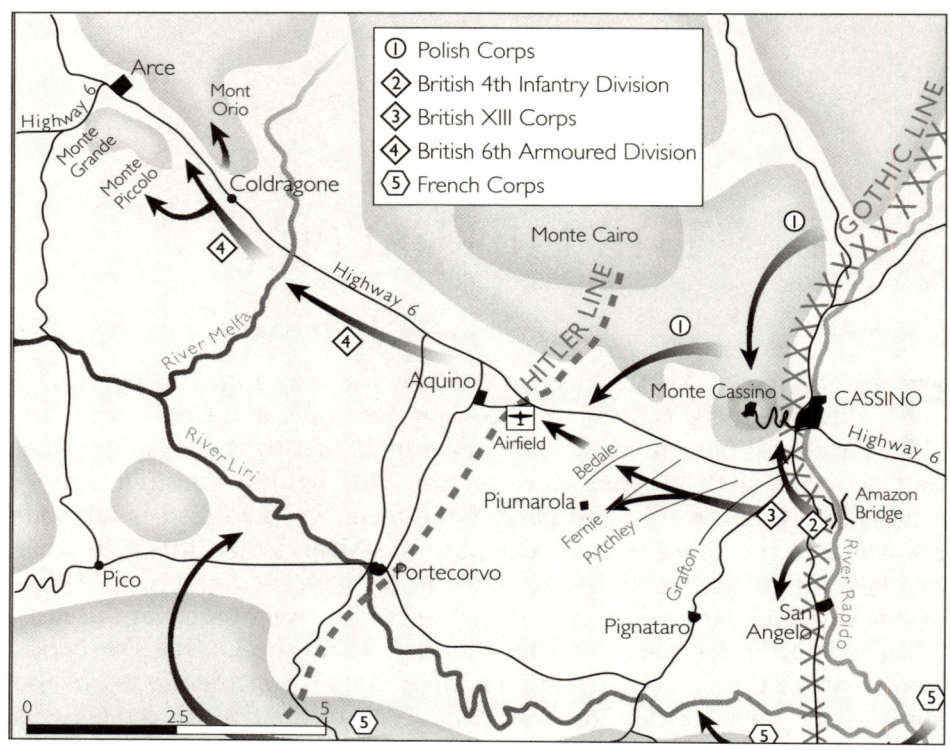

Map 7. The Liri valley

Division's role in Operation Diadem was initially one of support. Its armoured brigade was to supply tanks for the attacking infantry, with each of its armoured regiments supporting brigades, and individual squadrons supporting battalions. The 1st Guards Brigade would remain in Cassino during the attack and then assist with the capture of the town after 4th Division had crossed the Rapido and swung towards it from the south, taking the enemy holed up there from the flank.

Close infantry/tank cooperation was essential during the initial stages of Diadem and the armoured brigade spent its first few weeks in Italy exercising with 4th Division. A series of set-piece attacks with the infantry were simulated so that the armour could work with all of the battalions of the division. They practised attacking fixed enemy fortifications and close-fire support on specified targets. By the end of the period the two arms had an appreciation of each other's needs. A little later, starting on 30 April, 16th/5th Lancers conducted this training with the infantry of 78th Division. A simulated attack was rehearsed which used the combined weapons of tanks and infantry. During the training this attack was repeated eight times, each time with a different infantry battalion, so that every squadron went through the exercise twice, leaving each arm confident in the other's ability for the coming offensive.

Lt George Martin of the Lothians later explained how the tank commanders communicated with the infantry: 'An empty 50mm ammunition box was spot welded to the hull at the back of the tank. Into this was fitted a 'Tannoy' microphone and a handset, the lead passing through the engine compartment to connect up to the crew commander's radio unit. Should the infantry be held up by a well-sited machine gun post, an officer or NCO could, by going to the rear of the tank, indicate by using the radio link, the position of the machine gun to the tank commander, who could, by using high explosive or machine guns, or both, destroy the post.' This idea was good in theory and worked well in local actions and training, but in a major battle it proved to be hazardous and of limited value. Usually the box was blown off or was a tangled mass of metal as a result of blast or shrapnel.[1]

The enemy along the River Rapido opposite the area selected for the assault had had four months in which to establish a series of interlocking positions, linked by wire, minefields and concrete emplacements. These positions were manned by the Bode Blocking Group, a mixture of static troops and *panzergrenadiers* – the first to be used as 'cannon fodder', their resolve strengthened by the depth and strength of the fortifications; the second to form the mobile reserve required to seal off any attempted British breakthrough. Von Vietinghoff's plan was to use the Bode Group to hold the Allies and determine the location and direction of the attack while mobile reinforcements, some of them elite units, could be brought down into the line to seal off any penetration.

Details were later given of 26th Armoured Brigade's intended role in the battle within Lt Gen Kirkman's XIII Corps attack. The task given to the corps was a difficult one. It was ordered to strike across the Rapido river in one of the most heavily defended sections of the line, right under the watchful gaze of the enemy on Monte Cassino. Kirkman intended to launch his attack with two separate assaults: the British 4th Infantry Division on the right, the Indian 8th Infantry Division on the left. The Canadian 1st Armoured Brigade would support the Indian Division; 26th Armoured Brigade would do the same with 4th Division. The first phase was to assault the river and break into the enemy defences. Bridges would then be built that were capable of carrying tanks and follow-up infantry across to break through the German line. As the bridgehead was enlarged, 78th Division would be introduced into the battle. The two assaulting brigades of 4th Division, 10th and 28th Brigades, would have 17th/21st Lancers with them in support. Its 12th Brigade was to form the reserve, assisted by the Sherman tanks of 2nd Lothians and Border Horse. The 16th/5th Lancers would support 78th Division when they had crossed over the river. The 6th Armoured Division's artillery would be pooled with the guns of two armies to form the largest concentration of gunfire seen thus far in the war.

Corps reserve was to be provided by a battlegroup from 6th Armoured Division, known as the Divisional Armoured Reconnaissance Group. The 6th Armoured Division had been ordered to provide a mobile strike force of all arms to be held ready to exploit the situation should the enemy defences in the Liri valley disintegrate and the corps achieve a sudden breakthrough. It was to provide the means of maintaining the impetus while 26th Armoured Brigade was recalled from its various commitments with other divisions and regrouped for the pursuit. This battlegroup consisted of 1st Derbyshire Yeomanry, 10th Rifle Brigade, 72nd Antitank Regiment RA, 625th and 627th Field Squadrons RE and the self-propelled battery of 51st Light Antiaircraft Regiment RA.[2]

The battle began at 2300 hr on 11 May, with a bombardment of over 1,000 guns on Eighth Army's sector and over 600 guns on Fifth Army's part of the line. The sky was lit by a thousand flashes and the shells screamed over towards the enemy in a continuous stream. Surprise was complete: the enemy knew that an attack was coming, but they did not know where or when it would fall. They never expected that the Allies would launch simultaneous assaults all along the line.

While the guns shelled the enemy and machine-gun fire and mortars raked the far side, the two brigades of 4th Division put in their assault across the river. As expected, the German reaction was fierce, but in spite of the heavy fire the assault boats ferried sufficient troops across to form a bridgehead, albeit shallow and very exposed. The sappers then tried to erect Bailey bridges to carry more troops and tanks over, but all their efforts were frustrated by enemy interference. Dawn came and exposed the vulnerability of the forward battalions, none of which had gained more than 500 yards. They were penned in close to the river and overlooked by enemy OPs on the high ground around Monte Cassino. Field regiments of artillery worked ceaselessly throughout the day to shroud the area in smoke so as to give the infantry some cover from enemy view as they plugged away at the fortifications in the gloom. All that the tanks of 26th Armoured Brigade could do was to fire across in support and wait for the bridges to be built.

The next day, 12 May, the armour continued waiting on the near bank out of sight of the enemy, but close enough to be able to come forward to fire on line-of-sight targets as requested. After dark, word was received that the first bridge was almost ready. C Squadron of 17th/21st Lancers moved forward, groping its way through the darkness, smoke and fog to reach the bridging site, only to find that the Bailey had been built, but all the bulldozers on the spot had been knocked out. The approaches on either side had not been completed and bridging operations had come to a halt. Troop leader Lt Wayne, in his first action, went forward to speak with the Royal Engineer officer in command and learned of the problem.

Wayne offered to help the sappers get the bridge across and with his tank he gently pushed the metal Bailey bridge over the river and into place, then volunteered to cross over and reconnoitre the exit. By 0445 hr, the bridge, now labelled Amazon Bridge, was ready for traffic and Wayne led his troop across and into the battle.[3]

The remainder of C Squadron crossed over the river in batches in what was left of darkness to join up with 10th Infantry Brigade. Visibility was poor – barely 20 yards – and the whole area near the Rapido was covered with irrigation ditches which made all cross-country work difficult. Many tanks were bogged-down in the soft ground or disabled by mines. As it became light, requests from the infantry battalions increased as they set about targeting troublesome German positions.

The 2nd Lothians and Border Horse also crossed over the river that day in support of 4th Division. In one of the leading tanks was Lt George Martin: 'Once on the bridge I looked for our objective. To get clear of the bridge was of major importance. A clear view ahead was not easy: shells landing in the field to our front threw up soft earth and before the smoke cleared others were landing! Those landing in the river threw up cascades of water as they exploded. The "heavies" came in with a rush like an express train and seemed to lift half the water in the river over the bridge and the tank as we crossed; to our great relief the nearest fell about six yards away.'[4]

Lt Allan Waterston, also with the Lothians, recalls a near miss just over the river when supporting 12th Brigade during an attack.

> On the second day of the battle one of my troop's tanks was knocked out while supporting the West Kents onto a ridge. Fortunately the crew baled out safely, but they were so fast that I did not see any of them on their feet and so I went to check that there were no injured in the tank. After climbing up to peer into the driver's hatches and the turret, I made my way back to my own tank. On the way I passed a vertical wooden post which was suddenly cut off by an armour-piercing solid shot passing about three inches above my head. This was very probably fired by the same gunner who had knocked out the tank and who had used the post on which to lay the cross wires of his sights ready for my passing. It was bang on for line, but just too much elevation! The loss of one tank meant that for the rest of the battle we reverted to being a three-tank troop: a much tighter formation to control. With four tanks in diamond formation, all with 75mm guns and two Brownings, one always anticipated being shot up the backside however well trained the crew of whichever tank happened to be 'tail end Charlie'.[5]

Throughout the day the bridgehead was covered by acrid smoke, drifting over the hedges and lanes of the battlefield, some of it being laid by the artillery to shroud the area and some from the shellfire from both sides. The lodgement on this the second day was still surprisingly small, barely a mile square. *Panzergrenadiers* were now backing up the German infantry in defence, ensuring that each field and bombed-out building was held by a determined force. There were no quick fixes for the attacking troops; the tremendous barrage, the overwhelming superiority of numbers, the presence of tanks and the continual pounding of artillery fire into the bridgehead appeared to have done little to lessen the enemy's hold on his line. It would take a lot more hard fighting before the Gustav Line was breached.

During 14 May, 8th Indian Division on the left of XIII Corps's front was progressing a little better. It had two bridges over the river and the tanks of 1st Canadian Armoured Brigade into its bridgehead. On 4th Division's front, the towering influence of Monastery Hill overlooking its area was continuing to make progress slow and cautious. Vast numbers of smoke shells were fired to try to keep German vision from Monastery Hill at a minimum, but it was impossible to shield every part of the battlefield all of the time. The amount of enemy shellfire aimed at 4th Division clearly showed that they still had a number of working OPs on this high ground.

By 15 May the two assaulting divisions had become exhausted by the break-in battle, but the lodgement was now large enough for a new division to deploy through and to begin smashing the main part of the German defence line. More bridges had been constructed and the build-up of strength was well under way, although great traffic jams of vehicles were beginning to become a problem in the congested bridgehead over the Rapido. Space was very limited on both sides of the river and the movement of battalions over very short distances often took hours.

Observation across the flat countryside enabled the enemy to sight and range his artillery and mortars to cover each lane and field. Antitank guns guarded every conceivable position and every means of approach. Progress through the great depth of the Gustav Line defences was proving to be a slugging match between tanks and guns and infantry and mortars. The attack had attracted more enemy units into the Liri valley: 90th Panzergrenadier Division was moving into the line and the front had been patched up with miscellaneous troops of 1st Parachute Division, including its Reconnaissance, Engineer and Machine Gun Battalions. Also located on the battlefield were two battalions of 114th Jäger Division, two from 5th Mountain Division and remnants of 15th Panzergrenadier Division. Both sides were steadily gaining strength, exchanging blow for blow in a stand-up fight. This was a battle of attrition in its severest form; the victor would be the side who kept its nerve and could plug away for longest.

The infantry of 78th Division was committed into the bridgehead on 15 May with 26th Armoured Brigade under command.[6] Its 11th Brigade attacked on the right with 17th/21st Lancers intending to make contact with the Polish II Corps when they had managed to capture and get beyond Monte Cassino, while 38th (Irish) Brigade moved on the left with 16th/5th Lancers in support. Because of the poor visibility caused by the close countryside and the smoke of battle, limited objectives were chosen which committed the advance to bounds of no more than 1,000 yards. The tanks and infantry could then easily reorganise on these lines to be ready for the next push. Maj Gen Keightley had decided to control his division's move forward in four bounds which, cavalryman that he was, he called after famous hunts: Grafton, Pytchley, Fernie and Bedale. The first of these objectives, 'Grafton', was the road which led from Cassino to the village of Pignataro.[7]

C Squadron of 17th/21st Lancers supported 5th Northamptons in their attack on 'Grafton'. It had been originally thought that 10th Brigade of 4th Division was already on the line, but this proved to be false and the tanks and infantry had to prepare a rather hasty attack on the objective, which moved off at 1230 hr. The armour led the way, with infantry following up close behind. After a short while they ran into an enemy strong point at a slight feature labelled K30. The area was marshy and two tanks were immediately bogged down, engaged by antitank fire and knocked out, as were two others that came forward in support, leaving two men dead and six wounded. The position was too strong to take on the move, so a set-piece attack was organised.

After a fifteen-minute artillery barrage, the Northamptons went in with the tanks of A Squadron and overran the position, capturing forty of the enemy and taking only light casualties. The whole of the 'Grafton' objective was secured a short time later. The 16th/5th Lancers had reached their part of the line in the early afternoon, after an advance in which the high spot was an attack on an enemy-held farmhouse position by supporting fighter-bombers who dropped their bombs just 300 yards ahead of the leading troops, killing the whole of the enemy garrison. Attacking with 6th Royal Inniskillings, the Lancers took the objective with the loss of four tanks.

Progress beyond 'Grafton' was difficult. Enemy resistance was increasing the further that the advance got into the Gustav positions. Other moves that day were postponed so that a fresh coordinated attack could be planned for 16 May. While these plans were being discussed between the CO of 16th/5th Lancers, Lt Col Loveday, and the commanders of 6th Royal Inniskilling Fusiliers and 2nd London Irish Rifles, a 150mm shell fell among them, killing or wounding everyone. Lt Col Loveday and Lt Col Ion Goff of the London Irish Rifles survived for a few hours, but eventually died of their wounds the next day.

On 16 May an attack was launched on 'Pytchley'. The objective was a ridge about a mile forward of the Pignataro–Cassino road, which included the village of Sinagogga. The advance moved off after a heavy artillery barrage had been put down on the enemy by seven field regiments. The infantry of 2nd London Irish Rifles followed close behind the falling shells and were among the Germans almost before they had realised that the barrage had moved on. Those in the buildings were a different matter and the London Irish CO, Lt Col John Horsfall, was pleased with the support he got from the Lancers as he travelled forward through the attack in one of 16th/5th's Shermans:

> Wherever we saw our men held up the supporting 16th/5th tanks worked up to them and literally pulverised the opposition by direct fire at close range. I must say that the tank's 75mm was a marvellous gun, and a single shot from it was sufficient to bring down a large part of the front wall of a house. Also the tactical co-ordination of the tank troops was very impressive. In a number of instances the enemy were trapped in their basements and cellars with tanks on top of them before they knew what was happening. In other cases I noticed the garrison run for it after a few direct hits – those of them who were still in a position to do so. While this stage lasted I think a good many of our opponents were shot down under fire from the tanks' Besas.[8]

The advance continued through to Sinagogga with increasing casualties for the London Irish. The village was finally taken after heavy hand-to-hand fighting. A counterattack by a few enemy tanks failed to evict the London Irish and the German armour was seen off by 16th/5th Lancers.

To the right 17th/21st Lancers were assisting 2nd Lancashire Fusiliers of 11th Brigade to attack their side of the 'Pytchley' line. The Lancers' history talks of the attack being a great success and the Lancashire Fusiliers being full of fight, remarking that it was one of the best actions of the battle: 'The infantry and tanks only met at midnight, arranged and planned the battle in the dark, and attacked at dawn. B Squadron lost two tanks to antitank guns on the right flank, but these and an SP were both knocked out. A Squadron had been busy during the night towing four 17-pounder antitank guns up to the infantry and thus strengthen the centre of the attack. B Squadron had a particularly hard time during the day; its tanks were heavily engaged by antitank fire and at one point it was held up by an antitank feature and under considerable shell fire. It prompted its commander, Maj Buxton to remark: "This is real war, and makes Africa seem like a picnic."'[9]

It was at this moment that the Lancashire Fusiliers needed tank support most of all, for their advance company was being attacked by enemy Panzer IVs. C Company of the battalion was suffering appalling casualties, with its strength quickly reduced from ninety to fifty. Lt Col Mackenzie directed both medium and field artillery to support the company, in the hope of holding the attack until 17th/21st Lancers could get forward. 'It was a very tense time,' recalled the CO. 'We could only wait and hope. But when news eventually arrived, it was of a miracle.'[10] The miracle that Mackenzie was alluding to came in the shape of Fusilier Jefferson, a company runner, up with the leading troops. He took a handheld PIAT antitank weapon and stalked two Panzer IVs, moving in the open in full view to engage the leading tank. He scored a direct hit and the panzer burst into flames, killing the crew. Then Jefferson turned on the second tank and drove it off the battlefield. For this action Fusilier Jefferson was awarded the Victoria Cross.

'Pytchley' was taken by early afternoon and the Irish Brigade then had to beat off a quick enemy counterattack. Another counterattack came a few hours later, put in by some paratroopers from GenMaj Heidrich's division, which delayed further moves and caused temporary confusion. The Germans were supported by a great number of machine guns, but the attack lacked the strength to regain more than just a small amount of ground, although it created turmoil right up to brigade HQ level.[11] Before nightfall the London Irish were patrolling towards the 'Fernie' objective and the Lancashire Fusiliers were digging in.

While the two sides in the Liri valley were locked in ferocious combat, trying to beat each other into submission, events elsewhere along the Gustav Line were beginning to reap some dividends. The Americans and the French to the south had broken through and were advancing up the coast and across the Arunci Mountains. Gen Juin's French Expeditionary Corps was making the most spectacular progress. His four divisions were relishing the fight with the Germans, wearing the enemy down with brave and determined attacks. Juin's North African tribesmen and the French colonials seemed to be in their element, killing Germans and taking one peak after another to sweep across the mountain tops towards the last high ground that looked down into the Liri valley from the south. Juin's forces were beginning to get into a position above the valley behind the enemy who were holding the British XIII Corps. They were also closing in on the flank of the German second line of defence, the Hitler Line.[12]

To the right of 78th Division and the tanks of 6th Armoured Division, 4th Division had swung to the right and lay poised on the southern outskirts of Cassino, blocking the road from the town into the Liri valley. It was waiting for the moment when it could attack Cassino from the southern flank. Up in the mountains on the other side of Monte Cassino, Gen Anders' Polish Corps was still licking its wounds after trying to capture Monastery Hill in an attack which coincided with the launching of Operation Diadem on 12 May. The attempt had been unsuccessful and had been beaten back with heavy casualties. Anders was told to stay put, but to be ready to attack once again when the troops in the Liri valley had got beyond the base of Monte Cassino. On 16 May, that point had been reached.

As 78th Division swung westwards along its advance, it began to veer away from 4th Division near Cassino. A wide gap now began to open up adjacent to the ground held by Heidrich's paratroopers. Into this gap the corps commander, Lt Gen Kirkman, now sent the mobile reserve, the Divisional Armoured Reconnaissance Group, the strike force containing the Derbyshire Yeomanry and 10th Rifle Brigade. Capt James Wilson, now Adjutant of 10th RB, later recalled crossing into the bridgehead: 'The narrow Liri valley lanes were choked with transport; visibility was limited and the situation confused. The close country made map reading a nightmare; one seldom knew for certain one's position and for the companies up front, fighting a tenacious and determined opposition, it was harder still.'[13]

The amount of transport across the Rapido was proving to be a great problem. Vehicles were stuck nose-to-tail in monster traffic jams that packed vulnerable transport together in lanes overlooked by the enemy. All divisions were to blame; the mechanised nature of the units had led to a mushrooming of their transport requirements. For example, the newly deployed Divisional Armoured Reconnaissance Group had 630 vehicles in its train. This number consisted of 520 vehicles in F and A1 Echelons and 110 vehicles in A2 Echelon. Since all this threatened to make the group completely unwieldy, its composition was slightly modified by leaving out one field squadron and the SP battery of 51st Light Antiaircraft Regiment RA.[14]

The attack on 'Fernie' started at first light on 17 May. The bridgehead was now three miles deep and XIII Corps was beginning to flex its strength, advancing on a three-division front with 4th on the right, 78th in the centre and 1st Canadian Division on the left; 8th Indian Division was now in reserve. Up in the mountains to the right, the Polish II Corps had been ordered to make another attempt to take Monastery Hill. The offensive was starting to swing Alexander's way, although in front of 26th Armoured Brigade German resistance was as ferocious as ever.

This was the day that the Gustav Line was broken. Multiple attacks all along the enemy line wore the Germans down to a point where they began to crack. The tanks of 26th Armoured Brigade were with the infantry of 78th Division in the vanguard of the advance fighting. The attack on 'Fernie' was led by 16th/5th Hussars in support of 1st Royal Irish Fusiliers. Just as it got under way, the commander of B Squadron was killed by mortar fire as he was mounting his tank after giving out orders. Then the programmed artillery concentration came down and the remainder of the squadron had to move off with the fusiliers to stay close to the rolling barrage. The tanks kept right up with the barrage as it lifted. At one point the forward troop actually reported that it was in the barrage, with the leading infantry close behind. When they reached the 'Fernie' line, based along the slight ridge of Massa Cerro, they rolled right over the enemy defenders just behind the artillery shells and pressed on to the final objective line, 'Bedale'.

Within fifteen minutes, B Squadron, together with more of the Irish Fusiliers, had joined the advance. The tanks and infantry continued through close country until they reached a patch of open ground 800 yards across. The tanks immediately broke cover and charged forward on to the objective with the infantry racing behind. Two enemy tanks guarding the position, turned and took flight. The left flank of the line 'Bedale' was taken and consolidated immediately. Further over to the south, the Lothians and Border Horse were probing forward and had come across the village of Piumarola, which was obviously held in some strength by the enemy. This area was still relatively unexplored and the Lothians were told to keep it under observation while the rest of the brigade came forward abreast of it.

Over to the right, 11th Brigade had also been fighting forward towards 'Bedale', with the Lancashire Fusiliers in the van supported by tanks of 17th/21st Lancers. The brigade's final objective involved a swing to the right towards Highway 6. This move left it with its flanks exposed, but the infantry and tanks pressed on without incident behind a rolling barrage. Enemy opposition was less than expected, although there were still defended farmhouses and machine-gun posts to be dealt with. The tanks made short work of these. By 1600 hr the battalion had reached its final objective; phase line 'Bedale' had been taken and Highway 6 was just a few hundred yards away.[15]

The 78th Division was now on the last of Keightley's phase lines and had broken through the defences of the Gustav Line. All opposition, however, did not end there for the enemy were still holding villages and farms and defending lanes and fields with as much vigour as they had in the more heavily fortified positions closer to the Rapido. Before 16th/5th Lancers could end the day's fighting, there was one more task to be undertaken. Over to the right of the Lancers was Piumarola and fire from this village now fell among the tanks and the Irishmen. An attack was ordered to be carried out by the regiment together with fresh troops from 6th Inniskilling Fusiliers; A Squadron of the Lothians was to supply a flank guard for the undertaking. The attack and capture of Piumarola was a textbook example of tank/infantry attack and the operation is described at length in the Lancers' regimental history.

The first move was made by an infantry patrol, screened by tanks, to determine the lay of the land and the enemy's positions. At least one Panzer IV was located, which withdrew into a wood on the right. The Lothians moved forward to seal off this flank and the patrol waited for the remainder of the Inniskillings and the whole of A Squadron to move up to a point 1,000 yards short of the village. A plan of attack was formed and orders were issued. A company of the Irishmen was to advance to the northern end of the village, accompanied by two troops of tanks. They would then swing round on to the far side of Piumarola. Supporting fire would be put down by the remainder of the Inniskillings and A Squadron of the Lancers, together with an artillery concentration on the village by 200 guns of corps and division.

The attack began at 1600 hr, with tanks and infantry moving across country to gain the road leading into the village from the north. Soon enemy shellfire aimed at the advancing troops ceased, a sure sign that they were approaching German positions. The forward infantry were held up by machine-gun fire from a farm building. A tank came forward and blew the farmhouse apart. White flags appeared and the Irishmen moved into the collection of barns and outhouses to mop up the area, finding at least twenty enemy dead. The attack moved on and reached a stream which proved to be too wide for the tanks to cross. The advance halted and was hit by a burst of enemy shellfire in which the Inniskillings' CO, Lt Col Bredin, was wounded in both legs and evacuated.

With the wide encirclement halted, the main advance switched to a move down the road into the village from the north. A bridge across the stream in front of Piumarola was crossed and tanks fanned out either side of the village. When these were in position they sealed in the enemy holding Piumarola, shooting down any Germans who tried to escape out of the far end. Then the tanks on the flanks provided fire support for an attack by armour and infantry straight down the main street. The village fell soon afterwards, though not without some casualties to the Irishmen. A total of 250 Germans were disposed of during the attack, 150 of whom were taken prisoner. They all belonged to 361st Panzergrenadier Regiment which had arrived from Rome only twenty-four hours before.[16]

That night the Luftwaffe was in action over the battlefield, putting in the heaviest raid that had been experienced for a considerable time. Some casualties were suffered by most of the units in the bridgehead, for all the forces over the Rapido were so closely packed together that the enemy could hardly miss finding a target. The air raids were laid on for a special purpose, for the advance in the valley and the progress of the Poles in the mountains had almost encircled 1st Parachute Division in Cassino and on Monte Cassino, and the time had come for it to pull out.

During 17 May, Gen Anders' Polish troops had been making good progress in the mountains behind Cassino and had almost reached Monastery Hill. In the Liri valley, 10th Brigade of 4th Division had crossed Highway 6 and was advancing towards the outskirts of the town. By 2050 hr there was still a gap a mile wide between the two forces through which the Germans in Cassino could escape. The bombing raid helped to cover this move.

Around midnight the gap had narrowed even more. Heidrich's paratroopers now began their withdrawal, relinquishing their hold on Cassino and its monastery. They had fought bravely against overwhelming odds for more than two months, defying all attempts by a complete Allied army to dislodge them. Now their task was completed and, in the darkness, they silently rose up from their positions and slipped away down into the Liri valley, not for a well-deserved period of rest, but to man the defences of the Hitler Line against a new onslaught.

The next morning, 18 May, the men of the Guards Brigade were met by the troops of 10th Brigade who entered the town unopposed. Up on the monastery the Polish and British flags could be seen flying from the top of the ruins. Cassino had at last fallen and men could once again move freely in the open. Soon the place was swarming with sightseers. Photographers, war correspondents, gunners, sappers, bomber pilots and generals wandered happily all around the town, until two pressmen trod on a mine and were blown to pieces. This prompted some German shelling and the crowds quickly thinned out and left Cassino to the guardsmen once more.

On 18 May, XIII Corps was five miles beyond the Rapido, through the Gustav Line and out the other side. Enemy resistance had eased and life in the crowded bridgehead became a little more bearable. No one, however, was fooled by this respite, for just a few miles further on was the Hitler Line. This line had been built by the enemy at his leisure. While the Gustav Line from the Garigliano to Cassino had been the front line, with its defenders holding back the Allies under almost continual bombardment, German engineers and four battalions of the Todt Organisation had been busy using copious amounts of concrete and steel to build this second line ten miles further back, intending it to be of even greater physical strength.

The Hitler (von Senger) Line stretched from Aquino, through Pontecorvo, along the River Melfa and over the Arunci Mountains. Some heavy weapons were built into the line – tank turrets were half buried in reinforced concrete pits, sited to provide armoured antitank positions – but to rearm the whole of the line in advance had proved to be impossible. To overcome this, the plan was that the gun emplacements, troop shelters, antitank and mortar pits should be prepared to receive the units holding the Gustav Line as they fell back, bringing their weapons with them. These troops were then to re-establish the weapons in the new concrete positions.

On paper the Hitler Line was a formidable obstacle. Several things, however, lessened the impact the line was to have on the Allied advance. First was the enemy's failure to implement its plan to withdraw into the line with its weapons. The strength of the Allies' advance through the Gustav Line had applied such relentless pressure that the Germans found it very difficult to disengage and make an orderly withdrawal. Much of their ordnance was left captured or broken on the battlefield. Another factor was the failure to execute the move soon enough; the rigid doctrine of fighting for every square metre of land had left little time to complete the manoeuvre. One obvious example of this was the delay in pulling

1st Parachute Division out of Cassino. Unit pride made the paratroopers hold on for longer than was prudent, resulting in them arriving on the Hitler Line just as the leading Allied troops were attacking. But perhaps the most overwhelming reason that the Hitler Line did not live up to expectations was that the French Expeditionary Corps was already behind the southern flank of the line. Before the line was fully manned, the French divisions led by the Goums had swept across the Arunci Mountains, over ground thought by the Germans to be impassable, and had started enveloping it from the west. Nonetheless, the German defenders elsewhere on the Hitler Line did not just roll over and let the Allies pass, as 26th Armoured Brigade and other armoured units found out to their cost.

On 18 May, 36th Brigade attacked westwards from Piumarola with 17th/21st Lancers in support. C Squadron led 8th Argyll and Sutherland Highlanders; B Squadron was up with 5th Buffs. The move started at 0900 hr and met no opposition. After reaching the first objective there was still little sign of the enemy so the advance continued, moving at the pace of the infantry, against negligible resistance. Maj Gen Keightley ordered that the pace be speeded up. The tanks pressed on, moving in bounds, halting from time to time and switching off their engines to listen. All was quiet; the enemy in front of them had melted away.

Over to the north, the Shermans of the Derbyshire Yeomanry were also probing cautiously ahead. They, too, found the enemy gone. At around 1430 the leading troop radioed back that it was on the outskirts of Aquino airfield and it was clear of the enemy, although some shellfire was straddling the tanks. Orders came to press on into the town, even though this area was known to be part of the Hitler Line. Keightley was of the opinion that the enemy might not have had time to occupy the line and that decisive action now could swing the battle. This belief was strengthened when three troops of the Yeomanry reported that they were about to enter the town. One Sherman was then knocked out by an antitank gun, but others moved into the streets of Aquino and actually got to the far side to report that the bridge over the Melfa was still intact.

This news was quickly acted upon and at 1900 hr Col Dawney, second in command of 26th Armoured Brigade, was put in command of the whole of the battlegroup of the Divisional Armoured Reconnaissance Force and ordered to move to the east of Aquino and seize the village in cooperation with 36th Brigade and 17th/21st Lancers. Meanwhile the Shermans in Aquino were coming under more fire and the troops left at the airfield were being engaged by antitank guns. The Germans had woken up to the presence of armour in Aquino and were retaliating. The riflemen of 10th Rifle Brigade who had come up with the leading Shermans were being met by accurate fire and forced to ground. As darkness fell, no further support had arrived up with the Derbyshire Yeomanry and so the leading tanks withdrew.

The next day a deliberate attack was made on Aquino by two battalions of 36th Brigade, 8th Argylls and 5th Buffs, supported by tanks of the Ontario Regiment from the Canadian 1st Armoured Brigade. The enemy had been busy during the night, for the probe made by the Derbyshire Yeomanry the previous day had exposed the vulnerability of Aquino, one of the key points along his new defensive line. Although the Germans were at that moment very hard-pressed to hold an attack being mounted by Canadian 1st Division, they had managed to reinforce Aquino with a large number of troops.

At 0500 hr an artillery barrage was laid on Aquino, but it was more than an hour before the infantry moved off, as a thick mist had descended over the battlefield and made mutual support difficult. Once they did get going, the two battalions ran straight into a complex network of wire, criss-crossed by enemy machine-gun fire from interconnected pillboxes. At about the same time the fog lifted and exposed the supporting armour. Antitank fire ripped into the forward Canadian tanks and every Sherman of the leading two squadrons was hit, with thirteen of them being knocked out. With the demise of the armour the infantry had lost the means of eliminating the concrete pillboxes and stopping the deadly machine guns. Accurate fire smashed into the infantry, pinning them down. Unable to move forward, they spent the whole of the morning scratching holes in the dirt in a desperate bid to get below ground. Both battalions lost their commanding officers that day to this murderous fire. At around 1300 hr the decision to pull back was made and the Argylls and Buffs made a controlled withdrawal to their start line. Further to the right, 11th Brigade sent a strong probing patrol towards Aquino supported by six Shermans from 17th/21st Lancers. It got to within 150 yards of the town before the main German defences opened up and hit four of the six tanks; the remainder of the force withdrew.[17]

Eighth Army commander Gen Oliver Leese decided that the Hitler Line could not be bounced by a rapidly assembled attack; it would need a massive set-piece assault to smash through the defences. He now ordered the Canadian I Corps to use its 1st Infantry and 5th Armoured Divisions to accomplish the task. The attack was to be launched on 23 May. With this decision made, 26th Armoured Brigade could be returned to the control of 6th Armoured Division along with all other units of Maj Gen Evelegh's force that were spread across the battlefield. The division was to be assembled once again as a proper armoured formation, ready to exploit the situation once the Hitler Line was broken.

At first light on 23 May, the Ayrshire Yeomanry were told to fire a smoke screen to cover the Canadian attack on the Hitler Line, but this was then cancelled at the last moment and changed to a four-hour concentration of 360 rounds per gun in a lengthy barrage in support of the infantry. Later that day, the Yeomanry were involved in firing a

'William', or army, target – a concentration of the 696 guns of the whole of Eighth Army against one specific location. The battalion history noted that this was the only time that the regiment fired such a target in the whole campaign.[18]

The Canadians broke through the Hitler Line in a protracted battle that was costly to both sides. Kesselring's determination to hold the line now left him at some disadvantage. Von Vietinghof's Tenth Army in the Liri valley was in great danger of being trapped, for it was being hemmed in on three sides. The French were advancing down from the Arunci Mountains and moving up the other side of the River Liri; the British were pressing inexorably up the valley and, to the Germans' rear, Clark's US VI Corps was breaking out of the Anzio beachhead, threatening to cut Highway 6 south of Rome. Time was running out; a protracted stand anywhere south of Rome could lead to the whole of Tenth Army being cut off.

Alexander had won the battle: Operation Diadem was a huge triumph. Kesselring now knew that his only option was to withdraw his forces to the north of the capital where they could regroup along another defence line. His immediate task now was to keep open the roads that led back to Rome and try to hold off the flank attack from Anzio. To buy some time, he also needed to delay the British and the French as long as he could.

Chapter Nine

THE CHASE BEGINS

Canadian I Corps's attack on the Hitler Line resulted in a breakthrough which rolled on over the River Melfa. The gap punched by the Canadian 1st Division in the German defences was exploited by the Canadian 5th Armoured Division. Its axis for the advance northwards was on the left of Eighth Army's front. With the Hitler Line now no longer a complete barrier, 6th Armoured Division could begin its drive along the right-hand side of the valley, using the route of Highway 6.

On 25 May, Maj Gen Evelegh's division began its pursuit of the retreating German Tenth Army. Although Evelegh had been in command for six months, this was the first time he had taken the whole of the Mailed Fist Division into action. Almost immediately there were problems. In the sector assigned to the division, 78th Division had not yet cleared Aquino of the enemy and there was no crossing-place established over the River Melfa. Army HQ therefore ordered Evelegh to break out through the Canadians' sector.

This produced another problem for Evelegh. In the Liri valley were four infantry divisions and three armoured divisions. The amount of transport supporting these divisions, hemmed in among the narrow lanes and roads of the valley, was enormous. Each of the infantry divisions used nearly 3,400 vehicles, and an armoured division about 3,000. In addition there were two corps headquarters together with their artillery, engineer and support vehicles. To complicate matters, 6th Armoured Division was now being asked to move from its assigned roads on to those of an adjacent corps and division. Not unexpectedly, there was some confusion and delay, and some very large traffic jams.

Once its leading vehicles had negotiated their way through the Canadian sector, they swung northwards behind Aquino back into the division's assigned route. Lt Allan Waterston recalls the start of this move through the early-morning mist and the fog of the previous battle: 'Things gradually began to move more quickly and it was with mixed feelings that we passed a number of knocked-out enemy tanks in the vicinity of Pontecorvo. There was relief that they could no longer threaten us, but we were not encouraged by the sight and smell of roast tank crews. Later we paused for a while on what had been the Hitler Line, where almost a whole squadron of Churchill tanks from the North Irish Horse had been destroyed by Panther tank turrets and guns mounted in concrete emplacements. It was a rude reminder of what could happen if the mist and smoke suddenly lifted.'[1]

In the lead were the Derbyshire Yeomanry and 10th Rifle Brigade. A minefield two miles east of Pontecorvo caused some delay, but the River Melfa was reached during the afternoon. Reconnaissance along the wooded banks of the river found a bridge still intact, although it was covered by enemy machine-gun fire. It was thought to be impracticable to try to take the bridge with the scouting light Honey tanks of the regiment while under fire, so a troop of Shermans came forward, supported by M10 self-propelled guns from 72nd Antitank Regiment. The four Shermans got across the bridge safely, but the first M10 to try was hit by an antitank shell while on the bridge and caught fire. As the bridge was mainly a wooden structure, this too went up in flames, resulting in its complete destruction.

The four Shermans stranded on the far bank spread out along the river, trying to locate and eliminate the enemy covering the crossing site. Almost immediately, one of the tanks was hit by the same antitank gun that had destroyed the M10. The remainder of the tanks were told to hold on to their small bridgehead while infantry came across to help flush out the enemy. The 10th Rifle Brigade was now ordered forward to cross the river. For some reason, probably traffic jams, it was almost seven hours before this attack could be launched. In the meantime the three Shermans had to deal with all kinds of enemy fire and were extremely short of ammunition.

The attack by B Company of 10th Rifle Brigade was a failure: heavy machine-gun fire from the wooded banks opposite swept the river and made all movement on the open water virtually impossible. After twenty minutes of trying the attack was called off. By this time it was virtually dark and there was no time to mount a stronger assault. The crews of the three stranded Shermans, after hanging on to their tiny lodgement for over seven hours against every form of enemy attack, were ordered to withdraw as near to the river bank as possible and destroy their tanks. After that they were to try to get back across the Melfa on foot, relying on darkness to give them cover. It was an ignominious end to their brave sortie.

The next day a patrol of the Rifle Brigade probed further downriver and initially drew fire; but an hour later all was quiet and Lt Victor Hannay waded over to find that the enemy had gone. The news was passed back to division and 3rd Grenadier Guards were sent over a shallow crossing-place to form a bridgehead. This ford was then improved by the sappers and the opposite banks reduced by bulldozers to allow the tanks of 16th/5th

Lancers to wade over and take up the pursuit, with the Grenadiers riding on their backs.

The halt on the River Malfa had delayed the start of the drive and allowed more of the enemy to escape. The setback was later commented on by Lt Gen James Wilson of 10th RB: 'The Germans still thought, wrongly, that Eighth Army's advance up the Liri valley was the main threat to their withdrawal; we, in turn, thought that 6th Armoured Division must have been committed with a pursuit battle in view. Our slow progress up to and across the River Melfa was, therefore, disappointing and an affront to our armoured "machismo". We had yet to understand the facts of Italian military life.'[2]

Maj Gen Evelegh was eager to speed up the advance and push on to get to the town of Arce. Highway 6 turns sharply south-west at that point and another road leads away to the north. It was along these routes that the enemy was escaping, trying to get beyond Rome. Further up these roads the enemy had to switch round to the eastern side of the capital, for Gen Mark Clark's VI Corps at Anzio was advancing eastwards and threatening to cut Highway 6 south of the capital. Arce had become of supreme importance and the capture of the road junction was a high priority. Gen Evelegh insisted that the town be seized with all haste.

Three and a half miles short of Arce the advance came to a halt just beyond the village of Coldragone. The armour was checked by a blown bridge and sappers could not get forward to deal with it because of heavy shellfire. This same fire was holding up the Grenadiers, and the guardsmen had gone to ground just behind a rise which looked down on the obstacle and along the straight road that led to Arce. There seemed to be no other immediate way forward, for the road ran through a narrow pass flanked by high ground. Evelegh decided that the Welsh Guards would advance through the Grenadiers and occupy this high ground either side of the road to allow the armour to continue towards Arce and capture the town.

At that time the Welsh Guards were way back down the divisional column. It was nightfall before they arrived, after a tiresome journey along crowded roads riding on the backs of the tanks of the Lothians and Border Horse. None of the battalion's wheeled transport had been able to move with them, so there was no hot meal waiting for the men as they prepared themselves for action. The guardsmen moved up to an assembly area behind the Grenadiers' positions and received their orders for the attack. The battalion was to advance along Highway 6 through Arce and occupy the high ground on the far side of the town, an advance of over six miles. The CO and his company commanders moved forward to try to get a look at the terrain over which they were to make the advance, but could not see beyond the rising ground ahead of them. They were told that intelligence had received information which led them to believe that Arce was being evacuated and that the hills flanking the pass before the town were not being held.

It was to be a night move, with the battalion setting off down the main road at 2300 hr. Lt George Martin and other tank crews of the Lothians were aware that the 'Tall Men', as the guardsmen were called, had not been fed and they decided to open carefully hoarded spare rations for them: 'With a willingness that did great credit to the tank crews, boxes were broken open and rations sorted. While the infantrymen rested, the tank crews rigged up tarpaulin shelters behind the tanks and set to work with stoves to warm up beans, stew, etc., with rice pudding and tinned fruit for the lucky ones.'[3]

Lt Allan Waterston in B Squadron of the Lothians had received his orders for the next morning's advance. The regiment would move through Arce after the Welsh Guards and continue the progress towards Rome. He was somewhat sceptical about the move, as he later wrote: 'I had never liked being involved in battles that began on the assumption that the enemy had withdrawn from a strong position, especially when the timetable for "hot pursuit" had already collapsed, so I went to bed that night somewhat apprehensive of the morrow.'[4]

The Welsh Guards were led down Highway 6 to carry out their attack by their CO, Lt Col Gurney. The battalion marched in single file on either side of the road, well strung out in a column that stretched for almost a mile through a very dark night. They were compelled to keep to the road by the close nature of the surrounding countryside. There was some occasional shelling, but nothing aimed specifically at the Guards. After an hour the column approached the area of the highway flanked by hills on each side. Gurney hesitated, for he was not actually certain that the enemy was withdrawing. If he believed the intelligence reports, he should be able to march his men straight into the town. If they were wrong, his force would be massacred.

Lt Col Gurney thought that to go on without further information would be reckless, so he decided the high ground on either side of the road would have to be checked out. He sent a patrol under Lt Hayley on to Monte Orio on the right and then ordered Maj Cobbold to make a reconnaissance in force with his No. 2 Company up on to Monte Piccolo which dominated the left side of the road. Lt Hayley's twelve-man patrol had to advance diagonally over open ground and cross a number of minor spurs before it could reach Monte Orio. The enemy watched them all the way and let them walk into a trap. Hayley was killed and most of the others wounded and taken prisoner; just three men returned to safety. The enemy were obviously on the mountain, but their strength was unknown. It was, however, vital that the hill be occupied and the pass opened, so the company commander, Maj Martin Smith, decided to attack and try to take the hill. His guardsmen fought a gradual advance over the foothills and along a spur which led to the summit throughout the whole of that day, braving snipers, machine-gun fire and heavy shelling. It was slow going and arduous work. By nightfall, the company, now reduced to the strength of just two platoons, had managed to establish itself just below the crest of the mountain, but the summit remained in enemy hands.

While Maj Smith's company was trying to clear the enemy from the right of the road, Maj Cobbold's men were attempting to do the same on the left. Their approach to the high ground was equally difficult, for the steep lower slopes of Monte Piccolo were terraced with strips of cultivated land, each rise edged with rocks and boulders. At the base was a wood, flanked by a lane and lined with a few houses. By the time that No. 2 Company had started to make its move, the early dawn was breaking on a bright May morning. It was hard work for the men, advancing in full fighting equipment, struggling over broken ground and up the terraced slopes. From the top of Piccolo the enemy watched their open advance below them with great interest.

Giving Cobbold's company some support were the tanks of the Lothians and Border Horse. Lt Allan Waterston's Sherman was among them: 'My troop moved forward over reasonably open ground without opposition or shelling until we found ourselves on a forward slope in broad daylight and with very little cover except for a few isolated trees and bushes. There was no point in going further as the ground fell away in front of us and then rose sharply in terraces up the steep flank of Piccolo. These were impassable for tanks. However, apart from being sitting ducks on a forward slope, we were in a perfect position to support our Guardsmen with fire when they began to struggle up the terraces.'[5]

The leading platoon of the Welsh Guards advanced through some shellfire and into the woods, but then lost its way, and on emerging from the trees began to veer across to far too the left. During this approach its radios failed and the guardsmen lost touch with Company HQ. Maj Cobbold decided to go after the platoon to lead it back onto the planned route. As the major approached the lane, he and his servant-orderly were killed by close-range fire from the houses. The platoon ahead of them was also engaged by the enemy; several guardsmen were killed and the remainder pinned down by small-arms fire. They could get no further forward and their way back was cut off by the enemy in the houses along the lane.

Lt Allan Waterston watched the Welsh Guards' advance from the safety of his tank and later described the attack.

> There was an initial hitch which caused me some concern. Our Guards had not had time to advance far enough for us to see them emerging

from the hollow in front of us but there was a great deal of activity on the crest of Piccolo. Men were walking about in the open and spreading along the ridge. In view of the uncertain state of affairs the previous evening I reported this activity on the wireless and asked for confirmation that the people I could see were not indeed guardsmen as the enemy was certainly not in the habit of wandering about on the top of exposed hill tops. For some time there was a good deal of humming and hawing over the air while I held my fire, but eventually somebody made up his mind and I was told that they must be Germans and that I had better get on with the war. Fortunately for my peace of mind, my doubts were dispelled a few moments later when I saw figures at the base of Piccolo who were clearly our 'Tall Men' starting to surmount the first terrace wall. 3 Troop opened a heavy fire on the crest which immediately sent the enemy to ground very smartly. Thereafter we kept up a steady barrage all along the summit ridge while the guardsmen gradually climbed higher and higher. In the end as they reached the topmost terrace we had to stop firing and then saw some figures coming down again rather faster than they went up.[6]

The other platoons of the Welsh Guards No. 2 Company had made a more successful start towards the summit, passing though olive groves and climbing the terraces one by one in the face of enemy resistance. Heavy machine-gun fire came at them from both the front and the flanks. Through this crossfire the platoons manoeuvred their way forward with great bravery. As soon as one enemy post had been eliminated from a fold in the ground, another sprang up on an adjacent spur. The enemy then started to slip around the exposed guardsmen, trying to outflank the attack. Lt Bankier, now in command of the company, realised that his men were hopelessly outnumbered and liable to be surrounded. It was certain that Monte Piccolo was too strongly held to be captured by his small force, so he ordered his men to fall back, down the hill. The withdrawal was very difficult, for the Germans covered most of the ground with accurate fire. The men could find some shelter behind the steps of the terraces, but as they continued their descent and came out on to the cultivated strips, they were once more in the open under observation from the enemy. Progress down was very slow; some of the guardsmen took all day and the following night to get back to the battalion. The 'reconnaissance' had been a disaster for the company, which had suffered almost fifty casualties during the attack, with two of its three officers killed and the other wounded.[7]

Lt Waterston of the Lothians continues with his account of the action.

By this time the sun was well up, the attack had evidently failed, my troop was sitting out in the open and it seemed very likely that even retreating enemy gunners would soon be taking us on. There was only one place where we could seek some cover and still do our job in support of the guardsmen withdrawing from Piccolo; that was in the vicinity of some farm buildings about one hundred yards to our left. I moved the troop and we tucked ourselves in as best we could behind the buildings. A major of the Guards with a ginger moustache and ruddy face, wearing his KD cap emerged at once and said to me very politely 'I trust your presence will not cause any unpleasantness', at which point most of the farmhouse roof disintegrated over our heads in a cloud of red dust and flying tiles. The gallant major disappeared from view. Suspecting that on his next appearance he would not be so polite I deemed it prudent to move the troop forthwith and we shifted back to where we had been all morning except that we did try to take advantage of what shadow there was under the few trees on the forward slope. The German gunners' observation officer must have watched us with some glee as we had no sooner halted than down came a very accurate 'stonk' on our new position, one round of which exploded on a branch about six feet above my head. I was a bit dazed but otherwise seemed unhurt; it was only when I saw the expression on the face of my gunner as he looked up from within the turret that I realised that there was something amiss and that there was a good deal of blood about which turned out to be mine. I decided that we had better get off the forward slope to sort things out but my experienced driver had already reached the same conclusion and started to reverse without orders from me. My other two tank commanders conformed and all three tanks reversed slowly on converging courses until they ended up colliding into an undignified huddle.[8]

On the main road that day, the remainder of the Welsh Guards were dug in, waiting for the two attacks on the hills on either side of the pass to make progress. While they waited, the enemy gave them no rest, shelling them unmercifully all morning. Casualties began to rise and a number of men were killed. Eventually, the battalion was withdrawn to the hamlet of La Cese, leaving No. 4 Company out on Monte Orio.

The 'reconnaissance in force' undertaken by the Welsh Guards had shown that both hills were held with some determination. It was clear that Arce and its approaches were set up to form a block on the British advance, buying time for the enemy retreating from the Liri valley and from the surrounding hills and villages. Maj Gen Evelegh's division was being checked by what was probably a relatively small force holding a superb defensive position across the important highway. It was frustrating for Evelegh because there was no immediate way round the obstruction. He was being kicked by his superiors to get on with the chase, but was stuck fast by a force of perhaps no more than a hundred enemy paratroopers backed by artillery. He now sent the other two battalions of the Guards Brigade to clear them out and take Monte Piccolo and the hill beyond it, Monte Grande. The entire XIII Corps waited on the outcome of this attack.

The 2nd Coldstream Guards were the first to advance, followed by 3rd Grenadier Guards in what was becoming a very untidy battle. The Grenadiers' own history admits that the attack started with many handicaps: 'The men felt lost: they could not see the objectives clearly through the thick foliage of the lower ground: there was no time to explain to every man exactly what was required of him: and during the preparatory phase of planning and giving orders they were exposed to heavy shell fire which prevented them from resting, and from assessing with calm and clarity the task by which they were confronted. In all this lay the seeds of their ill-success.'[9]

The Coldstream was to lead the night attack by making straight for Piccolo; the Grenadiers would start off behind them then move round the base of the mountain to get onto the slopes of Grande behind it. The two heights would then be attacked simultaneously. This time the attacks would have the full support of all the weapons of the division to shoot them in. Just after 2100 hr the two battalions moved off to reach their start line before the artillery barrage began. No. 2 Company of the Grenadiers were unfortunate to run into a salvo of enemy shells that caused at least twenty casualties before they had even been in contact with a single German. The company was disorganised by the shellfire and it took some time for Lt Denny to rally the survivors and reorganise at the foot of the hill.

At 0015 hr, the guns opened fire and the attacks began. The forward companies of the Coldstream moved slowly up the slopes of Piccolo, climbing over the terraces to be met with small-arms fire and grenades bouncing down from above. The German outposts that had caused so much trouble to the Welsh Guards the previous day then withdrew before the guardsmen up towards the summit, which was gradually disappearing under a great weight of shell fire. As the leading company approached the top, the artillery fire halted. By then the Germans had withdrawn further over the hill. By 0200 hr the Coldstream reported the hill cleared and were digging in on the reverse slopes.

No 1. and No. 3 Companies of the Grenadiers continued with their attack on Monte Grande, unaware that the delay of No. 2 Company at the base had left their left flank exposed. They pressed on up the terraces with such intent that they found themselves stumbling through some of their own artillery fire which was falling short of the top of the hill. By 0530 hr they had gained the crest to find that the enemy had moved down the slope behind it. Like the Coldstream, the Grenadiers reported the hill taken and started to dig in. Then came the enemy counterattack. The German paratroopers pushed up the far side of Monte Grande in some strength and forced the guardsmen under cover behind a stone wall which ringed the summit. A small hillock that overlooked the top of the hill was gained by the enemy, which enabled them to bring fire down on any guardsman who showed himself. The Grenadiers suddenly found themselves penned in on the summit.

The two sides on Monte Grande were in too close contact for artillery fire to be effective, so it was left to the guardsmen themselves to push back the Germans. Parties of the Grenadiers led by NCOs and officers sortied out from behind the wall, while others tried to pin down the enemy from their hastily erected stone sangars. Gradually the top of the hill was regained by the Grenadiers, but the enemy was still strongly emplaced on the reverse slope. Things continued to deteriorate when it was found that Germans were infiltrating around the left flank, through the position which should have been taken by the ill-fated No. 2 Company. Other Germans were slipping down the cleft between Grande and Piccolo. The Grenadiers were now in danger of being surrounded on the summit and cut off from the Coldstream and the rest of the division. At 0700 hr the colonel sent a message up to the two companies on the top of Monte Grande to pull back off the mountain while the near slopes were still open.

The Grenadiers withdrew over the open terraces pursued by Germans. To support the retreat 16th/5th Lancers harried the enemy with direct fire low over the heads of the guardsmen, and the guns of the Ayrshire Yeomanry plastered the top of the mountain with artillery fire. When the exposed companies had reached the level plain in front of the hills, the battalion regrouped and kept watch over the left flank of Monte Piccolo.

During the move to support the Grenadiers, several tanks from 16th/5th Lancers and one of the artillery OPs went forward to a small hill adjacent to the foothills of Monte Grande. They intended to get a good view of the Grenadiers' hill and act as forward control for the remainder of C Squadron. When they got onto the hillock, they found it already occupied by men from the German 1st Parachute Division. The enemy ambushed the armour, and the tank containing the squadron's second in command, Maj Eveleigh, was knocked out by a German 'Panzerfaust' handheld antitank weapon, killing the captain and his driver. One of the other tanks overturned while trying to escape, but the remainder managed to extricate themselves safely from the trap.

While the Grenadiers had been fighting a rearguard action on Monte Grande, the Coldstream on Monte Piccolo were dealing with their own German counterattack. The enemy was employing his usual tactics. The Germans on both hills had originally held their positions with a light screen of machine guns. They then allowed the initial attacks by the Guards to succeed with little opposition, before counterattacking with the bulk of their forces, just as the British were trying to get established. The Coldstream were hit by the same enemy onslaught that had struck the Grenadiers at around 0430 hr. At first it was just mortar and shellfire that struck the top of Monte Piccolo; then as the guardsmen were pushed back, the paratroopers closed in on the Coldstream. With Monte Grande in German hands the positions on Piccolo were now completely overlooked. The enemy attacked up their forward slope almost into the British line, but were repulsed by concentrated fire from the guardsmen and their supporting artillery. For the next few hours, the top of the mountain was alive with small-arms fire as the two sides struggled for possession of the heights. At 0800 hr a particularly determined attack almost swept the guardsmen from the summit. Fighting was hand-to-hand, with many of the enemy put to flight at the end of a bayonet. Dogged defence gradually allowed the guardsmen to gain the upper hand. Eventually the action died down a little, only to flare up throughout the morning as more of the enemy tried to get round the crest onto the Coldstream's reverse slope. Sniper fire seemed to come from all angles, but the battalion held.

Throughout these actions the guns of the Ayrshire Yeomanry kept up a steady concentration of shellfire to limit the enemy's movements. Communication between the guns and the forward OP on the mountain were complicated because of radio failures, but a little ingenuity found a way around these problems. Up on the crest Capt Chinner was able to radio back from his OP to Capt Box at the Coldstream battalion HQ on their net. Capt Box in turn relayed messages to L/Bdr Jones in the OP tank at the base of the hill, who was able to contact Lt Fisher at B Battery's Command Post, where the instructions were passed on to the guns. The Yeomanry used a prodigious amount of ammunition, as Lt Fisher later described: 'For about two hours the battery continued to plug away until ammunition began to run low; then we got another battery to take over. John de Burgh rushed off with the 3-tonners and found a dump near Aquino. We were able to get small amounts from here and there and went on firing all day. Another counterattack developed in the late afternoon and we got down to just ten rounds per gun.'[10] More ammunition arrived just in time to keep the guns firing, but it had been a difficult task to obtain it, for traffic jams in the rear meant that supplies to everyone were being held up and the ammunition at the dump was being strictly rationed.

At 1500 hr another strong attack came in on the Coldstream. Fortunately, it was spotted just as it started and the redoubtable guns of the Ayrshire Yeomanry broke it up. The 17th/21st Lancers also lent a hand from positions just 1,000 yards in front of Piccolo. They fired hundreds of rounds of high-explosive shells with remarkable accuracy at the Germans as they came over the hill. The attack was beaten off and the whole area slowly quietened right down, but the enemy remained in possession of a rocky outcrop on the edge of the spur, which was causing some discomfort. A request was passed back to battalion for more help to come up and capture it. No. 1 Company of the Welsh Guards led by Maj Gibson-Watt was given the task.

Down on the plain an Orders Group was called by Brig Haydon to organise the move. Lt Col Gordon Simpson of the Lothians and Border Horse was there and later recorded the scene in his diary: 'The "O" Group is fantastic – something rather like a scene from a film of the last war. A barn in a farm under fire – straw all round – in the middle the Guards' Brigadier with a map – in a circle round about all his COs, a few gunners, John Marling of the 17th/21st Lancers and myself. The orders are bad, I think, and David Gibson-Watt of the Welsh Guards is given orders to take the top of Piccolo in a certain way. David, and I will always admire him for this, argues with the Brigadier until the latter eventually climbs down and lets David do it his way – and why shouldn't he? It is his life and those of his guardsmen that are at stake. Just because it entailed altering an artillery programme by 15 minutes his way was said to be wrong.'[11]

The artillery preparation was duly put down and Gibson-Watt's company started up the hill just before 1800 hr. They passed through the Coldstream's positions and attacked eastwards along the ridge into the face of enemy machine-gun fire. The attack was pressed home with great bravery in what the Welsh Guards' history calls 'a text book demonstration of attack by fire and movement'. Men advanced firing Bren guns from their hips, throwing grenades and emptying sub-machine guns into trenches, sweeping across the broken ground at the enemy. The company lost twenty-two men killed and wounded in the attack, but it took the position.

By evening it seemed that the fighting was over, but everyone tensed themselves as night fell, expecting a renewed attack. None came and the next morning a Welsh Guards patrol reported seeing no enemy to its front. Other patrols checked the mountain and agreed; the enemy had slipped away during the night. Later that morning the advance resumed and the tanks of 26th Armoured Brigade motored through the pass up Highway 6 to entered Arce unopposed.

It had taken the division three days to get past the enemy position and finally seal off the road junction at Arce, three long days before Eighth Army could use Highway 6 and the smaller road which led off to the north from the town towards Sora. Maj Gen Evelegh's first battle in charge of the division had not won him any laurels. The price had also been high in men: the Welsh Guards had 112 casualties, the Coldstream lost 18 dead and 55 wounded, and 3rd Grenadier Guards 16 killed and 55 injured.

Before the advance resumed there were some adjustments to be made to ensure that the formation leading the pursuit group was correctly organised. Lt Gordon Simpson's diary recalls his frustration with these manoeuvres: 'Today is noted for two things: firstly, a "peace" march to make the divisional area look like a "square" instead of an "oval" on a Corps or Army map – and I may say it was more tiring and badly organised than anything I've ever done – and, secondly, the remark made by the General to the Welsh Guards while they were busy burying their dead and generally feeling pretty mournful and low, "Why only that number of casualties, that's nothing!"'[12]

The fighting in the Liri valley and the advance northwards against roadblocks, booby traps and delaying tactics by the enemy showed that there was no real role in Italy for an armoured division with equal balance between armour and infantry. The days of tanks charging across open plains, supported by motorised infantry, were over. The terrain in Italy did not allow large numbers of tanks to be employed en masse. It seemed clear that the campaign would see more and more of tanks supporting infantry, rather than the other way around. More infantry would be needed and the armour/infantry balance would have to be adjusted to suit these new conditions.

To meet these demands, 6th Armoured Division's organisation was changed by the addition of another infantry brigade. On 21 May, 61st Infantry Brigade was formed by Brig Adrian Gore, one-time commander of 10th Rifle Brigade, and on 29 May it came under command of 6th Armoured Division. The 61st Infantry Brigade was to include three battalions of the Rifle Brigade: 2nd, 7th, and 10th. The 10th Rifle Brigade was to move within the division across from 26th Armoured Brigade, retaining its organisation as a motor battalion. The other two battalions had been with Eighth Army in North Africa, both as motor battalions. For the past year they had been in Egypt, where they were redesignated as 'ordinary' infantry.[13]

James Wilson was the Adjutant of 10th Rifle Brigade and later recalled this reorganisation: 'It seemed in theory to give 10 RB the best of both worlds. We were to retain our vehicles, and the extra comfort and independence this implied. Equally we were to come under command of Adrian Gore who, as our former Commanding Officer, knew how to use a motor battalion properly. It was sad to leave 26th Armoured Brigade, but, on balance, it seemed a good deal, though, in the early stages, jealousy and patronage of the other two battalions, veterans of the desert with exceptional records, did not always make for easy relationships. In practice, 10 RB fell that summer between two stools. We lost some of our previous expertise at working with armour and were often too vehicle-bound when acting as infantry.'[14]

When 6th Armoured Division's advance resumed it was initially against negligible opposition. The retreat of the bulk of the enemy was by then well under way and had reached close to Rome. The Anzio beachhead had broken out of its confines, but its main thrust had not been directed towards Highway 6 to cut off von Vietinghof's fleeing Tenth Army; Gen Mark Clark was more intent on capturing Rome for himself and sent the bulk of his troops northwards instead of eastwards. As a result, most of von Vietinghof's forces were able to withdraw around the eastern side of the capital and put some distance between themselves and the Allies. Clark's decision also meant that the Americans and the French became tied up in traffic jams in Rome and were unable to stick close to the escaping enemy. Eighth Army did most of the pursuing until the various Allied corps and armies had got themselves sorted out.

It took many days and many miles before 6th Armoured Division met any major enemy formations. German resistance was confined to delaying tactics. Nonetheless, forward movement had to be undertaken with some caution. As the armoured advance ground its way forward, with each tank regiment taking its turn as the vanguard, a tank troop would be detached to reconnoitre along side roads to ensure that the enemy had not prepared an ambush from the flank. This task could often be dangerous, for the enemy frequently left a small party specifically to knock out any tanks that provided this flank guard. They would cover a bend in the road with an antitank gun, fire off a few shots at the first tank to appear, then retire along a prepared route to the next surprise position. The advance would slow, infantry would be brought forward and an attack prepared, only to find the enemy had gone.

Patrolling above the advancing armies were Allied fighter-bombers, shielding them from the rapidly diminishing Luftwaffe and trying to cause havoc among the fleeing Germans. Most of these attacks on enemy columns took place well in front of the roads packed with Allied traffic, but sometimes the most forward of the armour, those in the lead of the advance, came close to the area in which these aircraft were operating. Lt George Martin of the Lothians later remembered one such occasion:

We were in line ahead on a narrow sunken track, the banks not very high, waiting to move forward in support of the infantry; suddenly a Hurricane zoomed low over us and banking steeply had a good look at us. It was often difficult on the ground to identify the types of tanks so I doubted if the pilot, travelling at such speed, would see anything but armour and tend to assume it was German. We carried no identification marks on our tanks, unlike the Americans, so I began to wonder what he was going to do. Coming in at almost treetop level he roared over us from front to rear, turning in the distance he once again lined up his nose in our direction. At this moment I had the impression he was going to rake us with cannon fire. For just such occasions we carried canisters of yellow smoke. I hurriedly grabbed a canister and threw it out and was pleased to see smoke billowing upwards. With a sigh of relief I noticed the nose of the Hurricane lift sharply, bank steeply and roar away.[15]

Chapter Ten

The Advance through Italy

Gen Alexander wished to exploit the epic victory that he had gained in front of Rome by continuing to apply pressure to the retreating enemy, allowing him no respite or opportunity to regroup. He knew that Kesselring's forces were weak and disorganised and wished to prevent them withdrawing into the easily defended country of the northern Apennines. It was important that the advancing Allies did not lose contact with the Germans, nor allow them to hold up the advance to buy time in which to occupy a new stop-line.

GenFM Kesselring had for many months been preparing a new line of fortifications stretching across the whole of Italy from Pisa to Rimini, incorporating the high Apennine mountain range. On this new defence line, known as the 'Gothic Line', the German Commander in Chief (Italy) wanted to establish Tenth and Fourteenth Armies among concrete and steel barriers, well before the rain and snow of winter arrived. Kesselring hoped that the combination of strong fortifications, winter weather and the mountainous terrain would halt the Allies completely, just as it had done at Cassino. Gen Alexander hoped to forestall this plan by reaching the line early and forcing his way through it before the rains of autumn arrived.

The 6th Armoured Division's advance through Italy, like those of other divisions, was a long, arduous slog. In the early stages the fighting consisted of actions against the enemy rearguard often based around a blown bridge or across a narrow defile. After the division reached the River Tiber, opposition became more serious. Still no great numbers of the enemy were involved, but the positions where he chose to make a stand required complicated set-piece attacks to clear away his forces. Time after time these small actions consisted of the same sequence of events: the advance was brought to a halt; a plan was formed to get around the hold-up; a set-piece attack by artillery, tanks and guns was put in; objectives were taken; a slight pause, then a German counterattack with some ground retaken; another Allied set-piece attack, even larger than the first, was arranged only to find that the enemy had slipped away to man the next feature along the route. The advance north for Alexander's armies was costly, tedious and difficult.

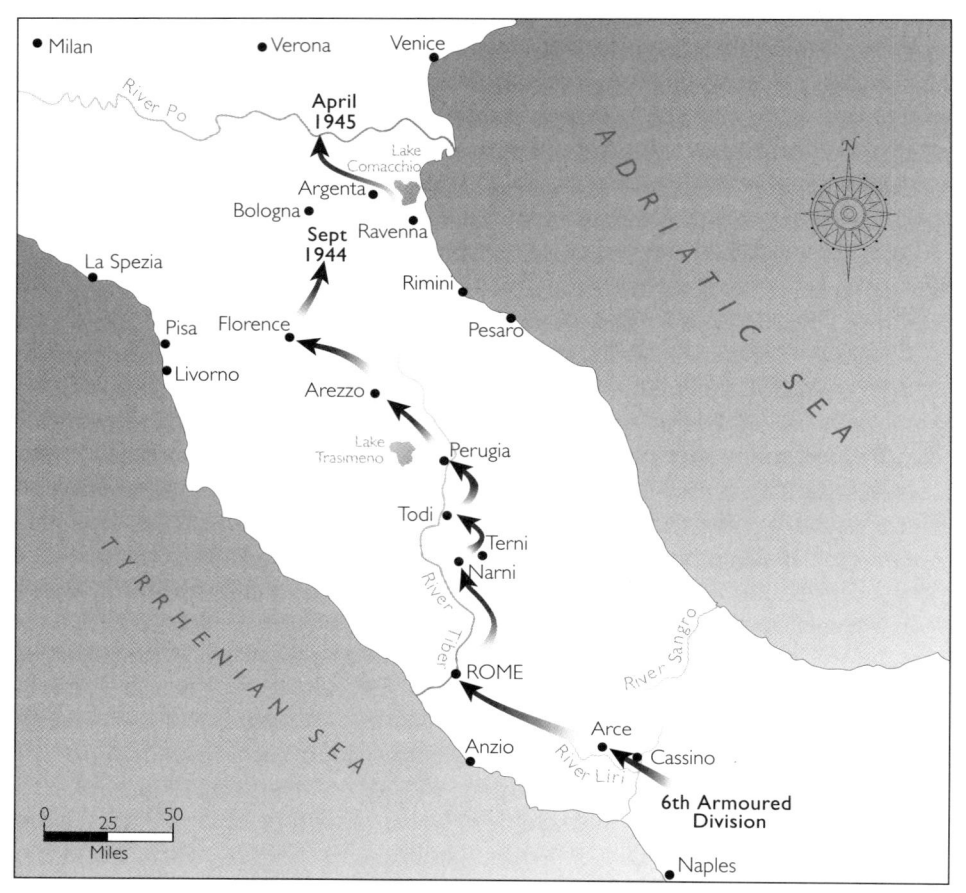

Map 8. The advance through Italy

At the start of the advance there was still an element of the chase in the moves, with an air of excitement in the leading groups. Lt Col Gordon Simpson recalled some of this in his diary entry for 5 June, when 2nd Lothians and Border Horse led 6th Armoured Division up to the area of the River Tiber in order to pick up Highway 3 which led north-east from the capital:

> Now starts a classic chase for which the 2nd Lothians will always be known. Without any breaks we go flat out along roads, tracks, Roman roads with their original paving stones, fields, ditches, little bridges, big bridges and up and down hills for getting on for forty miles. A chase if you like, but a hard and driving chase up to Route 3. We passed by guns in position firing, troops moving up, black men, Americans, German prisoners, corpses, burnt tanks and everything of war. We even ran into a few American MPs who helped us get through. It took some

people three days to do the same journey later, but we were on Route 3 quick enough to have a crack at a few odd Boches holding a position. There we harboured and everyone was pleased, but no one more than I, as I had cracked the whip and we had galloped.[1]

With the advance well under way towards the River Tiber, it was hoped that bridges might be captured intact to allow a quick and easy passage over the river. The enemy was trying to keep these bridges open for as long as possible to allow his retreating rearguards and parties of stragglers to withdraw across them. The bold dash to the Tiber was not fast enough, however, for when the division arrived on its banks they found the bridges blown and the enemy waiting on the far side of the river to resist any moves to cross it. Rather than make the assault, 6th Armoured was sent up its eastern bank and told to make for the two towns of Narni and Terni, through which the German divisions that had been holding the central part of the old front were still retreating. If these towns could be captured quickly, it was possible that the bulk of these German forces could be intercepted, but if the enemy could hold the route open long enough for his rearguards to fight clear, then the worst of the crisis facing Kesselring would be over. He would have pulled back all of his forces from the south into the more easily defended northern sector of Italy. The field marshal may have had to abandon huge areas of the country to the Allies, but the German armies would still be relatively intact and able to re-form along the Gothic Line.

The strip of land along the Tiber's left bank now became the focus of Eighth Army. A speedy advance along it could reap great dividends; for the enemy, his most important task was to prevent this happening. The Germans used two of their best divisions, 29th and 90th Panzergrenadiers, to fight delaying actions across Eighth Army's front. The two divisions were ordered to slow down the British advance, but not to get involved in battles to hold any given line, which might expose them to the risk of it being broken or outflanked. Such an outcome could precipitate a complete Allied breakthrough. Demolitions, mines, booby-traps and small rearguard actions were what was required.

The advance to Narni and Terni was made possible through the work of the Royal Engineers. Every bridge along the route was blown, every culvert demolished and every road and branch road blocked by felled trees. Stretches of tarmac roads were pock-marked with craters which forced vehicles off the road onto mined verges. The railway line along the route was blown every 50 yards, distorting rails and ripping apart sleepers. The division moved as fast as the engineers could repair the roads. Tanks led the advance and when they were forced to a halt by an obstacle, infantry would come forward to protect field squadrons of engineers as they brought lorry-loads of rubble or bridging material forward to deal with the hold-up. Bulldozers on low-loaders followed closely behind the forward troops so that they could be quickly offloaded to tackle a large crater or to carve a ramp down a steep bank to ford a stream.

The division, now transferred to Lt Gen McCreery's X Corps, advanced, with each of its armoured regiments taking the lead in turn, sometimes with the Guards Brigade up with the forward tanks and other times accompanied by the Rifle Brigade. With the self-propelled guns of 12th RHA and the Ayrshire Yeomanry not far behind, it meant that there was always some artillery to hand to deal with any stubborn groups of the enemy. Narni was reached and passed without any more difficulty than had been met at all the other enemy 'pinch points'. The tail of the escaping Germans was not far ahead.

The chase continued for Terni, with everyone going flat-out for the bridges. The Lothians and 10th RB made it to the town just in time to see the main bridge blown as they arrived. The enemy had left its destruction until the very last moment to enable as many of his troops to escape as possible. Some riflemen were actually in houses overlooking the crossing just as the last bridge erupted in a great explosion. The Royal Engineers now had to span the deep cut formed by the river – it passed through a wide gorge – with a high-level Bailey bridge long enough and strong enough to take tanks. It took just twenty-four hours for the sappers to complete this complicated task.

The enemy had achieved his primary objective in fighting the delaying actions east of the River Tiber, for by the time that 6th Armoured had fully captured Terni, all the German forces had passed through. Once more the wily Kesselring had engineered a remarkable escape and had shifted the bulk of his formations northwards towards the Gothic Line. While they were establishing and re-equipping themselves in that undulating course of fortifications in the mountains, some of his divisions were preparing to comply with Hitler's orders to fight to the last along any feasible line that could be held. The Führer had decreed that the Gothic Line was not to be regarded as the ultimate refuge behind which the German Tenth and Fourteen Armies should retire. Kesselring managed both to conform with this directive and man his new winter line by skilfully exploiting the easily defended country in front of the advancing Allies and husbanding some of his units in reserve.

With Terni taken, 6th Armoured Division's next main objective was Perugia, a highly defensible city standing on a hill ten miles east of Lake Trasimene. The drive from Terni continued along two roads, with 1st Guards Brigade taking the most direct route to the city and 26th Armoured Brigade moving along the left flank, intending to swing around the outskirts of the city. The Guards advanced through country devoid of Germans and reached Todi without incident. Here they were met by cheering Italians welcoming them with wine and flowers. Both columns then pressed on and began to converge on the outskirts of Perugia, where the tanks ran into enemy artillery fire, the first they had encountered for five days.

On 18 June, 3rd Grenadier Guards were sent along the main route into Perugia together with 16th/5th Lancers, while 17th/21st Lancers and 2nd Lothians and Border Horse were to advance on the left to try to get behind the ancient city. The Grenadiers took the terraced ridge in front of Perugia known as Monte Corneo by late afternoon and looked across the two miles of open ground to the steep, grey walls, the towers and palaces of the city. The Grenadiers then moved down off the high ground and advanced towards the Assisi–Lake Trasimene road that skirted the southern edge of the town. Here enemy fire became more and more concentrated and, as darkness was falling, the battalion halted for the night.

During the hours of darkness, patrols went out to test the enemy's defences and to reconnoitre the ground over which the attack would continue at first light. Leading one of the patrols was Lt Viscount Lascelles, a nephew of the King who was later to become Earl Harewood. The lieutenant and his patrol were ambushed by enemy soldiers and Lascelles was wounded by, as was learned later, fire from a captured British Bren gun. He and several of his men were taken prisoner. A few days later, German propaganda made great play of the fact that the King's nephew had been wounded by a British bullet.[2]

The next day the Grenadiers attacked just after first light, but were checked by strong German resistance. A little later the enemy counterattacked and were held by an equally determined resistance, which included support from tanks. On the left of the Grenadiers, advances by both the Coldstream Guards and 17th/21st Lancers had got beyond the Grenadiers' positions and had begun to loosen the enemy's defences in front of Perugia. Further to the left, 61st Brigade were across the Perugia–Lake Trasimene road. The 10th Rifle Brigade had taken Monte Lacugnano the previous day and 7th Rifle Brigade was advancing the three miles further north for Monte Malbe. Fighting continued throughout the night as the division pressed on around the southern and western sides of the city.

Early the next morning a company of the Grenadiers took the crossroads immediately beneath Perugia without a fight. The previous night it had been a heavily contested junction covered by a welter of enemy fire; now all was quiet. The guardsmen looked up at the ramparts above them, but no shots rang out. Except for one crater in an outer street, the city was untouched. Was the enemy going to defend Perugia? Ahead the road leading up into the walled city was barred by fallen trees. At around 0800 hr a group of high-spirited Italians heaved aside the log-jam and came forward to greet their liberators. The enemy was gone, the city was open. With the Italians as guides, four jeeps of Grenadiers made the spiral ascent around the many hairpin bends that led up into the centre of the city. One of the officers in the party described their entry: 'All the doors and windows were flung open and a great crowd welled onto the street, converging on our dusty caravan. I had the impression of thousands of laughing faces, of people stretching out their hands to be shaken or even just to touch my grubby pair of shorts.'[3]

The capture of Perugia was most welcome news. It would no doubt have been a costly battle to seize the ancient fortified city from the enemy and would have destroyed much of its heritage. The open capture of Perugia seemed to illustrate that Kesselring was standing by his stated intention of trying to preserve as much of Italy's most famous historical sites from the ravages of war as was militarily practical.

The enemy had gone, but not very far, for his forces had withdrawn on to the ring of hills to the north of Perugia and these he did not intend to give up so easily. The 26th Armoured Brigade and 61st Brigade were already well aware of this fact. Both brigades had been working forward through difficult country on the west side of the city against tanks and antitank guns. The advance for the armour had at first been quick, with 17th/21st Lancers committing each of its three squadrons in turn. They moved comfortably along the railway line until they found a bridge over the main road intact, but wired for demolition. However, their move was met by a concentrated burst of artillery fire, which hit the charges and blew the bridge. The quick way around Perugia was now closed.

To the north of Perugia the country was thick and tangled, with the enemy difficult to locate. The next objective was the village of San Marco and the line of hills beyond. Once past these features, the way would be open to Lake Trasimene. The 3rd Welsh Guards were given the task of capturing San Marco, and 3rd Grenadiers were ordered to capture the heights of Monte Pulito, Coppo Canella and Poggio Montione beyond, while 2nd Coldstream intended to take Monte Pacciano.

For the Grenadiers, its attacks were completed and its objectives taken with few casualties. After a very heavy barrage just before dark on 22 June, the battalion had advanced against stunned and demoralised enemy troops to occupy the three hills and link up with the Welsh Guards. Further to the right, the Coldstream Guards had begun their assault on Monte Pacciano the day before and had almost gained the summit. The following day further attacks put the guardsmen on top of Pacciano and the enemy to flight. In between these two battalions, the Welsh Guards advanced on San Marco. The line of this attack was along the main road from Perugia, so the Welshmen were able to call on the support of B Squadron of 16th/5th Lancers.

The main road into San Marco was overlooked on either side by high ground. During the advance, the Guards battalion came under heavy shell and mortar fire as it moved between the hills. The supporting tanks could do little to help, so the leading company deployed over the ground to the right and left and swept along the hills, clearing out the enemy. The guardsmen worked steadily forward, flushing out snipers and destroying machine-gun posts, forcing the enemy from the hills and allowing the main body to continue along the road. Progress was good until the route passed through a narrow defile. Again, fire came at them from both sides, and again the infantry had to deploy off the road to clear out the enemy troops. Then the whole battalion was held up by a strong position based around a single house, fortified by enemy machine guns and supported by an enemy tank.

The Lancers were called forward and the house was blown to bits; the enemy tank retreated and the machine-gunners were killed or captured. So it went on; the approach to San Marco was a series of small actions to flush out the enemy and gain a few more yards. More often than not, the enemy defenders held up the advance until it was clear that the Guards were about to launch a determined attack, then, almost at the last moment, the Germans would slip away. The Welsh Guards were made to fight every yard of the way into San Marco, then fight for every building in the village. Enemy resistance was not intense or fanatical, but it was persistent and required all the talents of the guardsmen to clear it out. By the evening San Marco was free of Germans. With the high ground to the north of the village taken by the remainder of the Guards Brigade, the Welsh Guards' next task was to clear the road to the north that passed through these hills, most especially the northern slopes of Montione, the last of the peaks captured by the Grenadiers. It took two more days of intermittent struggle before the brigade could look out from these hills towards the blue waters of Lake Trasimene. Then it was time for the division to take a little rest.

The enemy had withdrawn over a hundred miles since the Gustav Line battles along the Liri and Garigliano rivers. Delaying tactics had kept the Allies at arm's length and had enabled GenFM Kesselring to bring the bulk of his armies into the Gothic Line. The period of fighting rearguards was at an end; the enemy's regrouping had been completed. The Germans now had main positions along the Trasimene Line, based around the lake, and a final winter line to fall back into.

While 6th Armoured Division was resting at Perugia, XIII Corps had got further ahead of X Corps and was therefore given the task of forcing the Trasimene position with its South African 6th Armoured Division and Maj Gen Keightley's 78th Division. When, after much heavy fighting, these two divisions had completed their objectives and cracked the Trasimene position, the Mailed Fist Division was transferred back to Lt Gen Kirkman's XIII Corps to exploit the breakthrough. Maj Gen Evelegh was now ordered to continue the advance past Cortona towards Arezzo and on to the River Arno.

By the time 6th Armoured Division had moved across to join in the drive for Arezzo, 78th Division had reached Cortona. Here 6th Armoured Division took over the advance with 26th Armoured and 61st Brigades. The 1st Guards Brigade was left to hold the line of Lake Trasimene against possible enemy counterattacks. On 4 July 16th/5th Lancers' battlegroup, consisting of the regiment, 10th Rifle Brigade, C Battery 12th RHA, 8th Field Squadron Royal Engineers and 111th Battery of 72nd Antitank Regiment RA, moved off towards Arezzo along Highway 71.[4] Expectations were high as the column bowled along the wide Chiana valley, which carried the road, a railway and a canal. At first the going was perfect for the armoured force, but six miles short of the town the ground on the right began to rise up into a long, undulating ridge which culminated in the peak of Monte Lignano, 1,000 feet above the level of the valley. The northern end of this range of hills dropped down into a defile – the l'Olmo Gap – formed by the ridge itself and another peak of high ground, Monte Castellare. The only practical way into Arezzo was through this gap. Holding the defile and the hills on either side was the German 15th Panzergrenadier Division.

The road to Arezzo became more cratered and the demolitions more frequent the closer the battlegroup approached to the ridge, slowing the advance almost to a halt. Shelling increased and small groups of the enemy began firing on the column, then antitank fire forced it to a complete standstill. The CO of the Lancers, Lt Col Gundry, sent his C Squadron around to the left over the railway line to see if it could find a route between the railroad and the canal which ran parallel to the road. In the meantime he tried to squeeze B Squadron forward between the road and the railway line, the road itself being impassable until the obstructions were cleared. Enemy fire checked both of these moves and, as light was beginning to fade, the group withdrew to leaguer for the night.

The next day, the column continued its move, with the Derbyshire Yeomanry and the Lothians in the lead, followed by the infantry of the whole of 61st Brigade. After the advance had gone a short distance, fire from the ridge of high ground to the right forced it once again to a halt. The enemy had perfect observation over Highway 71 and the approach to Arezzo; no further movement was possible until these heights were cleared. Maj Gen Evelegh now came forward and deployed his three battalions of the Rifle Brigade, supported by a squadron of 17th/21st Lancers and a troop of Shermans from the Derbyshire Yeomanry, to sweep along the ridge and push back the enemy.

The first attempt to clear the area was made by 10th Rifle Brigade that evening. C Company gained a foothold near the summit of Monte Lignano, but were unable to clear the enemy from the crest or from his dug-in positions on the reverse slope. The same was true for B Company: it failed to get onto the summit of one of the other peaks along the ridge,

Monte Maggio, and was forced to dig in below the top. The 2nd Rifle Brigade came up onto the ridge the next day to occupy the ground between these two peaks and to strengthen the line. Further attempts to remove the enemy all failed. That evening 7th Rifle Brigade was committed into the battle: their night-time attack captured the summit of Monte Maggio and the German observation post was evicted, but the riflemen could not remove the Germans dug in near the top on the reverse slope.

The removal of one German OP improved matters slightly, but the overall struggle had resulted in something of a stalemate. Both sides were securely dug in on opposite slopes of the ridge, with the enemy still having fairly good observation over Highway 71 from the top of Monte Lignano. Each side shelled and mortared the other during the day and harassed positions with fighting patrols at night. Inevitably, the list of casualties slowly began to rise; the battle to take Arezzo was becoming another Cassino. Forward positions could only be supplied at night and even then it was a 2½-hour climb over rough ground. Everything had to be carried by hand; there were no mules available. Two complete companies were engaged each night, struggling through the darkness to resupply the line, further depleting the already overstretched riflemen.

On the night of 7 July, the enemy put in a counterattack on Monte Lignano and Monte Maggio. The attack on Lignano was beaten off before it could develop, without suffering any casualties. On Maggio it was different, for enemy infantry got to within 50 yards of 7th Rifle Brigade before they were spotted. The Germans were among the riflemen before they could react and fierce hand-to-hand fighting broke out among the slit trenches. Gradually the two companies holding the summit drew away, withdrawing 500 yards down the hill before they could reorganise, giving up the summit to the enemy. The next day passed quietly and patrols that night learned that the whole ridge was still in enemy hands and his defences had been thickened.

On the night of 9/10 July, 61st Brigade was relieved on the ridge by a brigade from 8th Indian Division. Intelligence suggested that the enemy in front of Arezzo had been strengthened. Elements of the German 305th Division were now holding the Monte Lignano ridge, with a battlegroup of 94th Division under command. The 15th Panzergrenadier Division were in Arezzo and along the River Arno. Evelegh's attempts to drive through to Arezzo had been stopped by the enemy on his right, and five days of fighting by 61st Brigade could not get the advance going again. It was clear to Lt Gen Kirkman that Arezzo could only be taken by a much larger assault. The 6th Armoured Division had already exhausted one of its infantry brigades and the other was holding the area of the south-west shore of Lake Trasimene. Kirkman requested Eighth Army's commander to reinforce his corps so that a much heavier attack could be made against the town. Reluctantly, Gen Leese agreed, and the decision was taken to bring forward 2nd New Zealand Division from its training area in the Liri valley, where it was rehearsing for the assault on the Gothic Line.

It would take four days for the New Zealanders to arrive and organise for the battle. During this period the enemy was allowed no respite, for as much artillery as possible was concentrated along the corps's front to maintain a heavy barrage and to provide counter-battery fire against enemy gun positions. The 6th Army Group RA moved up and joined in the shoot with six field, five medium, one heavy and two heavy-antiaircraft regiments of artillery. On the day of the attack, the field regiments would increase their rate of fire to 300 rounds per gun, per day in support.[5]

The plan for seizing Arezzo relied on the ridge to the east of Highway 71 being taken first. The 6th Armoured Division would attack the centre of the ridge at Monte Lignano, then the high ground either side of the gap with 1st Guards Brigade, after the New Zealanders had put in an assault on Monte Maggio and the near end of the ridge, so as to protect the armoured division's right flank. The 26th Armoured Brigade's tanks would then drive through the gap and make for the River Arno beyond Arezzo, driving down its right bank to seize the town from the rear. Simultaneously with this operation, the British 4th Infantry and the South African 6th Armoured Divisions would launch their own attack towards the River Arno further downstream.

After ten days stalled in front of Arezzo, 6th Armoured Division went back into the attack on 15 July. The operation began with a night attack by the Guards Brigade and 2nd New Zealand Division. The summit of Monte Lignano had been taken by the New Zealanders before dawn, but the Germans were fighting hard to hold on to the reverse slopes. The Guards' attack immediately met stubborn resistance and a protracted advance went on through the hours of darkness as 3rd Grenadiers led the brigade up the steep slopes. Once they had gained the top they swept northwards towards the gap. Just after dawn 2nd Coldstream came through to take up the advance and to capture the central part of the ridge. Close-quarters combat continued throughout the day as the fighting swung back and forth along the mountain tops, each side determined to gain victory over the other.

The 2nd Coldstream were in turn relieved by 3rd Welsh Guards on the ridge, allowing the momentum of the attack to roll on. By nightfall the ridge was in safe hands; German resistance had crumbled. On the right of the Guards, the New Zealanders had evicted the enemy from their half of the feature and were sweeping down the far side attacking towards the German gun lines. Just before dawn the next morning, a company of the Welsh Guards came down from the ridge, crossed over the gap and up on to Monte Castellare, where the guardsmen found the German trenches empty. The l'Olmo Gap was open.

The first tanks through the gap were those of 16th/5th Lancers. At first light they drove down the road towards Arezzo against negligible opposition and had entered the town by 1000 hr. The enemy holding Arezzo had withdrawn across the River Arno and were heading northwards into the Gothic Line. The other two armoured regiments advanced round the west flank of the town towards the River Arno, through thick vineyards, craters and demolitions, looking for a way across the river.

Up with 2nd Lothians was Lt Allan Waterston, who later recalled his actions on the River Arno:

After moving steadily across country and through trees, under a persistent but not 'personal' shell fire, we first crossed a very deep canal cutting by a bridge and then found ourselves on the south bank of the Arno. Surprisingly there was a Royal Engineer Sherman bulldozer already there cutting a track down the steep wooded bank to the river bed. I reported where we were and was given the OK by the squadron leader to try and cross over. The north bank seemed too steep at that point to climb out so the troop proceeded downstream in line ahead as there was little water in the river. As we approached a bend it struck me that we were in a rather vulnerable formation and managed to climb out on to the German bank where we continued our westward progress in rather more spread out fashion, but keeping a sharp eye open for a possible way back to the 'home' bank should the enemy suddenly react to our intrusion. In this way we came to the German end of the Ponte Buriano bridge and I halted my own tank at the end of the parapet with the houses of the village rather too close for comfort on my right. Through the binoculars we could see half a dozen Germans peeling potatoes in the garden of a house at the British end of the bridge. One of them looked up and seeing three Sherman tanks on 'their' side of the river they all took to their heels and fled into the trees except for one who mounted a bicycle and shot off up the road towards where we thought 'C' Squadron would be. Presumably our departed friends were those responsible for blowing the bridge as we now found that every arch appeared to be mined. There were piles of earth at the crown of each arch on both sides of the roadway all connected up with black shiny cable. We were just considering how best to cope ourselves or to call for the sappers when a group of excited Italian men rushed out of the houses and dashing onto the bridge set about hauling up the cable with complete abandon. This gave us quite a shock as we fully expected the whole thing to blow up in our faces. Fortunately nothing happened and one of the Italians climbed onto my tank and told me that he spoke English as he had had a hot dog stand in New York for many years. Through him we were able to confirm that the 'tedeschi' in the village had departed in haste.[6]

Before the day was out, tanks were across the River Arno and the division was consolidating a bridgehead. The fighting in front of Arezzo had been protracted against a stubborn enemy defence, but the final battle for the town had been short and effective. Faced with a determined attack, the enemy had withdrawn, satisfied with the respite he had gained by frustrating the British advance for eleven days – eleven more days in which to improve the manning of his mountain line. The next orders for the division were to continue the advance along Highway 69 down the Arno valley to Florence, the last city before the Gothic Line.

The division was not too far into its advance before it realised that the enemy was disposed to hold the length of the River Arno and Highway 69 in some strength. Further trouble came from the mountains on the right, which rose in height up to the 4,500 feet of the Pratomagno. The division advanced as the flank defence of XIII Corps and the main effort to reach Florence was made by other divisions over to the west. Both XIII and X Corps continued the attacks towards the mountains, on a wide front, overcoming many minor German defensive lines in the process. Florence was declared an open city by the Germans and it was hoped that they would leave its bridges over the Arno intact, but when the South Africans reached the city on 3 August, they found all the bridges blown save the Ponte Vecchio. No attempt was made to force the River Arno as to do so would make the city a battleground. Florence was taken on 11 August after it had been almost completely outflanked.

Chapter Eleven

ITALY: THE SECOND WINTER

By the time Florence had fallen on 11 August, 6th Armoured Division was getting tired. Most of its units had been in action for three months; some had been in almost constant contact with the enemy since January. This period coincided with changes being made throughout the whole of Alexander's command. The long-awaited invasion of southern France was scheduled for 15 August and Gen Mark Clark's US Fifth Army had to provide the manpower to undertake the landings. His US V Corps and the French Expeditionary Corps were both transferred to Gen Dever's US Seventh Army to carry out the amphibious assault. This left Clark with just five experienced American divisions and two untried units: US 92nd Division and 1st Brazilian Divisions. Alexander had decided that, as the main assault on the Gothic Line would take place on the Adriatic side of the country with Eighth Army, British XIII Corps, which included 6th Armoured Division, should be transferred to Gen Clark's US Fifth Army.

Other changes in command were also being implemented. Lt Gen Allfrey was to lose his V Corps and be replaced by the commander of 78th Division, Charles Keightley. His infantry division had performed well under his command and he was being given a just reward by being promoted to lieutenant general. At the age of 43 he had become the youngest lieutenant general in the whole British Army and the only one of that rank who had not seen service in the First World War.[1]

Maj Gen Evelegh did not fare so well. The swap of divisions between Keightley and Evelegh was in part to allow each to command a division outside their normal specialism and to be judged for corps command. Keightley was the winner of the contest for promotion and on 24 July, Maj Gen Evelegh was posted to the War Office in England and replaced by Maj Gen Gerald Templer. Many in the division were sad to see Evelegh leave, but they thought it was the right decision. As one officer put it, 'He was a tired man; 6th Armoured Division was in a rut and required a new mind to remove its developing pessimism and loss of dash.'[2]

Maj Gen Templer was transferred across from command of 56th (London) Division. He had seen a great deal of active service and

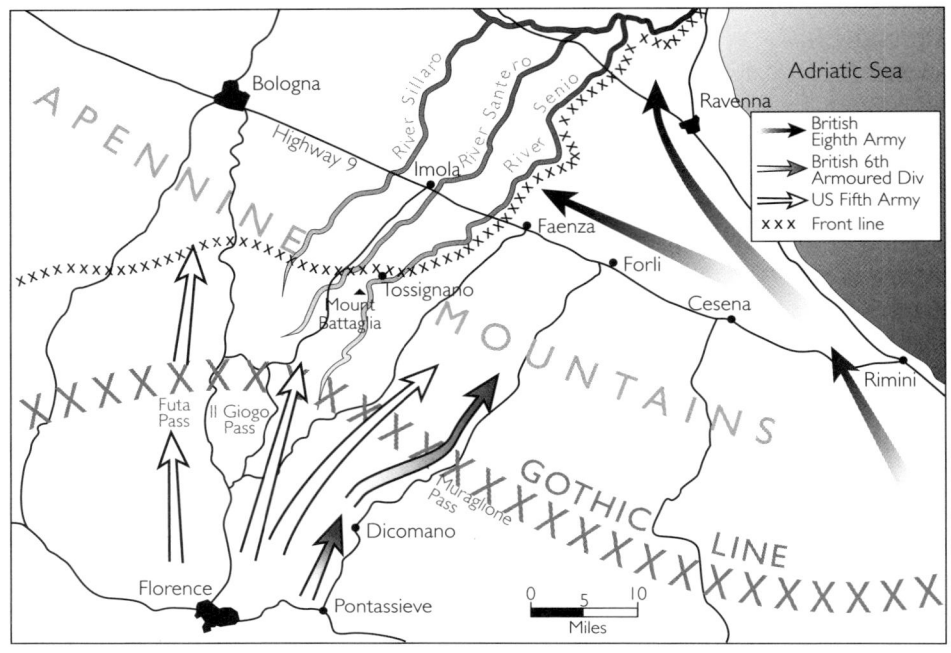

Map 9. The mountain line, September–October 1944

had led 56th Division at Salerno and through the early battles in Italy, before landing with them at Anzio. His stay with 6th Armoured Division was, however, rather short: he arrived on 25 July and left on 5 August. The reason was described by James Wilson of 10th Rifle Brigade: 'Gerald Templer was a new broom if ever there was one. We were just beginning to feel the impact of his very different style when he was wounded by a mine on the side of the road, set off by a Guards Brigade lorry. In the back of the vehicle was a grand piano, liberated by the Grenadier Guards. Out flew the instrument, pinning Gerald Templer beneath it; when, ten minutes later, he was extricated, there was no question of his continuing in command and he was evacuated back to England.'[3]

Templer was replaced at the head of 6th Armoured Division by Maj Gen Horatius 'Nap' Murray. Murray was an infantryman who had served in command of 1st Gordons in the Western Desert. He was wounded at Alamein and was out of action until the campaign in Sicily, where he was promoted and recalled to lead 153rd Brigade. He returned home to the UK with his brigade in early 1944 to take part in the landings in Normandy as part of 51st Highland Division. The nickname 'Nap' (short for Napoleon) was conferred upon him early in his career because of his dedication to soldiering. Murray was an officer who had seen much continuous action during the war and brought with him a realistic outlook to the difficulties of fighting in Italy.

When Florence had finally fallen, 6th Armoured Division was at Pontassieve on the River Arno, eight miles to the east of the city. With XIII Corps's main effort being developed to the north-west of Florence, the division was pulled out of the line for a short rest and refit. Maintenance tasks that had been neglected for months were completed, reinforcements inducted into various units and training exercises organised to make the division ready for the tasks that awaited it up in the mountains on the Gothic Line.

The way northwards from Florence and the River Arno was barred by the Apennine mountain range which ran completely across the Allied front. The Gothic Line in this sector was built in depth among these peaks, some of which rose up to 5,000 feet high. The centre section of the Allied front faced forty miles of mountainous ground interlocked with enemy strong points. On the far side of the high ground the flat Lombardy plain stretched northwards to the valley of the River Po. Once through the mountains and the Gothic Line, the ground became much more suitable for armoured warfare, or so it was thought.

Eighth Army was making its main attack through the Gothic Line to the east of these mountains near the Adriatic coast. This sector gave better ground for manoeuvre, but was defended by even thicker enemy fortifications. To assist this operation, Gen Clark was ordered to press on through the mountains to try to attract enemy forces away from Gen Leese's efforts.

There were two main routes for Gen Clark's attack northwards from Florence, the most important of which was along the road to Bologna through the Futa Pass, with a secondary line of advance through the Il Giogo Pass to Imola. Both of these passes were heavily fortified, for the Germans also knew that these were the prime routes through the mountains. There were other roads across the high ground and each of them had some part of Fifth Army pushing up them. On Clark's extreme right flank, 6th Armoured Division was to move northwards on Highway 67, which led over the mountains to Forli, by way of Dicomano and the Muraglione Pass.

The Gothic Line here in the mountains did not rely too heavily on fixed concrete fortifications. There was little need for them, for nature had already created a formidable natural defensive zone for the Germans. The line consisted mostly of well-sited artillery observation posts overlooking the roads through the mountains. Every bridge, culvert and viaduct was mined for demolition; every sharp bend and every cutting had been prepared for destruction. The road itself, however, was kept open to the rear to provide supply lines for the enemy. The most forward of these obstacles were covered by companies or platoons of infantry. As the Allies approached, the mines would be blown and the attackers drenched by artillery, mortar and small-arms fire from well-sited positions. 'The only way to unlock this combination was for infantry, supplied by mules and jeeps, to clear the heights, for engineers to bridge the obstacle and for tanks and infantry to regain contact at the next obstacle.'[4]

The advance into the mountains was extremely slow: as the infantry cleared the high ground on each side of the road, the route below was repaired by the sappers but neither could advance until the other had done its work. Tank support off the road was almost impossible; the few tracks that existed were often too narrow, generally terraced into the hillside and unable to take the weight of a 35-ton Sherman. Engineers were the key to all progress; everything depended on them. Sappers and their equipment were worth more than tanks during the advance and there was never enough of them to meet demand. During this period their numbers were swelled by the transfer of large parties of men from the division's antiaircraft and antitank battalions to help with manual labour and road-building tasks.

The division advanced towards Forli up Highway 67, starting on 25 August. Each of 26th Armoured Brigade's regiments took it in turn to provide tank support for the move, with 61st Brigade supplying the infantry. The 1st Guards Brigade had been transferred on to the mountains in the east, forming a loose contact between the division and other units of Eighth Army. The advance moved at a pace limited by the speed of reconstruction work by the Royal Engineers and the progress that the infantry could make sweeping along the high ground on the flanks. It took a month for the division to get its leading units up through Dicomano and Muraglione Pass – a month of filling and pounding cratered roads, repairing and rebuilding blown bridges, firefights with an evasive enemy and depressing bouts of inclement weather. By October the summer sun was gone and the weather had started to deteriorate quite badly, with high winds, driving rain and endless mud everywhere.

The enemy let the division progress up into the mountains, holding the advance at arm's length as it laboured through demolitions and ambushes, but slipping away when stronger attacks were put in. There was a method to this strategy: the Germans were allowing the Allies to penetrate into the mountains through the southern slopes of the Apennines, drawing them on to the high ground for the winter, leaving them with long and difficult supply routes through the mountains, but allowing themselves shorter approaches through the foothills bordering the long, straight Rimini–Forli–Bologna road, Highway 9.

Gradually the wire, pillboxes and trench systems of the Gothic Line were met and entered. Here progress became even slower against fixed defences, until the advance was finally halted some fifteen miles from Forli and the entry on to the Lombardy plain. The division had arrived almost on the other side of the mountains, near enough for observers to look down tantalisingly on the open plain, but here the enemy put a final stop to the advance of 6th Armoured Division with a fierce and determined resistance.

The employment of an armoured division in such a mountainous region was impractical. The road to Forli was never going to be opened, despite much wishful thinking by high command, without the sustained and strengthened commitment of an overwhelming infantry force. The offensives being undertaken by the British Eighth Army on the Adriatic side and, to a lesser extent by the Americans through the mountains between Florence and Bologna, meant that there was nothing to be gained by a major offensive in 6th Armoured Division's sector. The division's role was therefore to threaten a move, hold the line and harass the enemy.

The American attack in September had managed to get through the Il Giogo and Futa passes, but became bogged down on the peaks that overlooked both roads. One of the most significant, the key position of Monte Battaglia, located between the Bologna and Imola roads that divide the valley of the Santerno from the valley of the Senio, had been captured after a spirited action by the US 88th Division. This division was now required for the continuation of Clark's attack up Highway 65 to Bologna, so 1st Guards Brigade was switched across to the American sector on 30 September to hold the mountain in order to release 88th Division.

The Guards' tenure of Monte Battaglia was one of the most desperate and depressing periods of the war for them. The mountain could be reached only by a minor road from Firenzuola. Five miles short of Battaglia, wheeled transport could go no further. Here the infantry dismounted from their lorries and, accompanied by porters and mules, ascended the narrow track leading up the mountainside. Constant rain and the passage of men and mules had turned the tracks into rivers of glutinous mud. Men's boots, no matter how tightly they were laced, would be pulled away from their feet. The round trek from Brigade HQ to the front-line positions and back, a distance of no more than three miles, sometimes took ten hours for the supply train to complete. Once the troops had reached the most forward area, which was perched precariously on the top of the mountain and fed by a narrow, knife-edge causeway, they were confronted by a scene of complete devastation. Every feature had been blown apart by shells; what few trees there were had all been stripped and truncated by shrapnel. Water-filled shell-holes littered the area; rusty ration tins mingled with the corpses of Americans and Germans, joining with the stench of human faeces and rotting food to assault the senses. After the long journey the guardsmen picked their way across this dead landscape and found their foxholes, filled with water and lined with mud. Within minutes their blankets, boots and equipment were all sopping wet.

The three Guards battalions held the long ridge of Battaglia overlooked by the Germans on three sides. Life was made almost intolerable by rain. By day the men lay in open slit trenches, soaked to the skin and pounded by enemy shellfire. The Grenadiers lost an average of ten men a day to this fire and the casualties among the Welsh Guards and the Coldstream were equally depressing. The night brought little rest, since it was then that the supply trains struggled up the mountain and the Germans increased their shell and mortar fire to interfere with the moves. Every man remained alert, for the enemy had used these diversions to creep up and launch violent attacks. Six or seven times the Germans had been repulsed by the Americans, but still they seemed determined to regain the hill. While the brigade was on top of Battaglia, it too had to deal with many German fighting patrols and enemy attacks.

One such event against the small house containing the tactical HQ of 3rd Grenadiers was witnessed during the night of 9 October by Maj Knob of the Ayrshire Yeomanry, who was in the building with his battery's OP; he later described the event: 'At 2 a.m. the sentry on the door opened fire with his tommy-gun, and a German Schmeisser replied. Bullets tore through the windows and the light went out. German hand grenades were thrown into the smashed windows and the floor was covered with men groaning and screaming. The noise, dust and smell of explosives was overwhelming. The survivors manned the door and windows with tommy-guns and Sergeant Dunn positioned himself on the roof armed with grenades. It seemed obvious that the enemy would follow up their advantage with a quick rush, but instead they made off, perhaps missing the chance of a valuable capture in the person of the CO of the Grenadiers, Colonel Nelson.'[5]

All three sentries were killed in the raid; eleven Grenadiers were injured and only three men escaped unhurt, including Col Nelson. Another attack by the enemy two days later, in much greater strength, caused even more concern and German troops again penetrated right up to the Grenadiers' HQ. Fierce fighting took place before the assault was beaten off, often at very close quarters. 'It is not too easy', remarked Col Nelson later, 'to command a battalion with a telephone in one hand and a revolver in the other.'[6]

The 1st Guards Brigade held this mountain until the end of October, when the guardsmen were brought down from the hills for a short rest. On 3 November they returned to the mountains to relieve 3rd Brigade of the British 1st Division. This time they had moved a little to the east to hold features above the Senio valley with even longer supply lines. Mules were known to drop dead with fatigue during their trek up to the front.

Back across on 6th Armoured Division's front, the need for more infantry to hold the positions won by the Americans took priority. The

61st Brigade was ordered on 15 October to take its three battalions of riflemen across to the west of the Guards Brigade to relieve the Irish Brigade of 78th Division, who had been helping Gen Clark's offensive. The brigade, together with the artillery of 12th RHA, moved into the line next to the Americans and endured the same privations and punishment as the Guards a few miles away to the east. The brigade held the line high in the mountains through the same bad weather and enemy harassment throughout the deteriorating autumn months, and survived on the wild terrain through a combination of courage and expertise.

The question of how to replace 61st Brigade's role as infantry in the division was solved by dismounting the tank men of 26th Armoured Brigade. Some of these tankers were ordered up into the hills as foot-soldiers, while a squadron from each regiment was ordered to use its 75mm tank guns as artillery.

Lt Col Val ffrench Blake of 17th/21st Lancers – wounded at Two Tree Hill in Tunisia but now back with his regiment in command – later recalled receiving this order:

> I doubt whether a more extraordinary order than this has ever been carried out by a cavalry regiment but, the orders having been received at 11.30 a.m., by 3 p.m. that afternoon the men of B Squadron were toiling up the mountain track with borrowed rifles; blankets and rations followed by mule, and I ferried up the Doctor and George Brooks, B Squadron's leader, in my jeep, covered in a pile of sooty cooking pots. The Doctor cooked a hot meal which was eaten after B Squadron's four hour climb and they were then guided two miles along the ridge to the 7th RB's positions. Meanwhile C Squadron took over the artillery tasks from 12th RHA, starting next morning to register targets with the aid of an officer from 57th Field Battery. Thirty targets were registered, and could be engaged without undue delay, in spite of the lack of any instrument for paralleling the guns rapidly.[7]

Their period as infantry lasted for about a week, for by the end of October the positions around Highway 67 were taken over by the Polish II Corps. The town of Forli on the other side of the mountain was on the point of being taken by Eighth Army, now commanded by Lt Gen McCreery. Its great offensive had penetrated the Gothic Line near the coast and was advancing along the edge of the plain beneath the mountains towards Bologna. This led to many of the enemy retiring from the hills and moving on to the plain to block Highway 9 in front of Bologna. Eighth Army's offensive eventually run out of steam before Imola amid the myriad watercourses, drainage canals and small rivers that crossed the flat terrain. It had become the victim of deteriorating weather, a lack of infantry, and increased enemy resistance. The front line now ran along the valley of the River Senio and then up over the Apennines in front of the US Fifth Army's mountain positions.

The three armoured regiments of 26th Armoured Brigade were ordered to perform a variety of tasks and were involved in several moves and countermoves across the region. The 17th/21st Lancers were withdrawn in early November and re-equipped with Staghound armoured cars for a special mission, which turned out to be an invasion of Yugoslavia. This operation was eventually cancelled on 5 December. A little later, the Lancers were told that they were going to Greece; this, too, was cancelled on 7 January, only three days before the regiment was due to embark. On 20 January, 17th/21st Lancers were sent back into the mountains as infantry.

The 16th/5th Lancers came out of the line just after 17th/21st Lancers and spent a period at Antella near Florence. Here the regiment was ordered to provide various parties of troops for other duties: fifty tank men spent time breaking stones and improving roads, while a party of seventy were used as stretcher-bearers for 78th Division. The remainder were involved in training and instructing tank crews on new weapons and engines. On 27 November the regiment moved to near Ancona on the eastern coast prior to a rumoured move to Greece. This in turn was cancelled and 16th/5th Lancers returned to the front line as infantry early in January 1945.

The 2nd Lothians and Border Horse were also temporarily dismounted and became infantry a little sooner than the other two armoured regiments of 26th Brigade when, on 25 November, they went into the line to relieve 56th Reconnaissance Regiment of 78th Division on the north side of the Santerno valley. The regiment remained holding the line, rotating the squadrons in the mountains in turn, until 25 January 1945 when it was moved to Bagno a Ripoli for a rest.

During this same period, the other armoured unit of the division, the Derbyshire Yeomanry, spent the time based in a village outside Florence. While there it had to provide a certain number of men as stretcher-bearers for the Guards Brigade holding the winter line in the hills, while others were employed as Military Police, controlling traffic on the tortuous mountain roads.

While these tank crews were in the line, they did not carry out any attacks, nor did they have to get involved in fighting patrols. It would have been a waste of well-trained men to use them in that way. They were there to hold the line defensively and to deter the enemy from making attacks. The real infantry, however, the men of the Guards and 61st Brigades, were required to tackle the enemy.

The 61st Brigade moved into the mountains overlooking the Santerno valley, to the left of 1st Guards Brigade on Monte Battaglia, in mid-October. The three rifle battalions each held part of the line above Castel del Rio. The town provided the administrative areas for both 78th and 6th Armoured Divisions and the rear areas for the battalions up at the sharp end. Castel del Rio became a favourite target for enemy gunners and was shelled sporadically throughout the winter. Only the enemy's shortage of ammunition saved it from being entirely obliterated. Each rifle company spent fourteen days up in the mountains and seven days at the battalion base. Life in the line for the troops settled down into something of a routine and became a round of monotonously holding exposed positions in often dreadful weather, interspersed with the nerve-tingling patrols across barren mountainside in the dark.

During this period there was a reorganisation in Allied command. Gen Alexander became Supreme Commander Mediterranean and was replaced as head of Fifteenth Army Group by Mark Clark. Lt Gen Lucien Truscott took over the US Fifth Army, and XIII Corps reverted to Eighth Army under its new commander, Lt Gen McCreery. Both sides knew that the offensive through the mountains had stalled completely and the Allies were expected to wait out the winter and prepare for the inevitable spring offensive. It therefore came as something of a shock to 61st and 1st Guards Brigades when they were ordered to attack and capture the town of Tossignano and Monte Penzola respectively in early December.

Eighth Army was going to launch one last attack to get across the Senio and Santerno rivers, while the US Fifth Army attacked simultaneously towards the west of Bologna. In concert with these attacks, 6th Armoured and 78th Divisions would attack down the Santerno valley towards Imola. The capture of Monte Penzola and Tossignano were 6th Armoured Division's contribution to this offensive. All of the attacks by both of the armies failed to gain any of the necessary objectives.

The Guards' attack on Monte Penzola was to help 61st Brigade capture the town of Tossignano. The mountain peak overlooked the Rifle Brigade's approach to the town, so the Coldstream was ordered to take Penzola first. The attack on the hill made use of the fact that the Guards Brigade already overlooked its rear slope from a ridge to the west. The plan, therefore, was for two flanking attacks to occupy the defenders, while S Company assaulted the summit from the rear. The Coldstream battalion history commented on the amount of preparation and thought that had been put in before the operation: 'The attack might have been a tactics problem at Sandhurst. It was small, it was isolated, there was time to prepare it, intelligence was complete and there were plenty of high-ranking officers to tell you if the plan was a good one.'[8]

The plan was an excellent one. The division's artillery laid down a good shoot; the flanking attacks occupied the enemy as intended and the assaulting company made the strenuous climb to the summit to attack the

German defenders in a determined final charge. The enemy was taken in the rear before they knew what had happened. A German counterattack was put in later to regain the mountain, most probably out of habit, but this was beaten off quite comfortably. The 61st Brigade's attack on Tossignano was not so successful.

The town of Tossignano lies on top of a hill dominating the Santerno valley. It was defended by a battalion of troops from the German 334th Division, thought by some to be the best division in Italy, next to the parachute divisions. The plan of attack was for 2nd Rifle Brigade, now down to just three rifle companies, to assault both of the narrow entrances that led into the town from the centre and the right simultaneously. Just prior to that, 7th Rifle Brigade would put in a diversionary attack from the left in order to draw the enemy's attention that way.

The assault began during the night of 12/13 December with a silent advance by 7th Rifle Brigade to occupy two hamlets to the west of the town. Then a company was sent directly forward towards Tossignano. As was expected, the Germans picked up these moves and thought that an attack was coming in on their right. They began to shell 7th Rifle Brigade with intense fire. While this was happening 2nd Rifle Brigade formed up and assaulted the town with two companies at 0200 hr behind a terrific barrage. The enemy replied in kind and many casualties resulted from this shellfire. By 0330, entry into the town had been gained by C Company in the centre, but the right-hand entrance was still under enemy machine-gun fire and unable to be penetrated by B Company. Some platoons from this company were switched from the right to the centre entrance and by dawn there were five platoons from the two companies sweeping through the town.

Once the riflemen had reached the middle of Tossignano, events took a turn for the worse. Mortar fire fell on the attackers and both company commanders were wounded. Communications with the guns in the rear and between companies became difficult because of the closeness of the buildings and the common problem of batteries going flat. Then the enemy counterattacked in some force and began pushing the riflemen down through the narrow streets towards the entrance. The men of 2nd Rifle Brigade were driven back and eventually confined in just a few houses on the edge of the town. Here they remained, fighting off a number of attacks throughout the day and into the night. Any attempt to reinforce them in daylight was beaten away by enemy fire. No artillery support could be given as the houses held by the surrounded riflemen could not be identified. All that the gunners could do was to shell the enemy gun positions behind Tossignano.

During the night, 10th Rifle Brigade were ordered forward and its D Company sent on ahead to try to gain access to the town and relieve

2nd Rifle Brigade. The approach march by D Company was long and difficult and it was almost dawn before it arrived on Point 222, a small hillock a few hundred yards short of the town. Here they found that the enemy held both the entrances, and the two companies of 2nd Rifle Brigade were cut off inside. Maj James Wilson commanded D Company during the attack and decided to send 14 Platoon under Lt John Goddard forward into the town to discover where 2nd Rifle Brigade's men were holding out, so that the town could be shelled without endangering them. The platoon successfully crossed the open ground and fought its way inside, losing just three men on the way. The riflemen's entry was followed by prolonged bouts of small-arms fire, then silence. A short while later, Point 222 was plastered by enemy mortar fire and swept by machine guns. Maj Wilson later described the intensity of this fire: 'Any movement brought down a hail of fire and our own gunners could not operate for fear of hitting 14 Platoon, who had gone into town not far from where the Spandaus were firing. "Pinned to the ground" is a military expression often used in training to describe this sort of situation; it was the only time in the war when I found myself so placed and I was too frightened to be frustrated by my impotence.'[9]

By now it was fully light. 'Suddenly the deadlock broke,' wrote Maj Wilson later. 'First there was an outbreak of firing from the houses in Tossignano nearest to us at Point 222. Next came the crash of what must have been bazookas fired at the buildings, two of which were soon afterwards observed to be in flames. Down the hill towards us burst about ten riflemen, all from 2 RB, while two others, one armed with a Bren, the other with a sub-machine gun, did their best from improvised fire positions in the rocks to cover the withdrawal. When the main party of the riflemen escaping from the town reached the open ground, the Spandaus opened up; three or four riflemen fell, while the rest found what shelter they could among the rocks at the bottom of the slope. Sergeant Watson put down some smoke with the scout section 2 inch mortar, under cover of which Lance Corporal Dyer, leader of the dash for freedom, made his way over the open ground and reached the relative safety of Point 222.'[10]

Cpl Dyer brought back news that all of 2nd Rifle Brigade's riflemen in the town had been killed or captured. His party were the only ones able to make the break; 14 Platoon had also succumbed to the enemy. It was now clear that the attack on Tossignano had failed. Preparations were made for a renewed assault, but these were later cancelled and eventually abandoned. Higher command now realised that the enemy's loss of Tossignano would result in his having to realign a long length of his front along the Santerno valley and it was obvious that he would put up a strong defence to prevent this happening. It was just not worth the effort at this stage in the campaign.

For 61st Brigade, the losses suffered in the Tossignano operation could not be easily restored. These totalled 13 officers and 207 riflemen, of which 2nd Rifle Brigade lost 7 officers and 147 other ranks. They came at a bleak period for the brigade and for 2nd Rifle Brigade in particular, for not all losses in Italy were being replaced. The strength of all units everywhere in the theatre was gradually being diluted through manpower shortages.

Snow began to fall in the mountains on 10 November, and by 22 December onwards it remained lying on the ground until the first thaw of spring. The 6th Armoured Division was told to remain in its present area and hold the line through the worst of these winter months. The only British mobile division in Italy was now as static as a division could be.

Chapter Twelve

THE FINAL BATTLE

At the end of February 1945, 6th Armoured Division came down from the mountains, leaving its now quiet positions for scratch groups of Italian infantry to hold. Maj Gen Murray brought his division on to the plain near the sea to rest and replenish its strength before the last great offensive in Italy. The armoured regiments were re-equipped with the latest tanks, receiving the improved 76mm Shermans. Each squadron was also re-equipped with a troop of the new Sherman Firefly, with its very potent 17-pounder gun able to engage even the heaviest German armour on equal terms, and the HQ Squadron was provided with two 105mm-gun tanks. The division then entered a period of training, concentrating on tank/infantry cooperation and contemplating the tasks that lay ahead, knowing that the end of the war was at last in sight.

The main Allied effort in Europe since 6 June the previous year had been in north-west Europe, with the bulk of all supplies heading for France and not Italy. Alexander's formations had been confined to a backwater. His armies had lost French and American divisions to take part in the landings in southern France, and in the New Year his forces were further weakened by the removal of five more divisions to the fighting on the borders of the Third Reich, including those in the Canadian I Corps. Alexander was then told to contain the German forces in Italy and exploit any weaknesses to prevent them being withdrawn elsewhere. Alexander was not content just to play this holding game and continued to plan for a new offensive to be launched when the weather improved.

Alexander's plan of attack was to assault the River Senio with an enlarged V Corps, now commanded by Lt Gen Keightley, which would then try to get through a gap to the east of Argenta, between the flooded ground beyond the river and the shores of Lake Comacchio. Once through this gap, Keightley's corps would fan out and make for the River Po. At the same time, the Polish II Corps would attack along Highway 9 towards Bologna. The Americans would launch their own operation three days later from out of the mountains, aiming to pass around the west of Bologna and then to swing part of their forces across to the north-east to meet up with the British V Corps before the River Po, thus encircling the

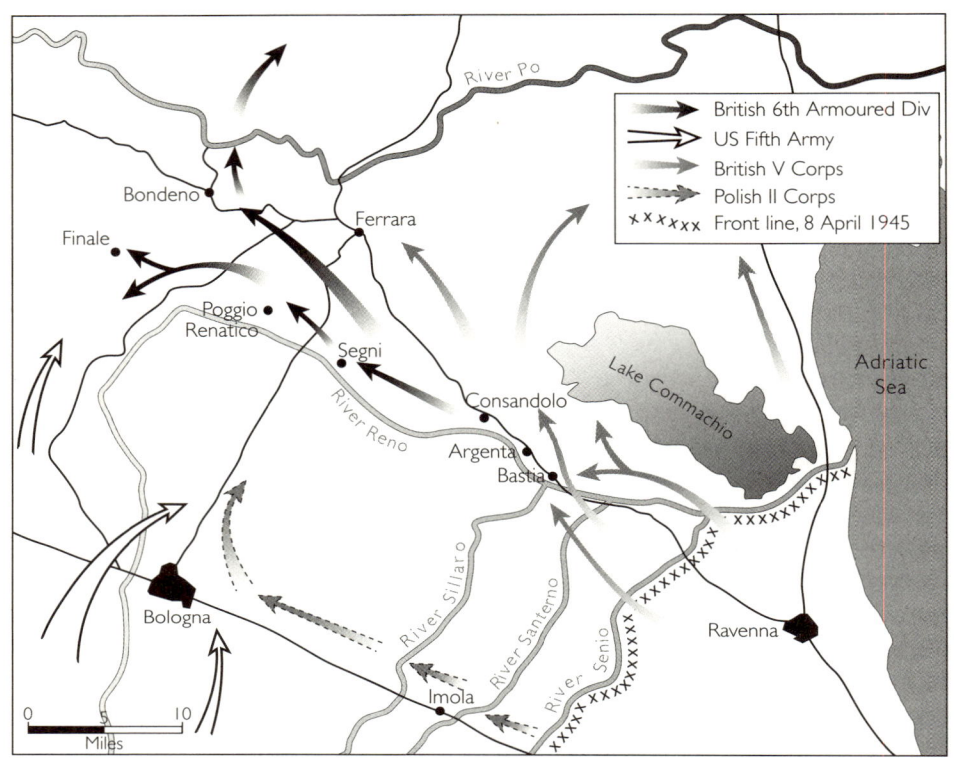

Map 10. The final battle, April 1945

Germans in front of that river. The start of this great offensive was set for 9 April.

The 6th Armoured Division's role in this battle was as Eighth Army's reserve. Gen McCreery had resolved to hold the division under his command until he decided on which axis it should be launched. The division would not be part of the original attack, for the first phase of the battle would be the demanding one of assaulting a German line that had been fortified over the previous five months. The first few days of fighting would be by infantry formations as they tried to break into and then through the defences along a series of waterways and rivers that crossed the area. After this phase everything depended on capturing a bridgehead across the River Reno and forcing a way through the heavily fortified Argenta Gap.

While the division reorganised and retrained ready for the battle, more changes were made to its make-up. The shortage of reinforcements coming into the theatre, coupled with the programme of returning home those men who had been abroad for more than a certain period, meant that something had to be done about the depleted state of the battalions. The 2nd Rifle Brigade had not recovered from its losses at Tossignano in

December, which had left it well below its normal complement. As 2nd Rifle Brigade was the senior battalion, it was decided that 10th Rifle Brigade should be disbanded and the two formations amalgamated. So it was that on 20 March 10th Rifle Brigade ceased to be. Changes had also been made that month to 1st Guards Brigade. On 3 March 2nd Coldstream Guards left the brigade to be combined with 3rd Coldstream in 24th Guards Brigade, replacing 5th Grenadiers, who had been disbanded and their guardsmen incorporated into 3rd Grenadiers. The Coldstream were replaced in 1st Guards Brigade by 1st Welch Regiment.

Alexander's last great offensive opened as planned on 9 April with raids by over 1,000 aircraft and the fire of over 1,500 guns. As expected, the fighting endured by the infantry was hard and costly, with both sides knowing that the result of the battle would be an end to the war in Italy. Lt Col Val ffrench Blake was to comment later: 'Every man knew that if he survived this battle he had probably survived the war; the courage and determination of all nationalities was astounding.'[1]

Keightley's V Corps was enlarged to five divisions plus 2nd Parachute Brigade and the six Italian battalions of the Cremona Group for the attack. It successfully breached the Senio line and then crossed the River Reno. By 18 April Argenta had been cleared. The time had come to release the armour and McCreery now transferred Maj Gen Murray's Mailed Fist Division to V Corps to continue the battle.

The 6th Armoured Division's entry into the fighting was not a great cavalry charge to exploit the breakthrough, for its progress up to the front from its holding ground in the rear was slow and very frustrating. The way through Argenta was restricted by great traffic jams and blocked by rubble-strewn streets. Both 56th and 78th Divisions were using the route to supply their own units at the front and the resulting transport problems were a nightmare. By late afternoon on 19 April, however, the Lothians and 16th/5th Lancers were both passing through the leading infantry with their support groups and preparing to move from Consandolo, ten miles north of Argenta.

The division's advance was led by 16th/5th Lancers Group which contained the regiment, supported by 1st King's Royal Rifle Corps, C Battery of 12th RHA, 111th Battery of 72nd Antitank Regiment RA and a troop of 8th Field Squadron RE. Each of the other two armoured regiments was also allocated support troops from these units, making them almost self-supporting for what were expected to be very mobile operations. Overhead were patrols of fighter-bombers on call to the division to attack any enemy strong points that held up the advance.

Capturing bridges over canals and waterways was now the overriding objective of the 26th Armoured Brigade. The advance of Eighth Army was confronted by these obstacles at every turn. The 6th Armoured Division was heading in a north-westerly direction, driving to meet up with the Americans, who were advancing round the west of Bologna. At the same time, the division was fanning out, pushing the enemy back towards the River Po. The Indian 8th Division was performing the same task along Maj Gen Murray's right flank, taking a more direct northwards route to the Po. The 2nd Lothians were also moving down this flank of the armoured division, widening the front of the advance.

The 16th/5th Lancers led the drive towards the Americans. The direction of the attack ran down the eastern bank of the River Reno. Across the initial part of the advance were two waterways, each of which received their water from the river. The first was the Po Morto de Primaro, the second the Fossa Cembalina. At their junctions with the Reno, both had a narrow passage at the foot of the great river's flood bank and both were guarded by a village: the first at Traghetto and the second at Segni. These two villages now became the division's first objectives. Five miles beyond Segni was the last bridge over the Reno at Poggio Renatico, the only escape route for the German forces facing XIII Corps south of the river.

The move did not get off to a flying start, for the ground over which the armour was advancing was very soft, criss-crossed with drainage ditches and scattered with lines of vines and olives, orchards and woodlands. Every so often there were 12-foot dykes to be negotiated, many of which were covered by small groups of the enemy. The infantry at first tried to move forward in their own vehicles, but these were soon abandoned because of the soft ground and the advance was forced to continue with the troops riding on the outside of the tanks. Eventually the infantry had to advance on foot on either side of the Shermans to be able to tackle the myriad of obstacles and the enemy interference that was slowing down the move.

This type of ground was later described by Col Gordon Simpson, CO of the Lothians: 'Some senior officers thought that tanks would run riot on the Plains of Lombardy as on the map they are quite flat. The trouble is that the drainage system, evolved after hundreds of years of cultivation, cuts up the plain into thousands of fields, some of an acre, others of hundreds of acres. Most of the drainage ditches are antitank obstacles. Another problem affecting mobility is that many of the roads are elevated with ditches on either side. No map can show all these potential tank traps.'[2]

On the right, 2nd Lothians Group was advancing on the bridge at San Nicolo Ferrarese across the Po Morto. It reached the village that night after a day of sporadic fighting, which caused the loss of four tanks, but found the bridge blown. On the left, 16th/5th Lancers had more luck in Traghetto, for they captured the village quite easily and by next morning had gained a bridgehead across the Po Morto. About a mile beyond Traghetto the advance ran into an enemy antitank screen and came to a halt. The 17th/21st Lancers were now called forward to take up the advance to Segni.

The country was a chequer-board of hedges, farms and orchards, with confined visibility and plenty of hiding places for the enemy. The tanks rolled forward, shooting up every thicket and building with gunfire and shell. The antitank screen was first softened up by fighter-bombers before the Lancers rushed the positions and continued the advance. Two squadrons were then deployed in the lead, with riflemen of 7th Rifle Brigade advancing alongside them. It was slow going and not without loss. Several villages were met and captured; the enemy was chased out of numerous buildings and a few antitank guns were overrun and taken. By nightfall the leading squadron was two miles short of Fossa Cembalina.

The squadrons were now beginning to tire and it was decided that the Lancers would harbour for the night under the protection of 7th Rifle Brigade and then resume the advance at first light the next morning to capture the crossing over the Fossa Cembalina. At 2300 hr, Lt Col ffrench Blake received orders to continue the advance in the dark. Maj Gen Murray urged his armour not to let up the pressure. Men were roused from their slumber and the advance continued. C Squadron reached the Fossa just before dawn, with C Company of 7th Rifle Brigade in support, and found the bridge blown. The riflemen waded across the wide ditch and captured forty surprised Germans on the other side. With a bridgehead across the Fossa, tanks moved to the left to try to force a way between it and the Reno at Segni.

The gap at Segni was reached and the village taken, but progress on the far side between the Reno on the left and a canal on the right was difficult. This gap was covered by antitank guns and it took several hours for the artillery to locate and destroy them. Other enemy guns fired across the open ground and movement in the open became hazardous. It was mid-afternoon before the advance resumed behind an artillery concentration, fired by most of the guns of the division. Fighter-bombers tackled the enemy guns emplaced further forward and also dispersed several German tanks that were advancing on to the battleground. At 1600 hr the Lancers and the riflemen had got across the open ground and were beginning to flush out scores of enemy infantry. B Squadron then took the lead and got back onto the road towards Poggio, urged on by its CO. The squadron was told to speed up and seize the next village of Gallo.

Gallo was reached and taken at 1730 hr. On the far side of the village a bridge over the canal was found intact and not primed for demolition. The news was passed back to brigade and the message came back: 'Push on to Poggio with all speed!' A fantastic opportunity had opened up for the division, as related by the commander of 17th/21st Lancers, Lt Col ffrench Blake:

This was the chance of a lifetime. Leaving B Squadron to guard the important bridge at Gallo, I brought up C Squadron from reserve and ordered them to go for Poggio Renatico at full speed down the road. The significance of Poggio was that it contained the only bridge over the Reno for the main road from Bologna to Ferrara and the Po crossings – the chief escape route for all the Germans retreating in front of US Fifth Army. Maj James Maxwell drove his leading troops on at a fine gallop, followed by RHQ and A Squadron. Machine-gun tracer streamed into farms and woods beside the road; many burst into flames, as they contained hidden stores of petrol. As we approached Poggio, surrounded by a mile of open fields, antitank fire began to come in from the town, which was on our left. The enemy fire came from an antiaircraft battery of four 88mm guns, but, unused to the antitank role, they did not score a single hit.[3]

C Squadron got into Poggio but was unable to clear the town because of antitank fire. A flanking movement around the houses by one of its troops also failed, losing its leading tank to an enemy infantryman armed with a bazooka. On the edge of town, RHQ, A Squadron and 7th Rifle Brigade were queued up along the road waiting for a breakthrough. None came and the force withdrew outside Poggio for the night.

A plan was made to capture the town and, at 0400 hr, 7th Rifle Brigade attacked a line of houses on the edge of Poggio. Tanks were then moved into this area to cover the open plain and at first light the riflemen began clearing the houses, supported by tanks as required. Throughout the day fighting went on, with the enemy shelling each sector as it was captured. Confused fighting broke out in several areas when more Germans came through Poggio, retreating over the bridge across the Reno. By nightfall the town had been taken and a further advance was considered by the Lancers, but was postponed until the next day.

Over to the right, 16th/5th Lancers had also been advancing across more open ground and had reached Mirabello, slightly ahead of the positions of 17th/21st Lancers. To their right, 2nd Lothians had just failed to capture the bridge at Bondeno after a dramatic entry into the town. Their leading tanks skirmished with two Tiger tanks and rushed the bridge, only to be followed over by the German tanks and destroyed along with the bridge. The Guards Brigade were also keeping pace with the advance and the Welch Regiment breached the German line to the north of 17th/21st Lancers in order to protect the armoured regiment's flank.

The next morning 7th Rifle Brigade was ordered to consolidate its hold on Poggio and to capture the bridge over the Reno. This it did just before first light and actually clashed with a patrol from the New Zealand Division which was advancing along the far bank of the river. The 17th/21st Lancers moved on westwards to San Agostino where it shot up columns of German transport moving northwards towards the River Po. B Squadron then continued the advance. At Pilastrello, the leading Shermans saw tanks coming up the road from the south and a 17-pounder shot was fired at them. Luckily it missed, for the tanks were Americans. The British Eighth and US Fifth Armies had finally linked up and the shot from the 17-pounder Firefly was the last to be fired by 17th/21st Lancers in the war.

A little further north, 16th/5th Lancers reached the appropriately named town of Finale, closing the German escape route and finishing their fighting war. The 2nd Lothians had continued moving northwards and had actually reached the banks of the River Po, the first tanks of Eighth Army to do so. Here they were told to halt and contented themselves with harassing the escaping enemy trying to flee across the river by any means possible.

Although this was the end of the battle for 26th Armoured Brigade, the rest of the division had not yet done with the enemy. The Guards Brigade reached the River Po on 24 April and, after a brief reconnaissance, 3rd Grenadiers made a rapid crossing during the night in amphibious craft, meeting only light opposition. Early the next morning the Welsh Guards and 1st Welch followed them over, then set off for the next water line, the River Adige, keeping up the pressure to prevent the enemy using the watercourse as a new defence line. Further upstream the New Zealand Division had made a simultaneous crossing of the Po and now they too dashed for the Adige.

Organised resistance south of the Po had virtually ceased by 25 April; most of the German tanks, guns and heavy equipment were left abandoned as the defeated Tenth Army retreated across the Po in congested ferries. The enemy had failed to get enough troops across the river to organise a defence along its banks or, indeed, along any other line during their retreat back towards the Alps. The New Zealanders beat the Guards Brigade to the River Adige and pinched it out of the battle, ending its participation in the fighting.

The remaining brigade of 6th Armoured Division, 61st Brigade, continued with the pursuit. The 2nd Rifle Brigade advanced to protect the right flank of the New Zealanders and immediately ran into trouble at Cavanazza just before the Adige. Several enemy counterattacks tried to retake the village, but all were beaten off. The position was reinforced by the arrival of 1st Welch and the enemy quickly moved away, back across the Adige. Then things began to speed up; 29 April was a day of fast motoring and surrendering Germans. Monselice was taken without respite and the tired riflemen pressed on towards Padua. Then there was a brief pause when an order arrived, halting the advance. The whole brigade now rested, but was suddenly roused at 0200 hr on 1 May and told to resume the chase. Padua was reached, then Trevisio. The German collapse was total; 2nd Rifle Brigade was offered the surrender of the whole of the German 65th Infantry Division. The next day, Col Fyffe went blindfolded behind German lines and negotiated the surrender of a further 6,000 of the enemy, including the whole of 715th Division's artillery. By then a surrender document had been signed on behalf of Gen von Vietinghoff, now Commander in Chief (Italy), stating that hostilities would cease in Italy on 2 May.

Prisoners were now beginning to appear in ever-greater numbers, embarrassing the Rifle Brigade and slowing down the advance. Italian partisans were killing any Germans they could find and enemy soldiers were eager to give themselves up to the riflemen. It was now important that British troops arrived in Austria to prevent the breakdown of law and order between the various factions that were roaming the area where Italy met Austria and Yugoslavia. On 4 May, 2nd Rifle Brigade was ordered to make for the Austrian border at full speed. Force was not to be used except in self-defence, but the road into the country was to be opened as soon as possible. The leading company, B Company, raced on for the border, finding its way around blown bridges, negotiating its way through partisan roadblocks and accepting the surrender of the German LXXXVII Corps on the way. On 8 May the rest of the battalion came up to join B Company and crossed over into Austria.

Also trying to find a way to the Austrian border was 7th Rifle Brigade. It followed behind Lt Gen Freyberg's New Zealand Division until Udine, where the New Zealand Division swung to the east towards Trieste to prevent Tito's partisans seizing the city. The 7th Rifle Brigade encountered some German resistance backed by tanks on 1 May, just before the ceasefire was made official. A few casualties were suffered, including one man killed, but one of the Rifle Brigade's antitank guns destroyed an enemy tank, the last kill of the war. A few miles further on 7th RB met with a group of 20,000 Croatian Chetniks and then had to prevent Marshal Tito's Serbian forces getting at them by blocking the roads and pushing the German sympathisers south towards Palmanova. The battalion then moved back to Tarvisio and crossed over with the rest of the brigade into Austria.

On 8 May the war in Europe against the Third Reich came to an end. The whole of 6th Armoured Division moved into Austria and became a force of occupation. Life then became very complicated. At a moment when all troops should have been celebrating the fruits of victory and being thankful for having survived years of battle, the division was plunged into political and emotional turmoil by having to deal with a devil's brew of humanity that even the great Solomon would have been at pains to sort out. Lt Col ffrench Blake, commander of 17th/21st Lancers, later summed up the problems:

The political situation was very complicated. The Germans were surrendering very quietly and efficiently; a large force of nearly ten thousand Croats under a German commander was only willing to surrender if the British would undertake not to hand the troops back to the Tito Government; the two Cossack divisions which had been fighting for the Germans were unwilling to return to Russia. There were also parties of Serbs and Chetniks running loose; Tito's troops were crossing the frontier, harassing Austrian property, and interfering in the process of surrender. The countryside was full of parties of armed men – violently opposed politically, short of food, and trying to get into neutral territory, where they would be under the protection of the Allies. Among them were also war criminals, young SS troops whose fanaticism might still be dangerous, spies, refugees, collaborators, communist partisans, and the whole contents of a world turned upside down. Everywhere, there could be found abandoned vehicles, guns and ammunition.[4]

Not surprisingly it took a great deal of tact, and some force, to sort out these problems, many of which ended in tragedy for the unfortunates who were sent back to their home countries, where they faced execution or persecution. Gradually, very gradually, the situation eased and the men of the Mailed Fist Division were at last able to experience the first summer of peace for six years.

One by one the men who had served abroad longest were sent home and each unit began to lose its wartime identity. It was decreed that 6th Armoured Division was to be manned only by Regular Army units, so the Territorial battalions had to leave. In mid-September the division moved back into Italy and much of its force was sent elsewhere or disbanded to be replaced by entirely new units. The wartime composition of 6th Armoured Division was changed forever.

Appendix

ORDER OF BATTLE
6TH ARMOURED DIVISION

GENERAL OFFICERS COMMANDING

Maj Gen John Crocker (27 September 1940–29 October 1941)
Maj Gen C.H. Gairdner (29 October 1941–19 May 1942)
Maj Gen Charles Keightley (19 May 1942–19 December 1943)
Maj Gen Vivian Evelegh (19 December 1943–24 July 1944)
Maj Gen Gerald Templer (24 July 1944–21 August 1944)
Maj Gen Horatius Murray (from 21 August 1944)

20TH ARMOURED BRIGADE
(16 October 1940–23 April 1942; disbanded)

1st Royal Gloucestershire Hussars
1st Northamptonshire Yeomanry
2nd Northamptonshire Yeomanry
10th Battalion, The King's Royal Rifle Corps
26th Armoured Brigade
16th/5th Lancers
17th/21st Lancers
2nd Lothians and Border Horse Yeomanry
10th Battalion, The Rifle Brigade (15 January 1941–29 May 1944)

6TH SUPPORT GROUP
(2 November 1940–31 MaY 1942; disbanded)

12th (Honourable Artillery Company) Royal Horse Artillery
51st Light Antiaircraft Regiment, RA
72nd Antitank Regiment, RA
162nd Regiment, RAC

38TH (IRISH) INFANTRY BRIGADE
(9 June 1942–16 February 1943)

2nd Battalion, The London Irish Rifles
1st Battalion, The Royal Irish Fusiliers
6th Battalion, The Royal Inniskilling Fusiliers

1ST GUARDS INFANTRY BRIGADE
(From 24 March 1943)

3rd Battalion, The Grenadier Guards
2nd Battalion, The Coldstream Guards (to 3 March 1945)
3rd Battalion, The Welsh Guards (from 1 March 1943)
1st Battalion, The Welch Regiment (from 9 March 1945)

61ST INFANTRY BRIGADE
(From 29 May 1944)

1st Battalion, The King's Royal Rifle Corps (from 8 March 1945)
2nd Battalion, The Rifle Brigade
7th Battalion, The Rifle Brigade
10th Battalion, The Rifle Brigade (30 May 1944–20 March 1945)

DIVISIONAL TROOPS

1st Derbyshire Yeomanry
12th (Honorable Artillery Company) Royal Horse Artillery (from 1 June 1942)
51st Light Antiaircraft Regiment, RA (from 1 June 1942)
72nd Antitank Regiment, RA (from 1 June 1942)
152nd (Ayrshire Yeomanry) Field Regiment, RA (from 15 June 1942)
5th Field Squadron, RE (19 November 1940–6 March 1944)
8th Field Squadron, RE
625th Field Squadron, RE (from 7 March 1944)
144th Field Park Squadron, RE
8th Bridging Troop, RE (from 25 December 1943)

Notes

CHAPTER ONE

1 H.F. Joslen, *Orders of Battle Second World War 1939–45*, HMSO, 1960. The 79th Armoured Division was an armoured division in name only: it never fought as a division in all of its existence, but was formed to provide a collection of specialised armoured weapons and equipment for specific tasks in support of the infantry.
2 James Wilson, *Unusual Undertakings*, Barnsley, Pen & Sword, 2002, p. 23.
3 Richard Doherty, *Clear the Way! A History of the 38th (Irish) Brigade, 1941–1947*, Dublin, Irish Academic Press, 1993, p. 6.
4 W. Steel-Brownlie, *The Proud Trooper: The History of the Ayrshire (Earl of Carrick's Own) Yeomanry*, London, Collins, 1964, p. 338.
5 Papers of Lt Col Val ffrench Blake and interview with the author.
6 Interview with the author.
7 D.G. Antonio, *Driver Advance: Being a Short History of the 2nd Lothians and Border Horse*, Edinburgh, Lothians and Border Horse Regimental Association, 1947, p. 32.
8 National Archives, WO 175/210.

CHAPTER TWO

1 Papers of Lt Col Val ffrench Blake and interview with the author.
2 Anon., *1st Derbyshire Yeomanry Scrapbook 1939–1947*, undated, p. 39.
3 Papers of Lt Col Val ffrench Blake and interview with the author.
4 James Colquhoun, *Action Front! A History of 'C' Battery in War and Peace*, Barnsley, Leo Cooper, 1992, p. 35.
5 Papers of Lt Col Val ffrench Blake and interview with the author.
6 Wilson, *Unusual Undertakings*, p. 33.
7 R.L.V. ffrench Blake, *A History of the 17th/21st Lancers 1922–1959*, London, Macmillan, 1962, p. 92.
8 *Blackwood's Magazine*, July 1943.
9 Wilson, *Unusual Undertakings*, p. 33.
10 ffrench Blake, *History of the 17th/21st Lancers*, p. 93.
11 Rick Atkinson, *An Army at Dawn*, London, Little, Brown, 2003, p. 189.
12 *Ibid.*, p. 191.
13 *Ibid.*, p. 203.
14 ffrench Blake, *History of the 17th/21st Lancers*, p. 99.
15 Wilson, *Unusual Undertakings*, p. 36.
16 Anon., *1st Derbyshire Yeomanry*, p. 42.

17 Ken Ford, *Battleaxe Division: From Africa to Italy with the 78th Division 1942–1945*, Stroud, Sutton Publishing, 1999, p. 31.
18 *Ibid.*, p. 33.

CHAPTER THREE

1 Antonio, *Driver Advance*, p. 11.
2 John Horsfall, *The Wild Geese are Flighting*, Kineton, The Roundwood Press, 1976, p. 26.
3 *Ibid.*, p. 28.
4 *Ibid.*, p. 28.
5 *Ibid.*, p. 29.
6 Papers of Lt Col Val ffrench Blake and interview with the author.
7 *Ibid.*
8 K.A.N. Anderson, 'Operations in North West Africa, 8 November 1942 to 13 May 1943', *London Gazette*, 1946.
9 The unfortunate GenLt Fischer was killed towards the end of the month, along with his Chief of Staff, when his command vehicle ran over an Italian mine. The 10th Panzer Division's new Chief of Staff was *Oberst* Count Claus von Stauffenberg, who was later involved in the bomb plot to kill Hitler on 20 July 1944. Von Stauffenberg actually placed the bomb alongside the Führer, but the resulting explosion failed to kill him.
10 The 5th Parachute Regiment was commanded by *Oberstleutnant* Walter Koch, hero of the daring capture of the Belgian Fort at Eben Emael in 1940. Then a *hauptmann*, Koch had led a Stürm battalion of 5th Parachute Regiment in an assault on the massive fortification which guarded the Albert Canal. Koch and his men landed on top of the fortress from gliders and proceeded to blow each of the giant steel cupolas holding the fort's main armament from the outside, using newly designed hollow explosive charges. The Belgian garrison holed up inside were powerless to stop them and the whole structure, the most powerful fort in the world, was rendered impotent within a few hours. It was perhaps the greatest *coup de main* of the war. Koch then took command of the regiment and led them through the campaigns in France and Crete. He and his regiment were some of the first troops to be rushed to Tunisia after the Torch landings, arriving in the capital just three days after the British had landed in Algiers. It was Koch and his paratroopers who played a large part in frustrating the British First Army's move on Tunis. He was a formidable opponent to set before 6th Armoured Division.
11 Wilson, *Unusual Undertakings*, p. 41.
12 Antonio, *Driver Advance*, p. 15.
13 Papers of Allan Waterston and interview with the author.
14 *Ibid.*
15 Frank Beckett, *Prepare to Move: With the 6th Armoured Division in Africa and Sicily*, Grimsby, Frank Beckett, 1994, p. 54.

NOTES

16 Quoted in Colquhoun, *Action Front*, p. 50.
17 Horsfall, *The Wild Geese*, p. 53.
18 Papers of Col Gordon Simpson and correspondence with the author.
19 Papers of Allan Waterston and interview with the author.
20 Doherty, *Clear the Way!*, p. 19.
21 Anon., *The London Irish at War*, London Irish Rifles Old Comrades' Association, undated, p. 53.
22 Quoted in Doherty, *Clear the Way!*, p. 37.
23 Anon., *The Royal Artillery Commemoration Book 1939–1945*, London, Bell & Sons, 1950, p. 261.

CHAPTER FOUR

1 Antonio, *Driver Advance*, p. 15.
2 Atkinson, *An Army at Dawn*, p. 370.
3 George Turnball, correspondence with the author and papers of the Lothians and Border Horse.
4 Erwin Rommel, *The Rommel Papers*, ed. B.H. Liddell Hart, London, Collins, 1955, p. 404.
5 Papers of the Lothians and Border Horse.
6 *Ibid.*
7 *Ibid.*
8 Rommel, *The Rommel Papers*, p. 405.
9 George Turnball, correspondence with the author.
10 National Archives, CAB 44/115.
11 In fact von Arnim did not agree with Rommel's attack and did little in the north to assist the field marshal in his intentions to drive on Le Kef.
12 Antonio, *Driver Advance*, p. 20.
13 Rommel, *The Rommel Papers*, p. 405.
14 Papers of Allan Waterston and interview with the author.
15 ffrench Blake, *History of the 17th/21st Lancers*, p. 119.
16 Antonio, *Driver Advance*, p. 21.
17 *Ibid.*
18 Papers of Allan Waterston and interview with the author.
19 Rommel, *The Rommel Papers*, p. 406.
20 Papers of the Lothians and Border Horse.
21 National Archives, CAB 44/115.
22 Papers of the Lothians and Border Horse.
23 *Ibid.*
24 Antonio, *Driver Advance*, p. 22.
25 Papers of Allan Waterston and interview with the author.
26 Papers of the Lothians and Border Horse.
27 Antonio, *Driver Advance*, p. 23.
28 Papers of the Lothians and Border Horse.

29 R.P. Pakenham-Walsh, *History of the Corps of Royal Engineers*, Chatham, Institute of Royal Engineers, 1958, vol. VIII, p. 402.

CHAPTER FIVE

1 Antonio, *Driver Advance*, p. 25.
2 ffrench Blake, *History of the 17th/21st Lancers*, p. 126.
3 Wilson, *Unusual Undertakings*, p. 45.
4 George S. Patton, *The Patton Papers 1940–1945*, ed. Martin Blumenson, Boston, Houghton Mifflin, 1974, p. 211.
5 N. Nicholson and P. Forbes, *The Grenadier Guards in the War of 1939–1945*, Aldershot, Gale and Polden, 1949, vol. II, p. 286.
6 Atkinson, *An Army at Dawn*, p. 470.
7 G.P.B. Roberts, *From the Desert to the Baltic*, London, William Kimber, 1987, p. 138.
8 *Ibid.*, p. 139.
9 ffrench Blake, *History of the 17th/21st Lancers*, p. 133.
10 *Ibid.*
11 C.N. Barclay, *History of the 16th/5th Queen's Royal Lancers 1925–1961*, Aldershot, Gale and Polden, 1963, p. 88.
12 Antonio, *Driver Advance*, p. 27.
13 *Ibid.*
14 John D'Arcy-Dawson, *Tunisian Battle*, London, Macdonald, 1943, p. 197.
15 Nicholson and Forbes, *The Grenadier Guards*, p. 124.
16 Steel-Brownlie, *The Proud Trooper*, p. 484.
17 Barclay, *History of the 16th/5th Lancers*, p. 89.
18 R.F. Johnson, *Regimental Fire! The Honourable Artillery Company in World War II 1939–1945*, London, HAC Regimental Committee, 1958, p. 213.
19 Barclay, *History of the 16th/5th Lancers*, p. 90.
20 ffrench Blake, *History of the 17th/21st Lancers*, p. 136.
21 Barclay, *History of the 16th/5th Lancers*, p. 91.
22 *Ibid.*
23 Patton, *The Patton Papers*, p. 218.

CHAPTER SIX

1 Steel-Brownlie, *The Proud Trooper*, p. 487.
2 Roberts, *From the Desert to the Baltic*, p. 144.
3 Steel-Brownlie, *The Proud Trooper*, p. 488.
4 *Ibid.*, p. 490.
5 *Ibid.*, p. 491.
6 *Ibid.,* p. 493.
7 This type of weapon was handheld and designed to be used at close quarters. Its effective range was limited, about 100 yards, so the brave infantryman using it had to get very close to an enemy tank to knock it out. The PIAT fired a 3lb bomb with a hollow charge, capable of penetrating 100mm of armour.

8 Brian Horrocks, *A Full Life*, London, Collins, 1960, p. 169.
9 C.J.C. Molony, *The Mediterranean and Middle East*, HMSO, 1973, vol. V, p. 451.
10 *Ibid.*
11 *Ibid.*
12 Anon., *1st Derbyshire Yeomanry*, p. 39.
13 Wilson, *Unusual Undertakings*, p. 50.
14 Steel-Brownlie, *The Proud Trooper*, p. 499.
15 Horrocks, *A Full Life*, p. 171.
16 L.F. Ellis, *Welsh Guards at War*, Aldershot, Gale and Polden, 1946, p. 127.
17 Papers of Allan Waterston and interview with the author.
18 *Ibid.*
19 *Ibid.*
20 *Ibid.*
21 Nicholson and Forbes, *The Grenadier Guards*, p. 338.
22 Wilson, *Unusual Undertakings*, p. 51.
23 Nicholson and Forbes, *The Grenadier Guards*, p. 340.
24 Anon., *1st Derbyshire Yeomanry*, p. 76.
25 *Ibid.*, p. 78.
26 Roberts, *From the Desert to the Baltic*, p. 147.
27 Kenneth Macksey, *Crucible of Power: The Fight for Tunisia 1942–1943*, London, Hutchinson, 1969, p. 301.

CHAPTER SEVEN

1 Ellis, *Welsh Guards at War*, p. 138.
2 *Ibid.*, p. 143.
3 National Archives, WO 170/1347.

CHAPTER EIGHT

1 G.W. Martin, *Cassino to the River Po*, Chesterfield, G.W. Martin, 1999, p. 14.
2 National Archives, WO 170/437.
3 ffrench Blake, *History of the 17th/21st Lancers*, p. 160.
4 Martin, *Cassino to the River Po*, p. 17.
5 Papers of Allan Waterston and interview with the author.
6 National Archives, WO 170/594.
7 Ford, *Battleaxe Division*, p. 162.
8 *Ibid.*, p. 166.
9 ffrench Blake, *History of the 17th/21st Lancers*, p. 165.
10 Ford, *Battleaxe Division*, p. 167.
11 National Archives, WO 170/594.
12 The Germans had earlier changed their name for this line to the von Senger Line, just in case it should prove to be incapable of holding the Allies, for nobody wanted the Führer's name associated with failure.

13 Wilson, *Unusual Undertakings*, p. 64.
14 National Archives, WO 170/437.
15 Ford, *Battleaxe Division*, p. 171.
16 Barclay, *History of the 16th/5th Lancers*, p. 128.
17 Ford, *Battleaxe Division*, p. 173.
18 Steel-Brownlie, *The Proud Trooper*, p. 524.

CHAPTER NINE

1 Papers of Allan Waterston and interview with the author.
2 Wilson, *Unusual Undertakings*, p. 67.
3 Martin, *Cassino to the River Po*, p. 25.
4 Papers of Allan Waterston and interview with the author.
5 *Ibid.*
6 *Ibid.*
7 Ellis, *Welsh Guards at War*, p. 154.
8 Papers of Allan Waterston and interview with the author.
9 Nicholson and Forbes, *The Grenadier Guards*, p. 439.
10 Steel-Brownlie, *The Proud Trooper*, p. 530.
11 Papers of Col Gordon Simpson.
12 *Ibid.*
13 Joslen, *Orders of Battle* p. 297.
14 Wilson, *Unusual Undertakings*, p. 67.
15 Martin, *Cassino to the River Po*, p. 28.

CHAPTER TEN

1 Papers of Col Gordon Simpson.
2 Steel-Brownlie, *The Proud Trooper*, p. 533.
3 Nicholson and Forbes, *The Grenadier Guards*, p. 453.
4 National Archives, WO 170/437.
5 Eric Linklater, *The Campaign in Italy*, HMSO, 1959, p. 320.
6 Papers of Allan Waterston and interview with the author. It is interesting to note that this medieval bridge at Buriano is in fact the one shown in the background of Leonardo da Vinci's great masterpiece, the *Mona Lisa*.

CHAPTER ELEVEN

1 Gregory Blaxland, *Alexander's Generals: The Italian Campaign 1944–1945*, London, William Kimber, 1979, p. 166.
2 Wilson, *Unusual Undertakings*, p. 75.
3 *Ibid.*
4 ffrench Blake, *History of the 17th/21st Lancers*, p. 185.

5 Steel-Brownlie, *The Proud Trooper*, p. 551.
6 Nicholson and Forbes, *The Grenadier Guards*, p. 283.
7 Papers of Lt Col Val ffrench Blake.
8 H. Michael and J. Sparrow, *The Coldstream Guards 1920–1946*, Oxford, Oxford University Press, 1951, p. 243.
9 Wilson, *Unusual Undertakings*, p. 93.
10 *Ibid*.

CHAPTER TWELVE

1 *Purnell's History of the Second World War*, ed. Barrie Pitt, London, 1966, vol. 6, p. 2420.
2 Papers of Col Gordon Simpson.
3 Papers of Lt Col Val ffrench Blake.
4 ffrench Blake, *History of the 17th/21st Lancers*, p. 227.

Bibliography

Anon. *1st Derbyshire Yeomanry Scrapbook 1939–1947*, undated

Anon. *The London Irish at War*, London Irish Rifles Old Comrades' Association, undated

Anon. *The Royal Artillery Commemoration Book 1939–1945*, London, Bell & Sons, 1950

Anon. *The Story of 46 Division 1939–1945*, undated

Antonio, D.G. *Driver Advance: Being a Short History of the 2nd Lothians and Border Horse*, Edinburgh, Lothians and Border Horse Regimental Association, 1947

Atkinson, Rick. *An Army at Dawn*, Little, Brown, 2003

Barclay, C.N. *History of the 16th/5th Queen's Royal Lancers 1925–1961*, Aldershot, Gale and Polden, 1963

Beckett, Frank. *Prepare to Move: With the 6th Armoured Division in Africa and Sicily*, Grimsby, Frank Beckett, 1994

Bethell, Nicholas. *The Last Secret: Forcible Repatriation to Russia 1944–47*, London, André Deutsch, 1974

Blaxland. Gregory. *The Plain Cook and the Great Showman: First and Eighth Armies in North Africa*, London, William Kimber, 1977

——. *Alexander's Generals: The Italian Campaign 1944–1945*, London, William Kimber, 1979

Brutton, Philip. *Ensign in Italy: A Platoon Commander's Story*, Barnsley, Leo Cooper, 1992

Bryant, Arthur. *Jackets of Green*, London, Collins, 1972

Carell, Paul. *The Foxes of the Desert: The Story of the Afrika Korps*, London, Macdonald, 1960

Colquhoun, James. *Action Front! A History of 'C' Battery in War and Peace*, Barnsley, Leo Cooper, 1992

D'Arcy-Dawson, John. *Tunisian Battle*, London, Macdonald, 1943

Doherty, Richard. *Clear the Way! A History of the 38th (Irish) Brigade, 1941–1947*, Dublin, Irish Academic Press, 1993

Ellis, L.F. *Welsh Guards at War*, Aldershot, Gale and Polden, 1946

ffrench Blake, R.L.V. *A History of the 17th/21st Lancers 1922–1959*, London, Macmillan, 1962

Ford, Ken. *Battleaxe Division: From Africa to Italy with the 78th Division 1942–1945*, Stroud, Sutton Publishing, 1999

——. *Cassino: The Four Battles*, Marlborough, Crowood Press, 2001

Fox, Frank. *The Royal Inniskilling Fusiliers in the Second World War, 1939–45*, Aldershot, Gale and Polden, 1951

Graham, D. and Bidwell, S. *Tug of War: The Battle for Italy, 1943–1945*, London, Hodder & Stoughton, 1986

Graves, Charles. *The History of the Royal Ulster Rifles*, Mexborough, Royal Ulster Rifles Regimental Committee, 1950

Hastings, R.H.W.S. *The Rifle Brigade in the Second World War 1939–1945*, Aldershot, Gale and Polden, 1950

Horsfall, John. *The Wild Geese are Flighting*, Kineton, Roundwood Press, 1976

Howard M. and Sparrow J. *The Coldstream Guards 1920–1946*, Oxford, Oxford University Press, 1951

Johnson, R.F. *Regimental Fire! The Honourable Artillery Company in World War II 1939–1945*, HAC Regimental Committee, 1958

Joslen, H.F. *Orders of Battle Second World War 1939–45*, HMSO 1960

Knox, B.M. *Brief Historical Notes on the Ayrshire Yeomanry 152nd Field Regiment RA 1939–45*, Stephen & Pollock, 1946

Linklater, Eric. *The Campaign in Italy*, HMSO, 1959

Macksey, Kenneth. *Crucible of Power: The Fight for Tunisia 1942–1943*, London, Hutchinson, 1969

Martin, G.W. *Cassino to the River Po*, Chesterfield, G.W. Martin, 1999

Molony, C.J.C. *The Mediterranean and Middle East*, HMSO, vol. V, 1973

Nicholson, N. and Forbes, P. *The Grenadier Guards in the War of 1939–1945*, Aldershot, Gale and Polden, vol. II, 1949

Orgil, Douglas. *The Gothic Line*, London, Heinemann, 1967

Pakenham-Walsh, R.P. *History of the Corps of Royal Engineers*, Chatham, Institute of Royal Engineers, vol. III, 1958

Parkyn, H.G. *The Rifle Brigade Chronicle for 1943*, London, Rifle Brigade Club and Association, 1944

——. *The Rifle Brigade Chronicle for 1945*, London, Rifle Brigade Club and Association, 1946

Patton, George S. *The Patton Papers 1940–1945*, ed. M. Blumenson, Boston, Houghton Mifflin, 1974

Playfair, I.S.O. and Molony, C.J.C. *The Mediterranean and Middle East*, HMSO, vol. IV, 1966

Quilter, D.C. *No Dishonourable Name*, London, William Clowes, 1947

Roberts, G.P.B. *From the Desert to the Baltic*, London, William Kimber, 1987

Rommel, Erwin. *The Rommel Papers*, ed. B.H. Liddell Hart, London, Collins, 1955

Scott, Daniell, D. *Regimental History: The Royal Hampshire Regiment*, Aldershot, Gale and Polden, vol. III, 1955

Steel-Brownlie, W. *The Proud Trooper: The History of the Ayrshire (Earl of Carrick's Own) Yeomanry*, London, Collins, 1964

Tolstoy, Nikolai. *The Minister and the Massacres*, London, Century Hutchinson, 1986.

Whiting, Charles. *First Blood: The Battle of the Kasserine Pass, 1943*, London, Leo Cooper, 1984

Wilson, James. *Unusual Undertakings*, Barnsley, Pen & Sword, 2002

Index

Adige river, 189
Alexander, Gen Sir Harold, 69, 72, 73, 78, 88, 89, 99, 100, 116–20, 125, 126, 128, 129, 138, 159, 171, 179, 183, 185
Algeria, 6–8, 11, 28, 58
Algiers, 9, 11
Allfrey, Lt Gen Charles, 29, 33, 43, 44, 50, 89, 98, 100, 119, 171
Amazon Bridge, 133
Anders, Lt Gen Wladislaw, 137, 140
Anderson, Lt Gen Kenneth, 7, 8, 20, 29, 30, 35, 49, 52, 57, 72, 89, 98, 99, 104, 106
Antonio, Sgt David, 37, 60, 63, 83
Anzio, 119, 126, 144, 147, 157, 171
Apennine Mountains, 115, 117, 129, 159, 173, 174, 178
Aquino, 141–5, 154
Arce, 147
Arezzo, 165–70
Argenta, 183–5
Arnim, GenObst Jurgen von, 36, 43, 49, 58, 69, 98, 99, 100, 102
Arno river, 165, 167, 169, 170, 173
Arunci Mountains, 121, 137, 141
Askew, Sgt, 108

Bald Hill, 19
Bankier, Lt, 150
Barbour, Lt, 123
Barlow, Lt Rudolf, 17, 18, 20
Barré, Gen, 12, 13, 30, 43, 46
Barstow, Lt Col, 40, 71
Barwell, Tpr Freddie, 108
Bayerlein, Obst, 61

Beckett, Frank, 39
Bedale Line, 135, 138
Bedford, Lt Col, 92
Beilby, Maj Tony, 54, 55
Beja, 11–13
Bey of Tunis, 111
Biferno river, 117
Bizerta, 11, 12, 89, 101, 102
Blade Force 7–27, 29, 63
Bliss, Lt, 24
Bode Blocking Group, 131
Bologna, 173–5, 177, 179, 183, 186
Bondeno, 188
Bordj, 87
Bordjgue, 22
Bou Arada, 28–48, 50, 69, 91, 92
Bou Ficha, 112, 113
Box, Capt, 92, 96, 97, 154
Brazilian 1st Division, 171
Bredin, Lt Col, 140
BRITISH FORCES
    V Corps, 29, 32, 43, 50, 89, 98–100, 119, 171, 183, 185
    IX Corps, 72–4, 88–91, 98, 99, 100
    X Corps, 119–21, 162, 165, 170
    XIII Corps, 129, 131, 134, 137, 138, 141, 152, 165, 170, 171, 173, 179, 186
    Fifteenth Army Group, 116
    Eighteenth Army Group, 69, 99
    First Army, 7, 8, 33, 35, 49, 52, 57, 73, 88, 89, 91, 99, 106, 113, 118
    Eighth Army, 6, 7, 9, 49, 61, 67, 69, 71, 72, 80, 86, 89, 91, 98, 102, 112, 113, 116–19, 126, 129, 132,

144, 145, 156, 161, 167, 171, 173–5, 177, 179, 184, 185, 189

Armour
1st Armoured Division, 1, 5, 89–94, 97, 98
2nd Armoured Division, 1
7th Armoured Division, 1, 99, 101, 118
9th Armoured Division, 1
11th Armoured Division, 1, 118
42nd Armoured Division, 1
79th Armoured Division, 1, 195
23rd Armoured Brigade, 119, 120
11th Hussars, 102
51st Royal Tank Regiment, 73, 78, 92
North Irish Horse, 146

Infantry
1st Division, 100, 176
4th Division, 99, 100, 130–5, 137, 138, 168
5th Division, 120
46th Division, 46, 50, 56, 58, 73, 89, 92–4, 121
56th Division, 99, 113, 172, 185
78th 'Battleaxe' Division, 7–13, 19, 23, 24, 26, 29, 35, 37, 46, 50, 69, 118, 119, 126, 130, 131–4, 137–9, 145, 165, 166, 171, 177–9, 185
Y Division, 69
10th Brigade, 131, 133, 135, 141
11th Brigade, 9, 11, 13, 19, 22, 23, 26, 27, 119, 134, 136, 139
12th Brigade, 131
28th Brigade, 131
36th Brigade, 9, 11, 19, 46, 142, 143
128th 'Hampshire' Brigade, 73, 75–8, 91, 93
138th Brigade, 91–3
201st Guards Brigade, 99, 101, 111
1st East Surrey Regiment, 19, 23, 25–7
1st Parachute Regiment, 12–13, 22, 23, 25, 27

2nd Lancashire Fusiliers, 27, 136, 137, 139
2nd Parachute Regiment, 23
2nd/5th Leicestershire Regiment, 50, 56, 58, 62–5
5th Buffs, 46, 47, 142, 143
5th Hampshire Regiment, 78, 121, 122
5th Northamptonshire Regiment, 25, 135
6th Royal West Kent Regiment, 46, 48
8th Argyll and Sutherland Highlanders, 19, 142, 143
Tower Hamlet Rifles, 4

Artillery
6th Army Group RA, 168
11th (HAC) RHA, 91, 100
17th Field Regiment RA, 35, 37
23rd Army Field Regiment RA, 62
58th Antitank Regiment RA, 62
71st Field Regiment RA, 58
93rd Antitank Regiment RA, 52
132nd Field Regiment RA, 24, 26
151st (Ayrshire Yeomanry) Field Regiment RA, 5
457, Light Battery RA, 24

Support
11th Field Ambulance RAMC, 26
86th Chemical Warfare Company, 62
Broich, GenMaj Friedrich von, 53, 54, 59, 61, 62, 64, 66, 67, 110
Brooke, Maj Gen Alan, 2
Buelowius, Gen, 49, 51–3, 67
Buxton, Maj, 136

Canadian I Corps, 143–5
Canadian 1st Division, 138, 143, 145
Canadian 5th Armoured Division, 143, 145
Canadian 1st Armoured Brigade, 131, 134, 143
Cap Bon, 99, 101, 102, 110–12
Casablanca, 9

Index

Cassino, 119, 120, 126–9, 137, 141, 159
Castel del Rio, 179
Castelforte, 124
Castle Hill, 126
Cavanazza, 189
Chetniks, 191
Chiana valley, 166
Chinner, Capt, 154
Chouigui Pass, 11, 13, 14, 16, 17, 19–23
Churchill, Winston, 4, 115, 116
Clark, Lt Gen Mark, 116–20, 125, 129, 147, 157, 171, 173, 177, 179
Coad, Sgt Bert, 16
Cobbold, Maj, 148, 149
Coldragone, 147
Commachio Lake, 183
Consandolo, 185
Cortona, 165, 166
Cossacks, 191
Coxen's Farm, 16, 20–2, 25
Cremona Group, 185
Croats, 191
Crocker, Lt Gen John, 2, 5, 72, 75, 76, 78–80, 88, 89, 91, 94, 97–9

D'Arcy-Dawson, John, 84
Daubin, Lt F., 21
Davie, Maj John, 113
Dawney, Col, 142
Denny, Lt, 152
Derrien, Admiral, 12
Dever, Gen, 171
Diadem Operation, 129, 130, 137, 144
Dicomano, 173, 174
Dimsdale, Maj, 105
Dipienne, 23
Djebel Aouareb, 74–7, 79, 80, 83, 88
Djebel bou Aoukaz, 100
Djebel Cherichira, 74
Djebel el Hamra, 47, 57
Djebel Houfia, 74, 75, 78
Djebel Kournine, 93–8
Djebel Mansour, 43

Djebel Medjanine, 41
Djebel Rhorab, 74–80, 82, 84
Djebel Rihane, 98
Djebel Rorouf, 103–5
Djebel Srassif, 97
Djebel Zaghouan, 89
Djebel Zuag, 68
Djedeida, 18, 19, 22
Dunphie, Brig Charles, 50, 52, 57, 58, 60–2, 67, 70
Dyer, L/Cpl, 181

Eastern Dorsal, 36, 43, 49, 72, 74, 86, 88, 89
Edwards, Capt, 47
Egypt, 9, 28, 69
Eilbote Operation, 36, 43
Eisenhower, Gen Dwight, 7, 28, 29, 69, 73, 88, 89, 116
El Bathan, 17, 19, 23, 25, 26
El Hamra, 58
Elliot Capt, 122
Enfidaville, 89, 98, 102, 113
Estéva, Admiral, 12,
Evelegh, Maj Gen Vivian, 10, 19, 20, 23, 118, 119, 129, 143, 145, 147, 151–3, 155, 165–7, 171
Eveleigh, Maj, 512

Faid, 36, 49
Fernie Line, 135, 138
ffrench Blake, Lt Col Desmond, 66
ffrench Blake, Lt Col Val, 5, 11, 14, 15, 33–5, 177, 185, 187, 188, 190, 191
Finale, 189
Firenzuola, 175
Fischer, GenMaj, 22–5, 38, 40, 43, 45, 53, 196
Fisher, Lt, 154
Florence, 170–4
Fondouk, 36, 69–88
Forli, 174, 175, 177
Fossa Cembalina, 186, 187

Fredendall, Maj Gen, 49, 57
Freeman-Atwood, Maj Gen R., 91
French Expeditionary Corps, 126, 129, 142, 144, 171
French IXX Corps, 74, 76, 89
Freyberg VC, Lt Gen Sir Bernard, 114, 129, 190
Frülingswind Operation, 49
Futa Pass, 173, 175
Fyffe, Col, 190

Gabes, 74
Gafsa, 49, 57, 74
Gairdner, Maj Gen C.H., 5
Gallo, 187
Garigliano river, 117–25, 129, 146, 165
GERMAN FORCES
  LXXXVII Corps, 190
  XC Corps, 12
  Afrika Korps, 49, 51, 53, 56, 58, 67
  Fifth Panzer Army, 36, 49, 69
  Tenth Army, 116, 144, 145, 159, 162, 189
  Fourteenth Army, 159, 162
  Panzer Army Africa, 49
  Panzer Forces
    10th Panzer Division, 22, 26, 30, 36, 49, 53, 54, 56, 58, 59, 61, 65, 66, 68, 72, 84, 91, 93, 98, 110,
    15th Panzer Division, 98, 99, 101
    15th Panzergrenadier Division, 134, 166, 167
    21st Panzer Division, 49, 51, 72, 84
    90th Panzergrenadier Division, 134
    361st Panzergrenadier Regiment, 140
    7th Panzer Regiment, 36, 38, 41
    190th Panzer Regiment, 20
    501st Heavy Tank Battalion, 48, 95
    Battlegroup Djedeida, 22
    Battlegroup Hüdel, 22–5, 27
    Battlegroup Lüder, 22, 23, 25
    Battlegroup Koch, 22, 25
    Panzergrenadier Regiment Africa, 52, 53

Infantry Forces
  5th Mountain Division, 134
  65th Division, 190
  90th Light Division, 103, 110, 113
  94th Division, 121, 167
  114th Jäger Division, 134
  305th Division, 167
  334th Motorised Division, 48, 99, 101, 180
  999th Light Africa Division, 76, 82
Parachute Forces
  1st Parachute Division, 125, 127, 128, 134, 137, 138, 140–2, 153
  5th Parachute Regiment, 36
  Herman Göring Division, 36, 39, 40, 91, 94, 98, 99, 101, 103, 110
Gibson-Watt, Capt, 105, 155
Goddard, Lt John, 181
Goff, Lt Col Ion, 135
Goodrich, Capt Gordon, 108
Gore, Lt Col Adrian, 52–6, 71, 78, 156
Gothic Line, 159, 161, 162, 165, 167, 169–74, 177
Goubellat, 30–3, 35, 89–93
Goums, 46, 48, 142
Grafton Line, 135
Graham, Maj Gen, 113
Grand Dorsal, 49
Grandstand Ridge, 33, 36, 37, 39, 40, 44, 92
Green, Maj, 123
Green Hill, 19
Grey-Turner, Capt Elston, 97
Griffiths, Lt, 108
Gundrey Lt Col, 166
Gurney, Lt Col, 148
Gustav Line, 117, 119, 120, 125, 126, 129, 134, 135, 137–9, 141

Hamilton-Russell, Lt Col, 60, 80, 81
Hammam Lif, 102–11
Hammamet, 102, 110, 112
Hannay, Lt Victor, 146
Harding, Lt Gen John, 129

Index

Haston, L/Sgt, 108
Hawkesworth, Maj Gen, 121
Haydon, Brig, 121, 126, 155
Hayley, Lt 148
Heidrich, GenMaj Richard, 128, 137, 138, 140
Heslop, Lt, 47
Highway 3, 160, 161
Highway 6, 125, 126, 129, 139, 140, 144, 145, 147, 157, 173
Highway 9, 174, 177, 183
Highway 65, 175
Highway 67, 174, 177
Highway 69, 170
Highway 71, 166–8
Hitler, Adolf, 12, 162
Hitler (Von Senger) Line, 137, 141–6, 199
Hobart, Maj Gen Percy, 2
Hodgson, Lt Col, 103, 105
Hooker, Lt, 18
Horrocks, Lt Gen Sir Brian, 99, 100, 104, 106
Horsfall, Lt Col John, 30, 31, 136
Hotel Continental, 127
Hughes, Maj, 39, 46–8
Hull, Lt Col Richard, 7, 11, 13, 23, 27

Il Giogo Pass, 173, 175
Imola, 173, 175
Indian 4th Division, 89, 99, 114, 126
Indian 8th Division, 131, 134, 138, 167, 186
Irwin, Brig Gen, 65, 66
Italian First Army, 69, 72, 86, 88, 101, 113

Jefferson VC, Fus, 137
Jeffreys, Lt Col, 44
Jefna, 19
Jones, L/Bdr, 154
Juin, Gen, 137

Kairouan, 36, 72–9
Kasserine, 49, 68, 69, 73, 74

Keightley, Lt Gen Charles, 5, 7, 30, 32, 35, 36, 41, 43, 50, 68, 69, 72, 73, 77, 78, 80, 84, 88, 93, 95, 98, 101, 102, 104, 106, 113, 114, 118, 119, 126, 135, 139, 142, 165, 171, 183, 185
Kesselring, GFM Albert, 19, 22, 67, 116, 117, 144, 159, 161, 162, 164, 165
Kirkman, Lt Gen, 131, 138, 165, 167
Knob, Maj, 176
Koch, ObstLt Walther, 36, 110, 196
Koeltz, Gen Louis, 76, 89

Lambert, Lt, 111
Lascelles, Lt Viscount, 163
Laverick, Pte, 26
Lee, Lt Col, 27
Leese, Lt Gen Sir Oliver, 125, 143, 168, 173
Le Kef, 49, 50, 52, 58, 67
Le Patourel VC, Maj, 27
Libya, 9, 11
Liri valley, 117, 119, 125, 129–45, 156, 165
Llewellyn, Capt, 104, 105
L'Olmo Gap, 166, 168
Lombardy Plain, 173, 174, 186
Longstop Hill, 29
Loveday, Lt Col, 135
Lucas, Maj Gen, 119

McCreery, Lt Gen Richard, 121, 162, 177, 179, 184, 185
Mackenzie, Lt Col, 136
MAILED FIST DIVISION (6TH ARMOURED DIVISION)
   Armour
   6th Armoured Division Armoured Reconnaissance Group, 132, 138, 142
   20th Armoured Brigade, 2
   26th Armoured Brigade, 2–4, 50, 52, 56–8, 62, 70, 75, 78, 80, 84, 86, 91, 93, 95, 100, 102, 112, 113,

126, 131, 132, 134, 138, 142, 143, 155, 156, 162, 164, 166, 168, 174, 177, 178, 185, 189
16th/5th/Lancers, 3, 51, 62, 67, 68, 82–8, 93–5, 100, 110, 112, 120, 130, 131, 135, 136, 138–40, 146, 147, 153, 163, 164, 166, 169, 178, 185, 186, 188, 189
17th/21st Lancers, 3, 7, 11, 14, 16, 20–7, 30–5, 46, 48, 58–60, 62, 63, 70, 79–88, 93, 94, 100, 109, 110, 112, 131, 132–6, 139, 142, 143, 154–5, 163, 164, 166, 177, 178, 187–91
2nd Lothians and Border Horse, 3, 6, 35, 37–43, 52–63, 65, 66, 70, 79–88, 93, 94, 109, 110, 112, 131–6, 139, 142, 143, 155, 163, 164, 166, 177, 178, 187–91

Infantry
1st Guards Brigade, 23, 50, 62, 67–9, 78–80, 84, 92, 94, 95, 103, 106, 110, 112, 115, 121, 123–8, 130, 152, 162, 165, 166, 168, 172, 174–9, 185, 189
38th Irish Brigade, 3, 4, 30, 31, 33, 38, 44, 69, 135, 137, 177
61st Brigade, 156, 162–4, 166, 167, 174, 177–80, 182
1st Kings Royal Rifle Corps, 185
1st Royal Irish Fusiliers, 3, 4, 30, 31, 33, 35, 36, 39, 40, 138, 139
1st Welch Regiment, 185, 188, 189
2nd Hampshires, 23, 25–7, 69, 70, 79
2nd Coldstream Guards, 29, 68, 69, 95–7, 105, 106, 111, 121–3, 127, 128, 152–6, 163, 164, 168, 176, 179, 185
2nd London Irish Rifles, 4, 33, 39, 43–5, 135–7
2nd Rifle Brigade, 156, 167, 180–2, 184, 185, 189, 190
3rd Grenadier Guards, 69, 96, 109–11, 121, 124, 127, 146, 147, 152–4, 155, 163–5, 168, 176, 185, 189
3rd Welsh Guards, 70, 78–80, 82, 103–6, 111, 121–5, 127, 147–56, 164, 165, 168, 176, 189
6th Inniskilling Fusiliers, 4, 33–6, 39, 40, 135, 139, 140
7th Rifle Brigade, 156, 167, 180, 187, 188, 190
10th Rifle Brigade, 3, 4, 7, 14, 16, 17, 23, 24, 36, 37, 52, 56, 64, 68, 71, 78, 82, 85, 95, 103, 106, 131, 138, 142, 146, 147, 156, 157, 162, 163, 166, 172, 180, 185

Artillery
12th (HAC) RHA, 2, 4, 7, 14, 20, 24, 25, 31, 37, 39, 40, 46, 52, 56, 58, 62, 63, 65, 66, 68, 71, 78–80, 83, 85, 87, 91, 111, 115, 162, 166, 177, 185
51st Light Antiaircraft regiment, RA, 3, 7, 30, 131, 138
72nd Antitank Regiment RA, 2, 7, 23, 24, 30, 46–8, 131, 146, 166, 185
152nd (Ayrshire Yeomanry) Field Regiment RA, 3–5, 31, 37, 69, 85, 92, 95–8, 103, 115, 121, 143, 153–5, 162, 176

Support Groups
5th Field Squadron RE, 3, 8
6th Armoured Division Provost Company, 8
6th Support Group, 2
8th Field Squadron RE, 3, 68, 166, 185
9th Tank Transporter Battalion, 8, 11
26th Armoured Brigade Company RASC, 8
144th Field Park Squadron RE, 3
165th Field Ambulance RAMC, 8
625th Field Squadron RE, 132
627th Field Squadron RE, 132

Index

Derbyshire Yeomanry, 2, 7, 11–14, 23, 25, 30, 31, 68, 101, 112, 113, 115, 131, 138, 142, 143, 146, 166, 178
Mairs, Sgt, 124
Maison Blanche, 9
Maitland, Capt E., 87, 88
Makins, Lt Col Sir Richard, 122
Mareth Line, 49, 51
Margaellil river, 82
Martel, Gen Gifford, 48
Martin, Lt George, 131, 133, 148, 157, 158
Martin, Maj, 104
Massicault, 11, 29, 90, 93, 94, 98–101
Mateur, 11, 13, 16, 19, 20–3, 25, 27
Maxwell, Maj, 81, 188
Medjerda river, 13, 18, 19, 22, 25, 27, 29
Medjez El Bab, 11, 13, 18, 19, 22, 25–7, 29, 30, 36, 89, 92, 99
Melfa river, 141, 142, 145–7
Menton, Obst, 53, 54
Messe, Gen Giovanni, 72–5, 77, 78, 84, 85, 88, 113
Metcalfe, Lt J., 82
Michols, Maj, 81
Middleton, Maj Cecil, 64
Minturno, 120
Mirabello, 188
Monastery Hill, 127, 129, 134, 137, 138, 140
Monselice, 189
Monte Battaglia, 175, 176, 178
Monte Casino, 117, 119, 120, 125, 126, 128, 129, 131, 132, 135, 137, 140
Monte Castellare, 166
Monte Cerasola, 121–4
Monte Corneo, 163
Monte Faito, 121, 124
Monte Fuga, 122
Monte Furlito, 121, 122
Monte Grande, 152–4
Monte Lacugnano, 163

Monte Lignano, 166–8
Monte Maggio, 167, 168
Monte Malbe, 163
Monte Orio, 148, 151
Monte Ornito, 121–3, 125
Monte Pacciano, 164
Monte Penzola, 179
Monte Piccolo, 148–55
Monte Pulito, 164
Monte Tuga, 124
Montgomery, Gen Sir Bernard, 49, 51, 72, 73, 89, 98, 102, 116, 117
Montione, 165
Moore, Lt Vin, 112
Morey, Lt P.J., 107
Munchar, 27
Muragliano Pass, 173, 174
Murphy, Maj Peter, 40
Murray, Maj Gen Horatius, 172, 183, 185–7

Narni, 161, 162
Naumann, Lt Tony, 15, 16
Nehring, Gen der PzTrp Walther, 12, 13, 19, 22
Nelson, Col, 176
New Zealand II Corps, 125, 126, 129
New Zealand 2nd Division, 89, 114, 126, 168, 188, 189, 190
Nicholson, Brig Cameron, 57, 62–7
Nix, Maj, 81

Ogilvie, John, 53, 55
Oran, 9, 11, 13
Oudna, 23
Oued Zarga, 27

Padua, 189
Palmanova, 190
Patton, Lt Gen George, 73–5, 88
Perry, Lt Col, 106
Perugia, 162–5
Pignataro, 135
Pilastrello, 189

Index

Pinchon, 74–6, 78, 86
Pirie, Capt, 56, 61–6
Piumarola, 138, 139, 140, 142
Poggio Renatico, 186, 187
Point 222, 181
Point 286, 43–5, 92
Point 279, 43–5
Polish II Corps, 126, 129, 134, 137, 138, 140, 177
Po Morto de Primaro, 186, 187
Po river, 173, 183, 186, 189
Poninville Hills, 111
Pont du Fahs, 30, 32, 41, 43, 45, 46, 89, 91
Ponte Buriano, 169, 200
Ponte Vecchio, 170
Ponticorvo, 141, 146
Pytchley Line, 135–7

Rapido river, 117, 120, 129, 131–4, 138, 140
Reno river, 184–8
Rimini, 174
Robaa, 43, 45, 46
Roberts, Brig G. 'Pip', 71, 78, 80–2, 84, 86–8, 93–5, 101, 102, 104, 113, 118
Robinett, Brig Gen Paul, 57, 67
Rome, 117, 120, 125, 144, 147, 148, 157, 159
Rommel, GenFM Erwin, 11, 28, 49, 51, 53, 54, 58, 59, 61, 65–7, 69
Roosevelt, President Franklin, 115
Russell, Brig Nelson, 33, 43, 45
Ryder, Maj Gen Charles, 73–7, 79,

San Agostino, 188
San Marco, 164, 165
Sangro river, 117, 119
Santerno river, 175, 178, 180
Sbeitla, 49
Sbiba, 50, 51, 69, 72, 74
Scott, Lt Col Pat, 31, 36
Sebret el Kourzia, 90, 93, 94

Sedjenane, 11
Segni, 186, 187
Senio river, 175, 176, 178, 179, 183
Serbs, 191
Setif, 12
Sidi Bou Zid, 49, 74
Sidi Nsir, 11, 13, 14
Siglin, Maj, 20
Simpson, Lt Col Gordon, 41, 155, 156, 160, 161, 186
Sinagogga, 135, 136
Smith, Maj, 104, 105
Smith, Maj Martin, 148, 149
Soliman, 110
Sora, 155
Souk el Arba, 13
Sousse, 86
South African 6th Armoured Division, 165, 168
Sponek, GenMaj Graf von, 113, 114
Stark, Col Alexander, 51–5, 57
Stauffenberg, Obst Count von, 196
Stewart-Brown, Lt Col, 96
Strang Steel, Maj, 16, 17
Strike Operation, 99, 101
Stuka Ridge, 37
Swiny, Maj, 45

Tebessa, 49, 57, 58, 67
Tebourba, 11, 13, 17, 19–27, 29, 36, 69
Templer, Maj Gen, Gerald, 171, 172
Terni, 161, 162
Thala, 49–68
Thomas, GenMaj Kurt, 76
Tiber river, 160–2
Tine valley, 13, 17, 20–2, 27
Tito, Gen 190, 191
Todi, 161, 163
Torch Operation, 7, 8, 11
Tossignano, 179–84
Traghetto, 186
Trasimene Lake, 163–7
Trevisio, 189
Trieste, 190